Software Preparation
Windows Computers

If you have any problem downloading the software, call Software Support (513)939-5305

To download the Solid Footing software and place the files on your computer's **C:** drive:

1. Use **Microsoft Edge** or **Internet Explorer** as your browser

2. Go to the website: **www.SolidFootingAccounting.com**

3. Click **DOWNLOAD Student Software**

4. Enter your **First Name** – enter your **Last Name**

5. Select **Solid Footing 10th edition** from the drop-down list

6. Click **Windows**

7. Enter your **Software ID Code** – code is 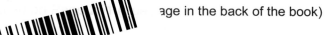 age in the back of the book)

8. Click **SUBMIT**

9. Confirm <u>Software</u> is **Solid Footing 10th** _____ ...mputer is **Windows** – click **Yes**

10. Read the <u>Ready to Download?</u> window – click **Yes**

11. Click **Open** (If you do not see "Open", click "Save" and then click "Open")

12. Click **Extract all**

13. When you are prompted to enter a Destination for the extracted files, delete the suggested destination in the **extract to** box, and enter just **C:**

14. Click **Extract**

15. Close all open windows – Close your browser

16. Your Solid Footing files are now on your computer in: **This PC** or **Computer**
    (C:) (drive)
    Solid Footing 10e (folder)

Read the information below and on Page *ii* to complete the software preparation process.

1. **Excel 2016** or **Excel 2013** or **Excel 2010 is required to run the Solid Footing software on a Windows Computer.**

   If you do not have Excel, see Page *iv* for information on how to copy your software to a USB flash drive, and then run the software on a computer that does have Excel.

   Caution: Do not use any application other than the three versions of Excel listed above to run the Solid Footing software on a Windows computer. If you use any other application, such as OpenOffice, Google Sheets, etc., to run the Solid Footing software, the software will not function correctly and your instructor will **not** be able to grade your Solid Footing projects.

2. Read the information in the box at the top of Page *ii* (the back of this page). After you read the information, then begin working on **Page 3** in your Solid Footing book.

Using **Excel 2016** or **Excel 2013** or **Excel 2010** to run the Solid Footing Software

The first time you open a Solid Footing workbook, there will be a series of two messages shown just above the workbook on the left side of the screen. The Protected View message will appear first and the Security Warning message will appear second. Do the following to Enable Editing and Enable Macros:

PROTECTED VIEW Be careful— .... | Enable Editing | ← **Click**

SECURITY WARNING Macros have been disabled. | Enable Content | ← **Click**

Needing to do the following is rare – If you do **not** see the "**Security Warning**" message and the buttons in the software do **not** work—then perform the following steps to change your Macro Security setting:

1. Open your Excel program.
2. Click **File** (upper left corner of the screen)
3. Click **Options** (last or second last choice on the left)
4. Click **Trust Center** (last choice on the left in the window)
5. Click **Trust Center Settings**

6. Click **Macro Settings**
7. Click **Disable all macros with notification**
8. Click **OK**
9. Click **OK**
10. **Exit out of Excel**

If Workbook Tabs are Not Visible

If you are not able to see the tabs at the bottom of a Solid Footing workbook, it is because the workbook needs to be maximized. To maximize the workbook:

⇨ Hold down the **Ctrl** key and Press the **F10** key

Software Preparation
Mac Computers

If you have any problem downloading the software, call Software Support (513)939-5305

To download the Solid Footing software and place the software on your Mac's desktop:

1. Use **Safari** as your browser

2. Go to the website: **www.SolidFootingAccounting.com**

3. Click **DOWNLOAD Student Software**

4. Enter your **First Name** – enter your **Last Name**

5. Select **Solid Footing 10th edition** from the drop-down list

6. Click **Mac**

7. Enter your **Software ID Code** – code is located on Page 251 (blue page in the back of the book)

8. Click **SUBMIT**

9. Confirm <u>Software</u> is **Solid Footing 10th edition** and <u>Type of Computer</u> is **Mac** – click **Yes**

10. Read the <u>Ready to Download?</u> window – click **Yes**

11. After the download is complete – Quit Safari

12. Click the **Downloads** folder in the Dock – drag the **Solid Footing 10e** folder to your Desktop

The Solid Footing software is now on your Mac computer. Follow the directions below to complete the software preparation process.

Excel 2016 or **Excel 2011 is required to run the Solid Footing software on a Mac Computer.**

If you do not have Excel, see Page *iv* for information on how to copy your software to a USB flash drive, and then run the software on a computer that does have Excel.

Caution: Do not use any application other than the two versions of Excel listed above to run the Solid Footing software on a Mac computer. If you use any other application, such as Apple Numbers, OpenOffice, Google Sheets, etc., to run the Solid Footing software, the software will not function correctly and your instructor will **not** be able to grade your Solid Footing projects.

Using **Excel for Mac 2016** or **Excel for Mac 2011** to run the Solid Footing software

1. To open a Solid Footing workbook – Double click the **Solid Footing 10e** folder – Double click the Solid Footing workbook you wish to open
2. **Enable Macros** – if when opening a Solid Footing workbook, Excel displays a question about macros—always click **Enable Macros**
3. Begin working on **Page 3** in your Solid Footing book

Tips:
  ▷ To exit out of **Full Screen mode** and display the **"Excel File Edit .."** menu across the top of the screen – press the **esc** key

  ▷ **If Workbook Tabs are Not Visible** – If the tabs are not visible at the bottom of a Solid Footing workbook, click the green circle in the top left corner of the screen.

Running the Software from a USB Flash Drive

You only need to read this page if you do **NOT** have Excel on your computer.

As indicated on Pages *i* and *iii*, Excel is required to run the Solid Footing software. If you do NOT have Excel 2010, 2013, or 2016 on your Windows computer – or Excel for Mac 2011 or 2016 on your Mac computer, then an alternative for running your Solid Footing software is to:

  ▷ Copy the Solid Footing 10e Folder from your computer to a USB flash drive.
  ▷ Take the USB flash drive to a computer that has one of the Excel versions listed above.
  ▷ Plug the flash drive into the computer – Run the Solid Footing software from the flash drive.

Copying the Solid Footing 10e folder to a USB flash drive:

On a Mac computer:

  ▷ *Plug* the flash drive into a USB port
  ▷ *Point* to the Solid Footing 10e folder on the desktop –
     Hold down **Control** key - *Click* – *Click* Copy "Solid Footing 10e"
  ▷ *Point* to the flash drive on the desktop – *Hold down* **Control** key - *Click* – *Click* Paste Item
  ▷ *Double Click* the flash drive – Confirm that the Solid Footing 10e folder is on the flash drive
  ▷ *Close* the window – *Point* to the flash drive – *Hold down* **Control** key - *Click* – *Click* Eject " "

On a Windows computer:

  ▷ *Plug* the flash drive into a USB port
  ▷ Not Windows 8 or 10.... ▶ *Select* Computer from the desktop or from the Start menu
     Windows 8 or 10 .... ▶ *Hold down* **Windows logo** key - *Tap* the **S** key
                                  Type This PC – *Press* **Enter** key
  ▷ *Double Click* C: (drive) – *Point* to the Solid Footing 10e folder – *Right Click* – *Click* Copy
  ▷ *Click* the flash drive – *Right Click* – *Click* Paste
  ▷ *Point* to the flash drive – *Right Click* – *Click* Eject

Running the Solid Footing Software from a USB flash drive on a Computer that has Excel

On a Mac computer

  ▷ *Plug* the flash drive into a USB port
  ▷ *Double Click* the flash drive on the desktop – *Double Click* the Solid Footing 10e folder
  ▷ *Double Click* the Solid Footing workbook you wish to open
  ▷ After you are finished working with the Solid Footing workbook – *Quit* Excel – *Close* the window – *Point* to the flash drive – *Hold down* **Control** key - *Click* – *Click* Eject " "

On a Windows computer

  ▷ *Plug* the flash drive into a USB port
  ▷ Not Windows 8 or 10.... ▶ *Select* Computer from the desktop or from the Start menu
     Windows 8 or 10 .... ▶ *Hold down* **Windows logo** key - *Tap* the **S** key
                                  Type This PC – *Press* **Enter** key
  ▷ *Double Click* the flash drive – *Double Click* the Solid Footing 10e folder
  ▷ *Double Click* the Solid Footing workbook you wish to open
  ▷ After you are finished working with the Solid Footing workbook – Exit Excel – *Point* to the flash drive – *Right Click* – *Click* Eject

Contents

Contents (continued)

Solid Footing

Building an Accounting Foundation

The purpose of Solid Footing is to help you learn how an organization's business transactions are entered into an accounting system and how the data in that accounting system is used to produce the organization's financial statements.

⇨ YOUR LEARNING PROCESS

▷ You will interact with the Solid Footing software to obtain an understanding of the material being presented.

▷ You will read the book to gain further insights into the new concepts.

▷ You will work end-of-chapter problems to test your understanding of the material.

▷ You will complete the Mini-Project at the end of Chapter 6 to test your understanding of the first six chapters.

▷ You will complete the **A**ccounting **C**ycle **P**roject to test your understanding of the entire accounting process.

STOP

Before you begin reading Chapter 1, be sure to perform the software preparation process.

To prepare the Solid Footing software, follow the directions on one of the **Software Preparation** pages located in the front of this book:

▷ Page *i*   Software Preparation – **Windows** Computers

▷ Page *iii* Software Preparation – **Mac** Computers

SOLID FOOTING'S AUTHOR

Dan Wiegand retired from the Department of Accountancy at Miami University, Oxford, Ohio. He holds a B.S. degree in accounting from Miami University and an M.B.A. degree in finance and accounting from Miami University. Dan was the coordinator of Miami's Introductory Financial Accounting course and taught Introductory Financial Accounting to over 10,000 students while at Miami. He also taught the accounting module in Miami's MBA program.

Dan came to Miami with over 30 years of business experience. He was an auditor with Ernst & Ernst, the Controller of a manufacturing corporation, the Vice President of Finance of two manufacturing corporations, the founder and President of a software development firm, and a seminar leader for over 80 continuing professional education programs for CPA's. On the CPA exam, Dan placed 2nd in the State of Ohio and received the Elijah Watts Sells Award for National Honorary Distinction. Dan served in the United States Army in Washington, D.C. and in Vietnam.

While teaching at Miami, Dan:

- ▷ Received the Farmer School of Business Teaching Excellence Award for his "outstanding gifts as a teacher, and his ability to use his years of experience in the practice of accounting to enhance students' understanding of fundamentals."

- ▷ Received the Outstanding Professor Award from Pi Sigma Epsilon (PSE).

- ▷ Received the Honored Professor Award from Miami University Associated Student Government for "making a remarkable commitment to students."

- ▷ Received the Outstanding Professor Award from the Miami Business Enterprises.

- ▷ Was nominated for the Ohio Society of CPA's Outstanding Ohio Accounting Educator Award.

- ▷ Was nominated for the Miami Alumni Association's Effective Educator Award.

- ▷ Five times received the "MBA boot camp award" that recognizes the outstanding professor in the summer MBA boot camp.

Dan is the author of three software-driven interactive accounting textbooks – projects, which are published by Micro Solve, Inc.:

- ▷ *Red Company - Financial Statement Analysis*

- ▷ *Solid Footing - Building an Accounting Foundation*

- ▷ *The Master Budget Project – Building a Master Budget Model*

Chapter 1
Stuff and Claims-to-Stuff

___

Before you begin reading this chapter:

⇨ Open the workbook **01-Stuff & Claims-to-Stuff** in the **Solid Footing 10e** folder

⇨ Enable Macros   For information on enabling Macros, refer to:
Pg *ii* Software Preparation – Windows
Pg *iii* Software Preparation – Mac

On your computer screen, observe the four tabs across the bottom of this workbook. The left most tab is labeled Stuff&Claims. If you do not see four tabs at the bottom of the workbook, refer to the information under the heading **If Workbook Tabs are Not Visible** on Pgs *ii* and *iii*.

🖱 Click the **Stuff&Claims** tab (if the Stuff&Claims tab is not selected).

You should see **Screen 1 A** in the upper left corner of the screen.

⇨ THE CASH BUCKET
___

Your introduction to double-entry accounting is going to be based on an accounting system you and your sister devised. If you do not have a sister—pretend.

Inside the front door of your house, you and your sister are going to keep a bucket of cash. The purpose of the bucket is to provide cash for going to the movies, restaurants, etc. The idea is for each of you to put a beginning amount of cash into the bucket. Each evening when either you or your sister leave to go out, you or your sister simply take some cash out of the bucket.

As you think more about your idea, you realize there are three things you and your sister need to know about the Cash Bucket. At any point in time:

1. How much cash is in the bucket?

2. What is the amount of your claim to the cash in the bucket? That is, how much of the cash is yours?

3. What is the amount of your sister's claim to the cash in the bucket? That is, how much of the cash is your sister's?

The system you devised to keep track of these three pieces of data is shown in the **01-Stuff & Claims-to-Stuff** workbook.

⇨ CASH BUCKET ACCOUNTING SYSTEM

Let's start running your system to see how it will keep track of the three things you want to know about the Cash Bucket.

To get the Cash Bucket started, you put $200 into the bucket. As soon as you put the cash into the bucket, you go to your accounting system to record the required data.

🖰 Click **I Put $200 Into the Cash Bucket**

Observe on the left side of your system you have an account, a place to keep track of the dollar amount of physical cash in the Cash Bucket. The first recording in your system is $200 to the Cash account. If you and your sister always make a recording in the Cash account each time money is put into or taken out of the Cash Bucket, then the balance in the Cash account will tell you the amount of physical cash in the bucket. Currently, the balance in the Cash account is $200, and the physical cash in the bucket is $200. For now, let's call the side of your accounting system where the Cash account is shown the **Stuff** side because it is keeping track of the dollar amount of actual stuff your organization owns. At this time, cash is your organization's only stuff.

On the right side of your system are two accounts. The accounts on the right side of your system are <u>not</u> tracking the dollar amount of stuff owned by your organization. (That is the job of the accounts on the left side of your system.) The accounts on the right side of your system are keeping track of the amount of your claim and the amount of your sister's claim to the stuff. Let's call the right side of your system the **Claims-to-Stuff** side. One account on the right side keeps track of the amount of your claim to the stuff. The other claim account keeps track of the amount of your sister's claim to the stuff.

At the same time you add $200 to the Cash account on the left side, notice you also add $200 to the My Claim account on the right side.

Following the plan you and your sister devised, your sister puts $150 into the Cash Bucket.

🖰 Click **Sister Puts $150 Into the Cash Bucket**

Now that both you and your sister have money in the Cash Bucket, let's look at some of the features of your accounting system:

▷ All accounts begin with zero balances because you just started your Cash Bucket Accounting System.

▷ The total of the account balances on the **Stuff** side of your system will always equal the total of the account balances on the **Claims-to-Stuff** side.

▷ The Cash account on the Stuff side always tells you how much money is in the Cash Bucket.

▷ The Cash account on the Stuff side is not tracking your claim or your sister's claim to the cash.

▷ The My Claim account shows how much your claim is to the stuff owned by your organization.

▷ The Sister's Claim account shows how much your sister's claim is to the stuff owned by your organization.

▷ The My Claim account and the Sister's Claim account are <u>not</u> keeping track of the dollar amount of stuff in your organization. That is the job of the account(s) on the Stuff side of your system.

So that you can show your sister the current condition of the Cash Bucket organization, you prepare a report from the Ending Balances in each account.

🖱 Click **Prepare the Report**

The report shows in a summarized form the information in the accounts. From the report you and your sister can very quickly see:

> ▷ Your organization has $350 of stuff.
> ▷ You have a $200 claim to the stuff.
> ▷ Your sister has a $150 claim to the stuff.

Why have we spent so much time on three accounts and two transactions? The reason is because the rest of this book rests on the concepts demonstrated by your Cash Bucket Accounting System.

⇨ DAD's LOAN TO YOUR ORGANIZATION

🖱 Click the **Dad's In** tab.

You should see **Screen 1 B** in the upper left corner of the screen.

Observe that there is a new account in your accounting system called Dad's Claim. You will use that account later in this section.

Also notice that a new name, Balance Sheet, has been given to the report on this screen. On the first screen, we called this report *Report of Stuff and Who has a Claim to the Stuff*. Balance Sheet is an appropriate name for the report because the report shows that the Stuff and the Claims-to-Stuff are in balance.

This new screen begins with no transactions recorded in your system. You will again need to record the two transactions showing that you and your sister put cash into the bucket.

🖱 Click the top two buttons to record those two put-cash-in transactions.

Your sister is leaving for the evening, and as she goes out the front door she takes $20 out of the Cash Bucket. You record the transaction in the accounting system before she leaves.

🖱 Click **Sister Takes $20 Out of the Cash Bucket**

Observe the following:
> ▷ Negative $20 is entered into the Cash account on the **Stuff** side of the system.
> ▷ Negative $20 is entered into the Sister's Claim account on the **Claims-to-Stuff** side of the system.
> ▷ The **Stuff** and the **Claims-to-Stuff** sides of your system are still in balance because you subtracted $20 from each.

You are leaving for the evening, and you take $15 out of the Cash Bucket.

🖱 Click **I Take $15 Out of the Cash Bucket**

Look at the accounts and observe the effects of your transaction on the system.

The following morning at breakfast, you convince your father to participate in the Cash Bucket. Dad agrees to loan the Cash Bucket $100. Dad is not an owner in the Cash Bucket organization. Rather, he is just making a loan to the organization. You and your sister sign an agreement with Dad called a Note. The note stipulates that Dad will be paid back over the next four weeks at the rate of $25 per week and that Dad will not charge interest. Dad puts his $100 into the Cash Bucket, and you make the required entries into your system.

🖰 Click **Dad Loans $100 to the Cash Bucket**

By looking at the balances in the accounts, you can see the following:

▷ Your organization has $415 of stuff.

▷ Dad has a $100 claim to the stuff.

▷ You have a $185 claim to the stuff.

▷ Your sister has a $130 claim to the stuff.

▷ The **Total Stuff** and the **Total Claims-to-Stuff** are equal.

A week goes by, and you and your sister have not taken any more cash out of the bucket. Per the agreement with Dad, it is time to make a $25 payment to him. You take $25 out of the Cash Bucket and give the $25 to Dad.

🖰 Click **$25 Payment to Dad Out of Cash Bucket**

Look at the accounts and observe the effects of the payment to Dad on the system.

You will now use the Ending Balances in each of the accounts to prepare the new Balance Sheet report.

🖰 Click **Prepare the Balance Sheet**

Observe that the Claims-to-Stuff area of the Balance Sheet has expanded to three line items. There are three line items because, in addition to your claim and your sister's claim, Dad now has a claim to some of the Stuff in your organization.

Look at the accounts in your system and the Balance Sheet, and answer the following questions. At this point in time:

▷ How much cash is in the Cash Bucket?

▷ How much total stuff does your organization have?

▷ How much is Dad's claim to the stuff?

▷ How much is your claim to the stuff?

▷ How much is your sister's claim to the stuff?

▷ What is the total claims to stuff?

▷ Is the **Stuff** side equal to the **Claims-to-Stuff** side?

⇨ USING ACCOUNTING TERMINOLOGY

⏏ Click the **Accounting Terms** tab.

You should see **Screen 1 C** in the upper left corner of the screen.

Looking at your screen and the information below, you can see the accounting terminology that is used for an organization's Stuff and Claims-to-Stuff.

Stuff and Claims-to-Stuff Terminology	Accounting Terminology
Stuff ⟶	**Assets**
Claims-to-Stuff of someone who is <u>not</u> an owner of the organization ⟶	**Liabilities**
Claims-to-Stuff of owners of the organization ⟶	**Owners' Equity**

⏏ Click the seven buttons on the left of the screen to record the six transactions previously described and prepare the Balance Sheet.

Observe that the recording is still the same—however; accounting terminology replaces the Stuff and Claims-to-Stuff terminology.

Look at the screen and observe the following points:

▷ Both Liabilities and Owners' Equity are claims accounts. The differences between Liabilities and Owners' Equity are:

- Liabilities are the claims of non-owners.
- Owners' Equity is the claim of owners.

▷ Dad's claim to the organization's assets is now in an account titled Note Payable. The balance in this account still represents Dad's claim to the assets. The account has been given this new name because your organization signed a note with Dad.

▷ Your organization's Balance Sheet contains new headings and titles.

▷ The Balance Sheet shows amounts for:

- Total Assets
- Total Liabilities (non-owner claims)
- Total Owners' Equity (owner claims)
- Total Liabilities and Equity (total claims)

——— The Accounting Equation ———

▷ In the accounting system: **Assets = Liabilities + Owners' Equity**

                                                  Stuff   =   Claims-to-Stuff

▷ On the Balance Sheet: **Assets = Liabilities + Owners' Equity**

⇨ GETTING READY FOR DEBITS AND CREDITS

You need to make one more change to convert your system to a traditional accounting system. You need to convert the accounts to the use of debits and credits.

🖰 Click the **Debits & Credits** tab.

You should see **Screen 1 D** in the upper left corner of the screen.

For now, ignore the Dr (debit) and Cr (credit) titles that are shown in each account. At first, the plus and minus signs will be discussed. After the "**+**" and "**–**" rules are presented, then the debits and credits will be examined.

In the first three screens, if you wanted to increase the amount in one of your accounts, you put a positive number into the account. If you wanted to decrease the amount in the account, you put a negative number into the account. Now you will make a change to each of the accounts that results in the following:

> ▷ Only positive numbers are put into the accounts.
> ▷ If the account is increased or decreased will be determined by whether you put the number on the left side or right side of the account.

Let's focus on the Cash account to see how this change works. Notice that the vertical line in the account has been moved to the middle of the account. The effect of this move is to create a left side and right side in the account.

Increase / Decrease Rules for All Asset Accounts
▷ If the amount is placed on the <u>left side</u> of the account, the balance in the account is <u>increased</u>.
▷ If the amount is placed on the <u>right side</u> of the account, the balance in the account is <u>decreased</u>.

To demonstrate these two rules for asset accounts, re-enter the six transactions you have previously recorded. For now, just focus on the Cash account. Do and observe the following:

🖰 Click **I Put $200 Cash into the Organization**

You want the balance in the Cash account to increase because putting $200 into the bucket increases the physical cash in the Cash Bucket; thus the $200 is entered on the left side of the Cash account. Observe that the balance in the Cash account went from $0 to $200. Also observe that the balance is shown on the left side of the account. This is consistent with the fact that the left side of an asset account is the positive side.

🖰 Click **Sister Puts $150 Cash into the Organization**

Observe where the $150 is put into the Cash account, and the effect it has on the balance in the Cash account.

🖰 Click **Sister Takes $20 Cash out of the Organization**

You want the balance in the Cash account to decrease; thus the $20 is entered on the right side of the Cash account. Observe that the balance in the Cash account is now a positive $330. This balance is the result of two left side entries reduced by one right side entry.

- Click **I Take $15 Cash out of the Organization**

  Observe where the $15 is put into the Cash account and the effect it has on the balance in the Cash account.

- Click **Dad Loans $100 Cash to Organization on a Note**

  Observe where the $100 is put into the Cash account and the effect it has on the balance in the Cash account.

- Click **$25 Payment made to Dad on the Note Payable**

  The payment is made to Dad by taking cash out of the Cash Bucket; thus the Cash account balance needs to be decreased. The $25 is entered into the right side of the Cash account and has the effect of decreasing the Cash account balance by $25.

While these new asset account rules seem simple, it is important that they become very intuitive to you. When you drive a car and need to come to a quick stop, you don't think *take my foot off the gas pedal—put my foot on the brake pedal.* You just press the brake pedal without thinking about it. Through practice, how to make an entry into your accounting system will become just as intuitive as driving a car.

Do the following to practice how to make an entry into an asset account:

- Click **Start Over**

- Click each of the transaction buttons, but before you click the button:

  ▷ Think about the transaction and picture cash flowing into or out of the Cash Bucket.

  ▷ Determine to which side of the Cash account the entry should be made.

  ▷ Determine what will be the effect on the balance in the Cash account.

Now let's develop the increase / decrease rules for the liability accounts and the owners' equity accounts. As previously discussed, all liability accounts and all owners' equity accounts are claims to asset accounts. The liability accounts track the claims of non-owners, and the owners' equity accounts track the claims of owners. Because both types of accounts are claims to asset accounts, they follow exactly the <u>same</u> increase / decrease rules.

Increase / Decrease Rules for All Liability and All Owners' Equity Accounts
▷ If the amount is placed on the <u>right side</u> of the account, the balance in the account is <u>increased</u>.
▷ If the amount is placed on the <u>left side</u> of the account, the balance in the account is <u>decreased</u>.

Let's again enter the six transactions to demonstrate these two rules for liability and owners' equity accounts. This time, just focus on the Liability or Owners' Equity account affected by the transaction. Do and observe the following:

- Click **Start Over**

🖱 Click **I Put $200 Cash into the Organization**

You want the balance in the My Equity account to increase by $200 because putting $200 cash into the organization increases your claim to the assets of the organization; thus the $200 is entered on the right side of the My Equity account. Observe that the balance in the My Equity account goes from $0 to $200. Also, observe that the balance is shown on the right side of the account. This is consistent with the fact that the right side of an owners' equity account is the positive side of the account.

🖱 Click **Sister Puts $150 Cash into the Organization**

Observe where the $150 is put into the Sister's Equity account and the effect it has on the balance in that account.

🖱 Click **Sister Takes $20 Cash out of the Organization**

Because this transaction decreases the assets of the organization by $20, somebody's claim to the assets must decrease by $20. Because your sister took the $20 cash out of the organization, it is her equity account that should decrease; thus the $20 is entered on the left side of the Sister's Equity account. Observe that the balance in the Sister's Equity account is now a positive (right side) $130. This balance is the result of the right side $150 entry reduced by the left side $20 entry.

🖱 Click **I Take $15 Cash out of the Organization**

Observe where the $15 is put into the My Equity account and the effect it has on the balance in that account.

🖱 Click **Dad Loans $100 Cash to Organization on a Note**

Observe that the $100 is put on the right side of the Note Payable account. Also observe that the balance is shown on the right side of the account. This is consistent with the fact that the right side of a liability account is the positive side of the account.

🖱 Click **$25 Payment made to Dad on the Note Payable**

This payment returns $25 cash to Dad and reduces his claim to the organization's assets; thus the Note Payable account balance needs to be decreased. The $25 is entered into the left side of the Note Payable account. This left side entry decreases the Note Payable account balance by $25.

Do the following to practice how to make an entry into a liability or owners' equity account:

🖱 Click *Start Over*

🖱 Click each of the transaction buttons, but before you click the button:

▷ Think about the transaction and picture whose claim account should be affected.

▷ Determine to which side of the liability or owners' equity account the entry should be made.

▷ Determine what will be the effect on the balance in the account.

⇨ DEBITS AND CREDITS

You should still have the Debits & Credits screen of the "01-Stuff & Claims-to-Stuff" workbook on your computer.

🖰 Click **Start Over**

If you understand the concepts presented to this point, then the transition to debits and credits will be easy.

Rather than calling the left side of <u>all</u> accounts the **left** *side*—let's call the left side of <u>all</u> accounts the **Debit** side.

Rather than calling the right side of <u>all</u> accounts the **right** *side*—let's call the right side of <u>all</u> accounts the **Credit** side.

Look at the four accounts in the Debits & Credits screen. Observe that in each account the left side of the account is labeled **Dr** for Debit and the right side of the account is labeled **Cr** for Credit. It makes no difference if the account is an asset account, a liability account, or an owners' equity account:

     ▷ The **left side** is <u>always</u> the **Debit side**.

     ▷ The **right side** is <u>always</u> the **Credit side**.

Asset Accounts – Debits and Credits

In the previous section, <u>Getting Ready for Debits and Credits</u>, the rules for which side of an asset account increases the account balance and which side decreases the account balance were given. Those two rules are repeated below. The only thing that has changed is that the word "Debit" replaces the word "left" and the word "Credit" replaces the word "right."

Increase / Decrease Rules for All Asset Accounts
▷ If the amount is placed on the ~~left~~ <u>Debit side</u> of the account, the balance in the account is <u>increased</u>.
▷ If the amount is placed on the ~~right~~ <u>Credit side</u> of the account, the balance in the account is <u>decreased</u>.

The two items below say the same thing as the two rules above:

     ▷ You **debit** an asset account to **increase** the account balance.

     ▷ You **credit** an asset account to **decrease** the account balance.

Liability Accounts and Owners' Equity Accounts – Debits and Credits

In the previous section, <u>Getting Ready for Debits and Credits</u>, the rules for which side of liability and owners' equity accounts increases the account balance and which side decreases the account balance were given. Those two rules are repeated on the next page. The only thing that has been changed is that the word "Debit" replaces the word "left" and the word "Credit" replaces the word "right."

Increase / Decrease Rules for All Liability and All Owners' Equity Accounts

▷ If the amount is placed on the ~~right~~ <u>Credit side</u> of the account, the balance in the account is <u>increased</u>.

▷ If the amount is placed on the ~~left~~ <u>Debit side</u> of the account, the balance in the account is <u>decreased</u>.

The two items below say the same thing as the two rules above:

▷ You **credit** a liability account or an owners' equity account to **increase** the account balance.

▷ You **debit** a liability account or an owners' equity account to **decrease** the account balance.

Remember that liability accounts and owners' equity accounts are both claims to asset accounts; thus it is logical that the same increase and decrease rules apply to both liability accounts and owners' equity accounts.

Using Debits and Credits to Make Entries

Let's enter those six transactions one last time. This time the entries will be discussed using the debit and credit approach. Do and observe the following:

🖱 Click **Start Over** (if there are any transactions in the accounts)

🖱 Click **I Put $200 Cash into the Organization**
   ▷ A $200 Dr is put into the Cash account. The balance in the Cash account goes from a $0 debit balance to a $200 debit balance.
   ▷ A $200 Cr is put into the My Equity account. The balance in the My Equity account changes from a $0 credit balance to a $200 credit balance.

🖱 Click **Sister Puts $150 Cash into the Organization**
   ▷ Observe the Dr to the Cash account and the Cr to the Sister's Equity account. The Cash account now has a $350 debit balance.

🖱 Click **Sister Takes $20 Cash out of the Organization**
   ▷ A $20 Cr is put into the Cash account. The balance in the Cash account is now a $330 debit. This balance is the result of two debits that total $350 reduced by a $20 credit.
   ▷ A $20 Dr is put into the Sister's Equity account. The Balance in the Sister's Equity account is a $130 credit. This balance is the result of a $150 credit reduced by the $20 debit.

🖱 Click **I Take $15 Cash out of the Organization**
   ▷ Observe the entries in the Cash account and the My Equity account. Notice the balances in those accounts.

- 🖱 Click **Dad Loans $100 Cash to the Organization on a Note**
  - ▷ Observe the Dr to the Cash account and the Cr to the Note Payable account. **The normal balance for a liability account is a credit balance. The normal balance for an owners' equity account also is a credit balance.**

- 🖱 Click **$25 Payment made to Dad on the Note Payable**
  - ▷ A $25 Cr is put into the Cash account. The balance in the Cash account is now a $390 debit. **The normal balance for an asset account is a debit balance.** This $390 debit balance is the result of three debits that total $450 reduced by three credits that total $60.
  - ▷ A $25 Dr is put into the Note Payable account. The balance in the Note Payable account is a $75 credit. This balance is the result of a $100 credit reduced by the $25 debit.

Additional Items to Observe on the "Debits & Credits" Screen

1. A Total Line is drawn across both the Dr and Cr columns to signify that the amount shown below the line is the new balance in the account.

   Let's examine the Cash account to demonstrate the use of a Total Line in an account.

   - ▷ The first amount shown in the Cash account is the beginning balance.
   - ▷ The next six amounts are transaction amounts, which either increase or decrease the Cash account.
   - ▷ A Total Line is then drawn across both the Dr and Cr columns. Below this line is the ending balance in the Cash account.

2. For each transaction you enter into your system, the total dollar amount of the debits equals the total dollar amount of the credits. This is <u>always</u> true for all entries you make into an accounting system.

3. Do not think of debits and credits as being good or bad. Debit is simply the left side of all accounts. Credit is simply the right side of all accounts. Do not confuse the way we use the word credit in accounting to the common use of the word *credit* in such terms as: **credit card** – **getting credit** – **credit your account**. In an accounting system, credit is nothing more than the right side of an account.

4. The Debits & Credits screen contains a new report at the bottom of the screen. This new report is called a Trial Balance. The Trial Balance is used by the accountant to prove that the accounting system is in balance—that the total debits equal the total credits.

   - 🖱 Click **Prepare the Trial Balance**

   The Trial Balance lists each account in the accounting system and the ending balance in each of the accounts. The debit and the credit columns are added-up, and if the totals are the same, then the accounting system is in balance. If the totals of the debit and credit columns are not the same, then the accounting system is out of balance and an error has been made.

   The Trial Balance is a report the accountant prepares for his/her own use before preparing the financial statements. The Trial Balance is generally not distributed outside of the accounting department.

5. The appearance of the Balance Sheet did not change as a result of using debits and credits in your accounting system.

    🖱 Click **Prepare the Balance Sheet**

    The Balance Sheet is one of the four primary financial statements that are prepared for use by individuals outside of the accounting department. Thus, the Balance Sheet does not assume that the reader of the report has any knowledge of debits and credits.

6. The collection of all of the accounts in your accounting system is called the **General Ledger**. Look at your computer screen and observe that your General Ledger currently contains the accounts: Cash, Note Payable, My Equity, and Sister's Equity.

⇨ CHAPTER 1 CONCLUSION

While the hypothetical Cash Bucket you used in this chapter might not be very realistic, it has been a very useful tool for introducing the key concepts that are in any accounting system. Everything that will be presented in the rest of this book and, for that matter, everything you will learn in any future financial accounting course is based on the foundation concepts presented in this chapter.

Use the "01-Stuff & Claims-to-Stuff" workbook to practice and review the concepts presented in this chapter. Start with the first tab in the workbook and work through all four screens.

For each screen do the following:

🖱 Click *Start Over* (if there are any transactions in the accounts)

⇨ For each transaction button on the screen:

▷ Determine what accounts are affected by the transaction.

▷ Determine how the accounts are affected.

🖱 Click each transaction button.

▷ Observe if the effect on the accounts is what you expected.

▷ Notice the effect the transaction has on the account balances.

🖱 Click the report button(s).

▷ Observe what information is shown on the report.

▷ Observe how the Ending Balance in each of the accounts was used to produce the report.

Note: When you are finished working with a Solid Footing workbook, you should quit Excel in the normal way. When you are asked if you want to save the changes, always select to **not** save the changes.

Chapter 1 Homework

Problem 1-1   The Coffee Can Accounting System

In this problem you are the only owner. You are saving for a trip by putting your money into a coffee can. When it is time to take the trip, the coffee can is a little short of the cash you need for your trip. Your Grandma Smith and Grandma Jones loan the coffee can the additional cash you need for the trip. Your Grandmas do not charge any interest on the loans. After you return from your trip, you continue to put money into the coffee can from wages you earn from your summer job. You then pay your grandmas with cash from the coffee can. After paying off the loans there is some cash remaining in the coffee can, which you will use for a future trip. Remove and use the forms on Pg 191 to complete this problem.

Requirement 1

    A. Label the accounting equation above the "T" accounts.

    B. You will utilize the following four accounts: My Equity, Note Payable-Smith, Note Payable-Jones, and Cash. Label the four "T" accounts using these account names.

    C. Put Dr and Cr Labels at the top of each "T" account. Also put "**+**" and "**-**" signs above the Dr and Cr Labels.

    D. Because you are just starting your Coffee Can system, put a beginning balance of zero in each account. Label these amounts as "Beg. Balance"

Requirement 2

    For each of the following transactions make the required entries in the "T" accounts:
        The description of the transaction that you write in the "T" account should be very brief.
        For example the description for transaction **A.** could be "I put in cash." There are no right or wrong descriptions for the transactions.

    A. You put $75 into the Coffee Can.

    B. You put $125 into the Coffee Can.

    C. Grandma Smith loans $300 to the Coffee Can.

    D. Grandma Jones loans $250 to the Coffee Can.

    E. You take all of the money out of the Coffee Can and go on your trip.
        Hint: It is OK for the My Equity account to have a debit balance at this time.

    F. You put $500 into the Coffee Can.

    G. You put $375 into the Coffee Can.

    H. You take cash out of the Can and pay off the total amount owed to Grandma Jones.

    I. You take cash out of the Can and pay off the total amount owed to Grandma Smith.

Requirement 3

    Compute an ending balance for each account. Be sure to place a Total Line in each account and the label "Ending Balance"

Requirement 4

    Prepare a Trial Balance.

Problem 1-2   True / False Questions

If this problem is assigned as a homework turn-in, remove and use the answer sheet on Pg 192 to record and turn-in your answers.

Circle **T**rue or **F**alse for the following questions:

T   F   **1.**   After certain types of transactions it is OK for the accounting system to have more Total Assets (stuff) than Total Liabilities + Owners' Equity (claims-to-stuff).

T   F   **2.**   Asset (stuff) accounts track the dollar amount of a physical asset and who has a claim to that physical asset.

T   F   **3.**   The main purpose of liability accounts is to keep track of non-owners' claims to an organization's assets.

T   F   **4.**   The main purpose of Equity accounts is to keep track of owners' claims to an organization's assets.

T   F   **5.**   In an accounting system, if Total Assets are not equal to Total Claims-to-Assets, then the Balance Sheet report will simply be relabeled as the UnBalance Sheet report.

T   F   **6.**   The Debit side of an asset account is the left side and the Debit side of a liability account is the right side.

T   F   **7.**   The Credit side of all accounts is the right side.

T   F   **8.**   In an accounting system that uses Debits and Credits, only positive numbers will be put into the accounts.

T   F   **9.**   The following is a correct summary of the increase / decrease rules for accounts:
   ▷ In all Asset accounts, if the amount is placed on the left (debit) side of the account, the balance in the account is increased.
   ▷ In all Liability accounts and all in Equity accounts, if the amount is placed on the right (credit) side of the account, the balance in the account is increased.
   ▷ In all Asset accounts, if the amount is placed on the right (credit) side of the account, the balance in the account is decreased.
   ▷ In all Liability accounts and all in Equity accounts, if the amount is placed on the left (debit) side of the account, the balance in the account is decreased.

T   F   **10.**   The Trial Balance lists all of the individual transactions that were entered into the Asset, Liability, and Equity accounts.

Problem 1-3   The Cash Bucket Accounting System

This additional problem is located in the **Word** file named Chapter 01 Additional Problem.doc. To print this additional problem, open the file using your Word application.

Chapter 2

Recording Asset, Liability, and Owners' Equity Transactions
Preparing the Balance Sheet

In the last chapter, you learned the basic concepts that will be used in the rest of this book. In this chapter, you will apply those concepts to a business organization.

⇨ GRAY CO. INTRODUCTION

In Chapters 2 through 6 of this book, you will be doing the accounting for Gray Co., Inc. Gray Co. is legally organized as a corporation. A corporation is a separate legal entity. Owners put money into a corporation, and to show that the owners have an ownership interest, the corporation issues shares of stock to the owners. The assets owned by a corporation belong to the corporation—not the individual owners. As you work through the transactions of Gray Co., the idea of a corporation will become clearer.

Gray Co. is a merchandising company. A merchandising company:

> ▷ Buys items from another company that manufacturers the items.
> ▷ Sells those items to the final consumer.

Costco is an example of a merchandising company. For example, Costco buys TVs from the manufacturer – displays the TVs in its stores – and sells the TVs to you, the final consumer.

In this chapter, you will be using the workbook entitled "02-Gray Co".

> ⇨ Open the workbook **02-Gray Co** in the **Solid Footing 10e** folder
> ⇨ Enable Macros

🖱 Click the **January** tab (if the January tab is not selected).

You should see **Screen 2 A** in the upper left corner of the screen.

This screen looks very similar to the last screen in your Cash Bucket system from Chapter 1. Let's look at what is new on this screen.

On the left side of the screen, there is a new area titled **General Journal**. In your Chapter 1 Cash Bucket system, you made entries directly into the accounts. In a traditional accounting system, the entry to record a transaction in the accounting system is first recorded in the General Journal. An entry in the General Journal is called a **Journal Entry**. The Journal Entry is then moved (copied) to the accounts in the General Ledger. The moving of the entry from the General Journal to the accounts is called **posting the entry**. If the accounting system is a computerized system, then posting is done automatically by the system. If the accounting system is a manual system, then the posting is done manually by the accountant. All entries <u>must</u> first be made in the General Journal and then posted to the accounts in the General Ledger.

Under the Assets heading are two new asset accounts, **Inventory** and **Equipment**. These new accounts will be discussed as entries are made to them. Under the Owners' Equity heading is a new account, **Common Stock**. You will use this new account when you record Gray Co.'s first transaction.

⇨ GRAY CO.'s JANUARY TRANSACTIONS

January 1 – Start Business

On January 1, 2017, Gray Co., Inc. starts into business. A group of investors put a total of $10,000 cash into Gray Co. To evidence their ownership in Gray Co., each investor receives shares of common stock issued by Gray Co.

Let's record this transaction into Gray Co.'s accounting system.

🖱 Click **Issue Stock**

Observe that an entry is made into the General Journal. Let's examine that entry:

▷ The amount of cash in Gray Co. increases as a result of the investors putting cash into the company; thus the $10,000 debit to cash. This transaction increases the Cash account by $10,000, and as a result, the total assets of Gray Co. are increased by $10,000.

▷ Someone's claim to the assets must be increased by $10,000 as a result of the total assets increasing by $10,000. Because the owners put the cash into the company, the owners' claim should be increased. In a corporation, the owners' claim to the assets is kept in the Common Stock account. A claim account is increased by a credit; thus Common Stock is credited for $10,000. The Common Stock account is a claim-to-assets account like the My Equity and Sister's Equity accounts in your Chapter 1 Cash Bucket system.

▷ The third line in your General Journal entry, "Issue common stock," is a brief description of the transaction. There is no specific format for the description, other than the description should be short and concise.

▷ The account being debited (Cash) is listed first, and the account being credited (Common Stock) is listed second. Also, observe that the name of the account being credited is indented. This pattern is the standard format used by accountants, and therefore will always be followed when making entries into the General Journal.

Observe that the entry was first made in the General Journal, and notice that the entry has not been posted to the accounts. Now let's have the General Journal feed the entry into the accounts.

🖱 Click **Post to Ledger** (under Issue Stock)

Look at the Cash account and the Common Stock account, and observe the results of posting your first entry.

January 5 – Bank Loan

On January 5, 2017, the bank loans $8,000 cash to Gray Co. The effect of this transaction is:

▷ An increase in Gray Co.'s cash.

▷ An increase in the bank's claim to Gray Co.'s assets. Because Gray Co. signed a note for the loan, you will track the bank's claim in a liability account called Note Payable.

᠆ᠿ Click **Bank Note**

The debit to cash increases the Cash account and the credit to note payable increases the Note Payable account.

᠆ᠿ Click **Post to Ledger** (under Bank Note)

Look at the Cash account and the Note Payable account to see the effect of posting this entry.

Look at Gray Co.'s accounts and observe the following:

 ▷ All accounts started with zero balances. The reason for this is because Gray Co. is a new company that just started business.

 ▷ The Cash account has an $18,000 debit balance. This balance is the result of two debit entries—one debit for $10,000 and one debit for $8,000.

 ▷ The Note Payable account has an $8,000 credit balance that represents the bank's $8,000 claim to Gray Co.'s assets.

 ▷ The Common Stock account has a $10,000 credit balance that represents the owner's $10,000 claim to Gray Co.'s assets.

January 10 – Purchase Equipment

On January 10, 2017, Gray Co. purchases some equipment (shelving, cash register, etc.) that will be used in its store. The equipment cost $5,000 and is paid for with cash. The effect of this transaction is:

 ▷ An increase in Gray Co.'s equipment (an asset).

 ▷ A decrease in Gray Co.'s cash (an asset).

᠆ᠿ Click **Buy Equipment**

The debit to equipment increases the Equipment account. The credit to cash decreases the Cash account. This entry is correct because Gray Co. now has $5,000 of physical equipment and $5,000 less cash.

᠆ᠿ Click **Post to Ledger**

Look at the Equipment account and the Cash account to see the effect of posting this entry.

The equipment purchase transaction is the first transaction that affected only one side of the accounting equation. This transaction only affected the Asset side. This transaction did not affect the claims-to-assets side (the Liability + Owners Equity side). Prior to the equipment purchase transaction, Gray Co. had $18,000 of total assets—all $18,000 was in the Cash account. After the equipment purchase transaction, Gray Co. still has $18,000 of total assets—$13,000 in the Cash account and $5,000 in the Equipment account.

January 31 – Purchase Inventory

On January 31, 2017, Gray Co. purchases some inventory that will be put on the shelves in its store and hopefully sold to customers. The inventory cost $7,000 and is paid for with cash. The effect of this transaction is:

 ▷ An increase in Gray Co.'s inventory (an asset).

 ▷ A decrease in Gray Co.'s cash (an asset).

🖰 Click **Buy Inventory**

The debit to inventory increases the Inventory account. The credit to cash decreases the Cash account. This entry is correct because Gray Co. now has $7,000 of physical inventory and $7,000 less cash.

🖰 Click **Post to Ledger**

Look at the Inventory account and the Cash account to see the effect of posting this entry. This is another transaction that only affected the Asset side of Gray Co.'s accounting system. Gray Co. exchanged one type of asset, cash, for another type of asset, inventory.

⇨ PREPARING A TRIAL BALANCE

These four transactions were the only transactions Gray Co. had in the month of January. Before preparing a Balance Sheet, you should make sure Gray's accounting system is in balance.

🖰 Click **Prepare the Trial Balance**

Observe that on Gray's Trial Balance, the total of the Debit column equals the total of the Credit column; thus Gray's accounting system is in balance.

⇨ PREPARING A BALANCE SHEET

Gray Co. prepares a Balance Sheet as of January 31, 2017, and gives the report to the investors who hold shares of Gray Co. common stock.

🖰 Click **Prepare the Balance Sheet**

Observe the following about the Balance Sheet:

▷ The heading tells the reader that the information given in the report is for one point in time—that point in time is as of January 31, 2017.

▷ The information shown in the report comes from the Ending Balances in Gray Co.'s General Ledger accounts.

▷ Gray Co. has three types of assets: Cash, Inventory, and Equipment.

▷ The total dollar amount of all of Gray Co.'s assets is $18,000.

▷ The bank has an $8,000 claim to the total assets.

▷ The owners have a $10,000 claim to the total assets.

▷ The assets and the claims to assets are in balance.

⇨ ASSUMPTIONS USED WHEN RECORDING TRANSACTIONS and PREPARING FINANCIAL REPORTS

You apply certain assumptions and principles as you record transactions and prepare financial reports. The following is a brief summary of some of those assumptions and principles.

PERIOD of TIME ASSUMPTION

For Gray Co., the period of time used when preparing financial reports is one month. This period of time is also known as the accounting period. The accounting period can be any length of time, but the periods of time most often used by companies are: a month, a quarter of a year, and a year.

During each accounting period, the accounting system goes through the same sequence of steps. This sequence of steps is called the Accounting Cycle. Gray Co.'s accounting system goes through the steps in the Accounting Cycle once each month because Gray Co.'s accounting period is one month long. The Accounting Cycle will be discussed in more depth in Chapters 4, 5, and 6.

ACCRUAL BASIS

Under the accrual basis of accounting—business transactions are recorded in the accounting period in which they take place even if <u>no</u> cash is received or paid out. For example, if an item is sold to a customer in one accounting period, but the customer will not pay for the item until some future accounting period, the sale transaction is recorded in the accounting period in which the item is sold to the customer. The February 10th sale on Pg 28 is an example of such a transaction.

ENTITY ASSUMPTION

The only transactions that you record in Gray Co.'s accounting system are those transactions related to the entity known as Gray Co., Inc. When Gray Co. receives cash from its new owners, that transaction is recorded in Gray Co.'s accounting system. The reason that transaction is recorded in Gray Co.'s accounting system is because an asset flowed into the Gray Co., Inc. entity.

If the same individuals who are owners of Gray Co. put money into another company, you would not record that transaction in Gray Co.'s accounting system because it did not affect the Gray Co., Inc. entity.

MONETARY UNIT ASSUMPTION

The only transactions that you record in Gray Co.'s accounting system are those transactions that can be stated in terms of dollars (a monetary unit). An example of an event that would <u>not</u> be recorded in Gray Co.'s accounting system would be when Gray Co. hires a new employee. The hiring of a new employee would not be recorded in the accounting system because no transaction took place that can be stated in terms of a monetary unit. When Gray Co. pays wages (dollars) to that new employee you record a transaction in the accounting system because that event can be stated in terms of a monetary unit (wages paid in dollars).

GOING CONCERN ASSUMPTION

As you record transactions and prepare financial reports for Gray Co., you are assuming that Gray Co. will be in business for a long time into the future. This is called the going concern assumption. Recording the $7,000 cost of the inventory purchased as an asset is an example of why the going concern assumption is important. By recording the inventory as an asset, you are making the assumption that Gray Co. will be in business long enough to sell that inventory to customers.

COST PRINCIPLE

When you record a transaction in Gray Co.'s accounting system you record that transaction at cost. For example, when you recorded Gray Co.'s purchase of inventory, you put $7,000 into the Inventory account because that was the cost paid by Gray Co. for the inventory. You did not try to determine if Gray Co. got a good deal or a bad deal on the inventory purchase. You did not try to determine what Gray Co. would ultimately receive when they sold the inventory to a customer. You simply recorded the inventory at the cost paid.

⇨ SUMMARY OF NEW AND REINFORCED CONCEPTS

Let's summarize the newly introduced concepts from this chapter and review the core ideas you learned in Chapter 1. Look at the screen for January and observe the following:

▷ All transactions are first recorded in the General Journal.

▷ Transactions are entered in the General Journal in date order; thus you can easily see the chronological sequence of business transactions by looking at the General Journal.

▷ By looking at an entry in the General Journal, you can see all of the accounts affected by a transaction.

▷ When an entry is made in the General Journal, the total dollar amount of the debits and the total dollar amount of the credits must always be equal.

▷ A transaction is never entered directly into the General Ledger accounts. A transaction is always first entered into the General Journal and then posted to the accounts. Think of the General Journal as the window into the accounting system.

▷ Entries made in the General Journal feed data into the General Ledger accounts, and the resulting balances in the General Ledger accounts are used to produce the financial statements. Thus, the accounts in the General Ledger are the focal point of any accounting system.

▷ The Trial Balance lists the General Ledger accounts and shows each account's ending debit or credit balance. The Trial Balance is prepared by the accountant to determine if the accounting system is in balance. The accounting system is in balance if the total debits equal the total credits. The Trial Balance is an accounting schedule prepared by the accountant for his/her own use. It is not a formal financial statement. The Trial Balance normally is not given to, or used by, anyone outside of the accounting department.

▷ The Balance Sheet is one of the primary financial statements. The Balance Sheet reports the Ending Balances in the Asset, Liability, and Owners' Equity accounts. The Balance Sheet is a point-in-time report.

▷ Gray Co.'s Accounting Period is one month long; thus Gray Co. completes the Accounting Cycle each month.

Chapter 2 Homework

Problem 2-1   OverPriced Jeans, Inc. Starts Business

On January 1, 2017, OverPriced Jeans, Inc. started business. OverPriced Jeans is a merchandising company that specializes in brand name overpriced jeans. OverPriced Jeans (OPJ) purchases jeans from various clothing manufacturers around the world, marks the jeans up about 500%, and then sells the jeans to various specialty stores located in malls. OPJ borrows money from two different banks: Big Bank and Little Bank. OPJ keeps some of its cash in Big Bank and some of its cash in Little Bank. Remove and use the forms on Pgs 193 to 195 to complete this problem.

Requirement 1

   A. OPJ has the following General Ledger accounts: Cash-Big Bank, Cash-Little Bank, Inventory, Equipment, Note Payable-Big Bank, Note Payable-Little Bank, and Common Stock. Label the "T" accounts using these account names.

   B. Because OPJ started business on January 1, 2017, put a beginning balance of zero in each account. Label these amounts as "Beg. Balance"

Requirement 2

   For each of the following transactions make the required entries in the General Journal:

   Jan 01   The new owners of OPJ invest $75,000 of cash in the business. $70,000 of the cash is deposited in Big Bank; the rest is deposited in Little Bank. OPJ issues shares of Common Stock to the new owners.

   Jan 02   Purchase $50,000 of equipment. The cash to pay for the equipment is taken out of Big Bank.

   Jan 05   OPJ gets a $65,000 loan from Big Bank and signs a note for the loan. The cash from the loan is deposited in Big Bank. The bank will not charge OPJ any interest on the loan for the month of January.

   Jan 10   OPJ gets a $60,000 loan from Little Bank and signs a note for the loan. The cash from the loan is deposited in Little Bank. The bank will not charge OPJ any interest on the loan for the month of January.

   Jan 20 $85,000 of jean inventory is purchased for cash. $50,000 of the cash to pay for the purchase is taken out of Big Bank; the remainder of the cash is taken out of Little Bank.

   Jan 25   Purchase $10,000 of equipment. The cash to pay for the equipment is taken out of Little Bank.

Requirement 3

   Post the entries from the General Journal to the General Ledger accounts.

Requirement 4

   Compute an ending balance for each General Ledger account.

Requirement 5

   Prepare a Trial Balance.

Requirement 6

   Prepare OPJ's Balance Sheet as of January 31, 2017.

Problem 2-2   True / False Questions

If this problem is assigned as a homework turn-in, remove and use the answer sheet on Pg 196 to record and turn-in your answers.

Circle **T**rue or **F**alse for the following questions:

T   F   **1.** In a traditional accounting system all entries must be first put in the General Journal.

T   F   **2.** Entries are posted from the General Journal to the Trial Balance.

T   F   **3.** The Note Payable account is increased by a Debit entry.

T   F   **4.** The Equipment account is increased by a Debit entry.

T   F   **5.** All entries must affect both the Asset side and the Liabilities + Equity side of the accounting equation for the accounting system to stay in balance.

T   F   **6.** The Inventory account is decreased by a Credit entry.

T   F   **7.** The Balance Sheet is a point-in-time financial report.

T   F   **8.** A company's Accounting Period must always be one month long.

T   F   **9.** The sequence of steps a company's accounting system goes through each Accounting Period is called the Accounting Cycle.

T   F   **10.** The largest transaction occurring during the Accounting Period is always entered first in the General Journal.

T   F   **11.** For each entry in the General Journal, the total dollar amount of the debits and the total dollar amount of the credits must always be equal.

T   F   **12.** The Balance Sheet is produced from the account balances shown in the General Journal.

T   F   **13.** The Balance Sheet is produced from the account balances shown in the General Ledger.

T   F   **14.** The primary reason the accountant prepares a Trial Balance is to determine if the accounting system is in balance.

Problem 2-3   Gray Co., Inc. Starts Business

This additional problem is located in the **Word** file named Chapter 02 Additional Problem.doc. To print this additional problem, open the file using your Word application.

Chapter 3

Recording Transactions Affecting Retained Earnings

In this chapter, you will continue to use the workbook that you used in the last chapter entitled "02-Gray Co". If this workbook is not open on your computer, do the following:

⇨ Open the workbook **02-Gray Co** in the **Solid Footing 10e** folder

⇨ Enable Macros

✌ Click the **Feb No Rev-Exp** tab

You should see **Screen 3 A** in the upper left corner of the screen. Make certain that you did **not** select the February tab, which is Screen 4 A.

There are three new accounts on this screen.

▷ **Accounts Receivable** under the Assets heading.

▷ **Interest Payable** under the Liabilities heading.

▷ **Retained Earnings** under the Owners' Equity heading.

These new accounts will be discussed when they are used to record Gray Co.'s February transactions.

Observe the beginning balances in the following accounts:

▷ Cash

▷ Inventory

▷ Equipment

▷ Note Payable

▷ Common Stock

These beginning balances, which are as of February 1, 2017, were the ending balances in these accounts as of January 31, 2017.

Notice the three new accounts have beginning balances of zero. This is the case because these new accounts had no transactions entered into them in the month of January.

⇨ GRAY CO.'s FEBRUARY TRANSACTIONS

As discussed in Chapter 2, Gray Co. is a merchandising company. The primary business of a merchandising company is to purchase inventory from suppliers and to sell that inventory to customers at a price higher than the purchase cost of the inventory. In January, Gray Co. purchased some inventory but did not sell any inventory to customers.

February 1 – First Sale of Inventory to a Customer

On February 1, 2017, Gray Co. makes its first sale of inventory to a customer. The inventory is sold to the customer at a selling price of $9,000. The customer pays Gray Co. cash for the purchase. The inventory sold to the customer cost Gray Co. $5,000. Let's see how the transaction will be recorded in the General Journal.

🖱 Click **Make 1st Sale**

Why didn't Gray Co. use Revenue and Expense Accounts?

Depending on your level of accounting knowledge you may be asking, *"Why didn't Gray Co. use revenue and expense accounts when journalizing this transaction?"* If you asked that question, please be patient. In this chapter, all transactions that increase or decrease the owners' claim to assets as a result of the operation of the business will be put directly into the Retained Earnings account. In the next chapter, you will be shown how revenue and expense accounts relate to the Retained Earnings account, and you will be shown how and why revenue and expense accounts are used during the accounting period.

Let's examine the sale entry you just made in the General Journal. The sale entry is easier to understand if you think of the sale of inventory by Gray Co. to the customer as really two transactions. The first transaction is when the customer pays Gray Co. for the item the customer purchases. The second transaction is when Gray Co. gives the item to the customer.

The first two line items of the entry in the General Journal record the customer paying Gray Co. for the purchase and the effect on Gray Co.'s accounts. The customer gives Gray Co. $9,000 cash; thus the $9,000 debit to the Cash account records the increase in Gray Co.'s cash asset. This $9,000 increase in cash causes Gray Co.'s total assets to increase by $9,000; thus somebody's claim to assets must also increase. It is the owners' claim to assets that increases as a result of this part of the sales transaction. The increase in the owners' claim to assets is put into **Retained Earnings**; thus a $9,000 credit to the Retained Earnings account.

Let's discuss the Retained Earnings account in more detail.

▷ Retained Earnings is an owners' claim-to-assets account.

▷ The Retained Earnings account is increased when the operation of the business results in an increase in the owners' claim to assets.

▷ The Retained Earnings account is decreased when the operation of the business results in a decrease in the owners' claim to assets.

As discussed in Chapter 2, the Common Stock account is an owners' claim-to-assets account. As discussed above, the Retained Earnings account is also an owners' claim-to-assets account. The following definitions should help you see why there are two owners' claim-to-assets accounts.

Common Stock Account – Retained Earnings Account

▷ When the owners' claim to the assets results from the owners putting money into the business, the claim is put in the **Common Stock** account.

▷ When the owners' claim to the assets results from the operation of the business, the claim is put in the **Retained Earnings** account.

The last two line items of the entry in the General Journal record Gray Co. giving the inventory item to the customer. When the item is taken out of Gray Co.'s inventory and given to the customer, Gray Co.'s Inventory account must be decreased by the cost of the item. The item given to the customer cost Gray Co. $5,000; thus the $5,000 credit to the Inventory account. This $5,000 decrease in inventory causes Gray Co.'s total assets to decrease by $5,000; thus somebody's claim to assets must also decrease. It is the owners' claim to assets that decreases as a result of this part of the sale transaction. The decrease in the owners' claim to assets is put into Retained Earnings; thus a $5,000 debit to the Retained Earnings account.

Let's now post the sale entry to the General Ledger accounts.

🖱 Click **Post to Ledger**

Observe the following:

▷ The Cash account increases by $9,000, and the Inventory account decreases by $5,000. The net effect on total assets is an increase of $4,000. This increase in total assets is the result of Gray Co. selling an inventory item that cost $5,000 to a customer for $9,000.

▷ The Retained Earnings account increases by $4,000 as a result of the $9,000 credit and the $5,000 debit. This reflects the increase in the owners' claim to assets as a result of <u>the operation of the business</u>. In this case, the operation of the business is selling inventory to a customer.

February 2 – Pay Rent for the Month of February

During January, Gray Co. rented a building from where it will run its business. The landlord, the owner of the building, gave Gray Co. free rent for January. On February 2, the landlord stops by the store to collect the rent for the month of February. Gray Co. pays the landlord $700 cash for the February rent.

🖱 Click **Pay Rent**

Because cash was paid out, the Cash account is credited to reduce the balance in the Cash account.

The rent that Gray Co. paid is only for one month, the month of February. Gray Co. will not prepare its next Balance Sheet until February 28, 2017, by which time all of the rent just paid will have been fully used up. The $700 decrease in cash causes Gray Co.'s total assets to decrease by $700. Because total assets decrease by $700, somebody's claim to assets must also decrease. It is the owners' claim to assets that decrease as a result of paying rent. The decrease in the owners' claim to assets is put in the Retained Earnings account; thus a $700 debit to the Retained Earnings account.

Let's now post the rent payment entry to the General Ledger accounts.

🖱 Click **Post to Ledger**

▷ Notice the Cash account decreases by $700 and no other asset account increases. As a result, total assets decrease by $700.

▷ Notice the Retained Earnings account decreases by $700 as a result of the $700 debit. This reflects the decrease in the owners' claim to assets as a result of <u>the operation of the business</u>. In this case, the operation of the business is paying rent.

February 7 – Pay Wages to Employees

On February 7, Gray Co. pays $1,000 to its workers for their first week of work.

🖱 Click **Pay Wages**

Because cash is paid out, the Cash account is credited to reduce the balance in the Cash account. The $1,000 decrease in cash causes Gray Co.'s total assets to decrease by $1,000; thus somebody's claim to assets must also decrease. It is the owners' claim to assets that decreases as a result of paying wages; thus a $1,000 debit to the Retained Earnings account.

🖱 Click **Post to Ledger**

Observe the effect on the Cash account and the Retained Earnings account.

February 10 – Sale of Inventory to a Customer on Credit

On February 10, 2017, Gray Co. makes a sale of inventory to a customer. The inventory is sold to the customer at a selling price of $4,500. The inventory that is sold to the customer cost Gray Co. $2,000.

This sale is very similar to the February 1 sale—with one important difference. This customer does not currently have the cash to pay for the purchase. The customer indicates that she will be able to pay a portion of the purchase price near the end of February and the remainder of the purchase price around the middle of March. Gray Co. decides to make the sale to the customer based on the customer's promise to pay in the near future. This is called making a sale on credit—or extending credit to a customer. For Gray Co., the customer's promise to pay in the future is an asset because it gives Gray Co. the right to receive cash at some future date. This asset (the right to receive cash in the future) is called an **Accounts Receivable**. Observe that Gray Co. records this sale when it occurs and not when cash is received, which is consistent with the accrual basis of accounting (introduced in Chapter 2 on Pg 21).

Let's see how this sale transaction would be recorded in the General Journal.

🖱 Click **Make 2nd Sale**

The first two line items of the entry in the General Journal record the customer giving Gray Co. her promise to pay in the future for the purchase. The $4,500 debit to the Accounts Receivable account records the increase in Gray Co.'s account receivable asset. This $4,500 increase in the Accounts Receivable account causes Gray Co.'s total assets to increase by $4,500; thus somebody's claim to assets must also increase. It is the owners' claim to assets that increases as a result of this part of the sales transaction; thus a $4,500 credit to the Retained Earnings account.

The last two line items of the entry in the General Journal record Gray Co. giving the inventory item to the customer. This portion of the sale entry is the same as the second portion of the February 1 sale entry. The only difference is that the cost of the inventory sold to this customer is $2,000. The $2,000 credit to inventory reduces the Inventory account, and the $2,000 debit to the Retained Earnings account reduces the owners' claim to assets.

Let's now post the sale entry to the General Ledger accounts.

🖱 Click **Post to Ledger**

Observe the following:

▷ The Accounts Receivable account increases by $4,500, and the Inventory account decreases by $2,000. The net effect on total assets is an increase of $2,500. This increase in total assets is the result of selling an inventory item that cost Gray Co. $2,000 to a customer for $4,500.

▷ The Retained Earnings account increases by $2,500 as a result of the $4,500 credit and the $2,000 debit. This reflects the increase in the owners' claim to assets as a result of the operation of the business. In this case, the operation of the business is selling inventory to a customer.

February 11 – Purchase Inventory

Notice the current balance in Gray Co.'s Inventory account is zero. Gray Co. started the month with $7,000 of inventory. On February 1, Gray Co. sold inventory to a customer with a cost of $5,000, and on February 10, Gray Co. sold the remaining $2,000 of inventory to another customer. Consequently, Gray Co. now needs to purchase additional inventory because the shelves in its store are empty.

On February 11, 2017, Gray Co. purchases additional inventory. The inventory cost $7,500 and is paid for with cash.

🖱 Click **Buy Inventory**

The debit to inventory increases the Inventory account. The credit to cash decreases the Cash account.

🖱 Click **Post to Ledger**

Look at the Inventory account and the Cash account to see the effect of posting this entry.

February 26 – Pay Wages to Employees

On February 26, Gray Co. pays $900 cash to its workers for their work during the last three weeks of February. Before you click the blue Pay Wages button and without looking at the wages payment entry on February 7, see if you know what will be the February 26 wages payment entry.

🖱 Click **Pay Wages**

Did you get the entry correct?

🖱 Click **Post to Ledger**

Notice the effect on the General Ledger accounts.

February 27 – Collect Cash from a Customer

On February 10, Gray Co. made a $4,500 sale to a customer and, at that time, did not receive cash from the customer. Instead of getting cash from the customer, Gray Co. received from the customer a promise to pay cash to Gray Co. sometime in the future. Look at the February 10 entry and observe that the customer's promise to pay was put into the Accounts Receivable account.

On February 27, this customer comes to Gray Co.'s store and pays $1,500 of the $4,500 she owes.

🖱 Click **Collect A/R**

Because the customer gives Gray Co. $1,500 cash, the Cash account is increased, debited, for $1,500. As a result of receiving the $1,500 cash from the customer, Gray Co.'s right to receive cash from the customer in the future is decreased by $1,500; thus the Accounts Receivable account is decreased, credited, for $1,500.

🖱 Click **Post to Ledger**

Look at the Cash account and the Accounts Receivable account to see the effect of posting this entry.

February 28 – Record the Interest Due on the Bank Loan

On January 5, Gray Co. went to the bank and got a loan for $8,000. You recorded that loan in Gray Co.'s accounts when you made January's entries. As an incentive for Gray Co. to make the loan, the bank did not charge Gray Co. any interest for the month of January; thus the total amount of the bank's claim to Gray Co.'s assets at the end of January was $8,000, which was the balance in the Note Payable account.

Interest on the bank loan started on February 1. At the end of February, Gray Co. owes the bank one month of interest. On February 28, Gray Co. calls the bank to find out how much interest it owes. The bank indicates that the interest on the loan for the month of February is $40, but that Gray Co. can wait until the end of March to actually pay February's interest. While no cash is paid to the bank at the end of February for February's interest, Gray Co. does need to make an entry for the interest owed to the bank. Observe that Gray Co. records the interest due on the bank loan even though no cash was paid to the bank—this is consistent with the accrual basis of accounting (introduced in Chapter 2 on Pg 21).

🖱 Click **Adjusting**

The $40 credit to the Interest Payable account records the bank's claim to Gray Co.'s assets that is the result of the interest on the loan. Observe the following:

▷ This entry increases the bank's claim to Gray Co.'s assets.

▷ Total assets do not change as a result of this entry.

As a result, somebody's claim to assets must decrease. It is the owners' claim to assets that must be decreased; thus the $40 debit to the Retained Earnings account.

🖱 Click **Post to Ledger**

Look at the Interest Payable account and the Retained Earnings account to see the effect of posting this entry.

This type of entry is called an adjusting entry. The entry is not the result of a transaction, but rather the result of the passage of time causing interest to be due to the bank. Adjusting entries are important because they "tune-up" the balances in the accounts prior to the preparation of financial statements. Chapters 7 and 8 will be devoted entirely to adjusting entries.

Prepare a Trial Balance

You have recorded all of Gray Co.'s February transactions and adjusted the Interest Payable account for the February interest owed to the bank. Before preparing the Balance Sheet, you need to make sure Gray's accounting system is in balance.

🖱 Click **Prepare the Trial Balance**

Observe that on Gray's Trial Balance, the total of the Debit column equals the total of the Credit column; thus Gray's accounting system is in balance.

Prepare the Balance Sheet

Gray Co.'s February Balance Sheet can now be prepared from the ending balances in the asset, liability, and owners' equity accounts.

🖱 Click **Prepare the Balance Sheet**

Observe the following about the Balance Sheet:

▷ The heading tells the reader that the information given in the report is for one point in time—that point in time is <u>as of February 28, 2017</u>.

▷ Gray Co. has four types of assets: Cash, Accounts Receivable, Inventory, and Equipment.

▷ The total dollar amount of all of Gray Co.'s assets is $21,900.

▷ The bank has a <u>total</u> claim to Gray Co.'s assets of $8,040. This total claim is shown in two line items: Note Payable $8,000 + Interest Payable $40.

▷ The owners have a <u>total</u> claim to Gray Co.'s assets of $13,860. This total claim is shown in two line items: Common Stock $10,000 + Retained Earnings $3,860.

▷ The assets and the claims to assets are in balance.

A Closer Look at the Change in the Retained Earnings Balance

During February, the balance in the Retained Earnings account goes from a beginning balance of zero to an ending balance of $3,860; therefore, you can see that the owners' claim to the assets increased by $3,860 as a result of the operation of the business during the month of February.

By looking at the credit and debit entries in the Retained Earnings account, and then tracing each entry back to the General Journal, you can determine the cause of each increase and the cause of each decrease in the owners' claim to the assets. On the top of the following page is a listing that shows each increase and each decrease in the Retained Earnings account. This listing also shows the cause of each increase or decrease.

Amount of Increase (Decrease)	Cause of the Increase (Decrease) to Retained Earnings
$9,000	**Sale** of inventory to a customer
($5,000)	**Cost of inventory sold** to the customer
($700)	Consumption of assets for **rent**
($1,000)	Consumption of assets for employee **wages**
$4,500	**Sale** of inventory to a customer
($2,000)	**Cost of inventory sold** to the customer
($900)	Consumption of assets for employee **wages**
($40)	Increase in the bank's claim to assets for February's **interest** on the bank loan

If you summarize the causes shown in the table above, the following report is produced.

What Caused the February Change in Retained Earnings

Sale of Inventory to Customers $13,500
Less: Cost of Inventory Sold to Customers .... (7,000)
           Assets Consumed for Rent .... (700)
           Assets Consumed for Wages .... (1,900)
           Increase in the Bank's Claim to Assets for Interest .... (40)
Increase in the Owners' Claim to the Assets during February....... **$ 3,860**

To the owners of Gray Co., the above report is much more informative than simply being told that during the month of February the owners' claim to the assets increased by **$3,860** as a result of the operation of the business.

Because Gray Co. had only eight entries that changed the Retained Earnings account during the month of February, the process of determining the cause of each entry was not a big job. Imagine how difficult the production of the above report would be if Gray Co. had 10,000 entries each month that changed the Retained Earnings account. There must be a better way to capture and summarize the data required for this report. In the next chapter, **Revenue** accounts and **Expense** accounts will be introduced, and they will solve the problem posed by a large volume of entries into the Retained Earnings account.

Chapter 3 Homework

Problem 3-1   OverPriced Jeans, Inc. Rips-Off Its First Customers

This problem will utilize the OverPriced Jeans company (OPJ) from Problem 2-1. Remove and use the forms on Pgs 197 to 200 to complete this problem. Notice that the beginning balances have been put into the General Ledger accounts. These beginning account balances were the January ending account balances from Problem 2-1.

Requirement 1

For each of the following transactions make the required entries in the General Journal:
(See the General Ledger on Pg 199 for the accounts in OPJ's accounting system.)

Feb 01   Take $4,000 cash out of Big Bank to pay for February's warehouse rent.

Feb 04   Sale of inventory to a customer – selling price $62,000 – cost of inventory sold $16,000 – customer paid cash which was deposited in Big Bank.

Feb 07   Take $10,000 cash out of Little Bank to pay employees for wages they have earned.

Feb 15   Sale of inventory to a customer – selling price $88,000 – cost of inventory sold $22,000 – customer will pay in the future.

Feb 18   Sale of inventory to a customer – selling price $110,000 – cost of inventory sold $28,000 – customer pays $40,000 cash which is deposited in Little Bank – customer will pay for the remaining amount of the sale in 30 days.

Feb 22   Purchase additional inventory – pay $17,000 cash out of Big Bank for the inventory.

Feb 27   Take $23,000 cash out of Little Bank to pay employees for wages they have earned.

Feb 28   Adjust the Interest Payable-Big Bank account to record the $600 of interest owed to Big Bank for February – interest will be paid in June.

Feb 28   Adjust the Interest Payable-Little Bank account to record the $450 of interest owed to Little Bank for February – interest will be paid in March.

Requirement 2
Post the entries from the General Journal to the General Ledger accounts.

Requirement 3
Compute an ending balance for each General Ledger account.

Requirement 4
Prepare a Trial Balance.

Requirement 5
Prepare the "What Caused the Change in Retained Earnings" report.

Requirement 6
Prepare OPJ's Balance Sheet as of February 28, 2017.

Problem 3-2   True / False Questions

If this problem is assigned as a homework turn-in, remove and use the answer sheet on Pg 201 to record and turn-in your answers.

Circle **T**rue or **F**alse for the following questions:

T   F   **1.** The Retained Earnings account is an asset account similar to the Inventory account.

T   F   **2.** The Retained Earnings account is similar to the Common Stock account, in that they are both owners' claim-to-assets accounts.

T   F   **3.** The Retained Earnings account tracks the owners' claim to assets that result from the operation of the business.

T   F   **4.** The Retained Earnings account is increased by a debit and decreased by a credit.

T   F   **5.** When a transaction increases a company's Accounts Receivable account the Retained Earnings account must be decreased to keep the accounting system in balance.

T   F   **6.** A transaction which decreases the Retained Earnings account must always decrease an asset account to keep the accounting system in balance.

T   F   **7.** The Common Stock account tracks the owners' claim to assets that result from the operation of the business.

T   F   **8.** The collection of cash from a customer will always result in an increase in the Retained Earnings account.

T   F   **9.** The payment of wages to employees for work they performed during the current accounting period will result in a credit to the cash account.

T   F   **10.** The Common Stock account is decreased by a debit; while the Retained Earnings account is increased by a debit.

Problem 3-3   Gray Co. Makes Its First Sale

This additional problem is located in the **Word** file named <u>Chapter 03 Additional Problem.doc</u>. To print this additional problem, open the file using your Word application.

Chapter 4

Recording Transactions in Revenue and Expense Accounts
Preparing the Income Statement

In this chapter, you will continue to use the workbook that you used in the last chapter entitled "02-Gray Co".   If this workbook is not open on your computer, do the following:

⇨ Open the workbook **02-Gray Co** in the **Solid Footing 10e** folder

⇨ Enable Macros

🖰 Click the **February** tab.

You should see **Screen 4 A** in the upper left corner of the screen.

At the end of the last chapter, after all entries had been recorded for the month, the following report was created to explain what caused the Retained Earnings account to increase by **$3,860** during the month of February.

What Caused the February Change in Retained Earnings

1.	Sale of Inventory to Customers	$13,500
2.	Less: Cost of Inventory Sold to Customers	(7,000)
3.	Assets Consumed for Rent	(700)
4.	Assets Consumed for Wages	(1,900)
5.	Increase in the Bank's Claim to Assets for Interest	(40)
	Increase in the Owners' Claim to the Assets during February....	**$ 3,860**

On your computer screen, five new accounts are under the Owners' Equity heading. These accounts are listed below. Notice how each new account relates to a line item on the above report.

1. Sales Revenue

2. Cost of Goods Sold (an expense account)

3. Rent Expense

4. Wages Expense

5. Interest Expense

⇨ UNDERSTANDING REVENUE AND EXPENSE ACCOUNTS

The following is the relationship of the new revenue and expense accounts to the line items on the *What Caused the February Change in Retained Earnings* report.

Sales Revenue

The first line item on the report is "Sale of Inventory to Customers." The $13,500 amount shown for this line item is calculated by adding together all the credit entries in the Retained Earnings account that relate to customer sales. In this chapter, rather than putting those credit entries into the Retained Earnings account, you will put those credit entries into the Sales Revenue account.

Cost of Goods Sold (an expense account)

The second line item on the report is "Cost of Inventory Sold to Customers."
The negative $7,000 amount shown for this line item is calculated by adding together all the debit entries in the Retained Earnings account that relate to the cost of the inventory items sold to customers. In this chapter, rather than putting those debit entries into the Retained Earnings account, you will put those debit entries into the Cost of Goods Sold account.

Rent Expense

The third line item on the report is "Assets Consumed for Rent." The negative $700 amount shown for this line item is determined by identifying the debit entry in the Retained Earnings account that relates to the payment of rent. In this chapter, rather than putting that debit entry into the Retained Earnings account, you will put that debit entry into the Rent Expense account.

Wages Expense

The fourth line item on the report is "Assets Consumed for Wages." The negative $1,900 amount shown for this line item is calculated by adding together all the debit entries in the Retained Earnings account that relate to the payment of wages to employees. In this chapter, rather than putting those debit entries into the Retained Earnings account, you will put those debit entries into the Wages Expense account.

Interest Expense

The fifth line item on the report is "Increase in Bank's Claim for Interest." The negative $40 amount in this line item is determined by identifying the debit entry in the Retained Earnings account that relates to recording the bank's claim to Gray Co.'s assets for interest on the loan. In this chapter, rather than putting this debit entry into the Retained Earnings account, you will put that debit entry into the Interest Expense account.

At the end of each month, using a process you will learn in the next chapter, the ending balances in the revenue and expense accounts will be emptied into the Retained Earnings account. As a result of this month-end process, the revenue and expense accounts will always start each new month with zero balances. Because the beginning balances in the revenue and expense accounts will always start at zero, the ending balances will always be the total of the transactions entered into the accounts during the month.

As you will see when you complete February using these revenue and expense accounts, the ending balances in these accounts will be the amounts needed to produce the *What Caused the February Change in Retained Earnings* report.

⇨ USING REVENUE AND EXPENSE ACCOUNTS

You will again enter Gray Co.'s February transactions; this time, the entries that went directly into the Retained Earnings account in Chapter 3, will now be placed in the newly introduced revenue and expense accounts.

> Observe in all of the transactions below that when the Retained Earnings account is replaced by one of the new revenue or expense accounts, the Retained Earnings account is shown as follows: ~~Retained Earnings~~.

February 1 – First Sale of Inventory to a Customer

On February 1, 2017, Gray Co. makes its first sale of inventory to a customer. The inventory is sold to the customer at a selling price of $9,000. The customer pays Gray Co. cash for the purchase. The inventory sold to the customer costs Gray Co. $5,000. Let's record the transaction using the Sales Revenue account and the Cost of Goods Sold account.

🖰 Click **Make 1st Sale**

The first two line items of the entry in the General Journal record the customer paying Gray Co. for the purchase. The customer gives Gray Co. $9,000 cash; thus the $9,000 debit to the Cash account records the increase in Gray Co.'s cash asset. This $9,000 increase in cash causes Gray Co.'s total assets to increase by $9,000; thus somebody's claim to assets must also increase. It is the owners' claim to assets that increases as a result of this part of the sale transaction. The increase in the owners' claim to assets is put in the ~~Retained Earnings~~ **Sales Revenue** account; thus a $9,000 credit to the ~~Retained Earnings~~ **Sales Revenue** account.

The last two line items of the entry in the General Journal record Gray Co. giving the inventory item to the customer. When the item is taken out of Gray Co.'s inventory and is given to the customer, Gray Co.'s Inventory account must decrease by the cost of the item. The item given to the customer costs Gray Co. $5,000; thus the $5,000 credit to the Inventory account. This $5,000 decrease in inventory causes Gray Co.'s total assets to decrease by $5,000; thus somebody's claim to assets must also decrease. The owners' claim to assets decreases as a result of this part of the sale transaction. The decrease in the owners' claim to assets is put in the ~~Retained Earnings~~ **Cost of Goods Sold** account; thus a $5,000 debit to the ~~Retained Earnings~~ **Cost of Goods Sold** account.

Let's now post the sale entry to the General Ledger accounts.

🖰 Click **Post to Ledger**

▷ Observe that the Cash account increases by $9,000 and the Inventory account decreases by $5,000. The net effect on total assets is an increase of $4,000.

▷ Observe that the ~~Retained Earnings~~ **Sales Revenue** account is credited for $9,000, and the ~~Retained Earnings~~ **Cost of Goods Sold** account is debited for $5,000. The net effect in these two accounts is a $4,000 increase in the owners' claim to assets as a result of <u>the operation of the business</u>.

February 2 – Pay Rent for the Month of February

On February 2, the landlord stops by the store to collect the rent for the month of February. Gray Co. pays the landlord $700 cash for the February rent.

🖑 Click **Pay Rent**

Because cash was paid out, the Cash account is credited to reduce the balance in the Cash account.

The rent that Gray Co. paid is only for one month, the month of February. Gray Co. will not prepare its next Balance Sheet until February 28, 2017, by which time all of the rent just paid will have been fully used up. The $700 decrease in cash causes Gray Co.'s total assets to decrease by $700. Because total assets decrease by $700, somebody's claim to assets must also decrease. It is the owners' claim to assets that decrease as a result of paying rent. The decrease in the owners' claim to assets is put in the ~~Retained Earnings~~ **Rent Expense** account; thus a $700 debit to the ~~Retained Earnings~~ **Rent Expense** account.

Let's now post the rent payment entry to the General Ledger accounts.

🖑 Click **Post to Ledger**

    ▷ Notice the Cash account decreases by $700 and no other asset account increases. As a result, total assets decrease by $700.

    ▷ Notice the ~~Retained Earnings~~ **Rent Expense** account is debited for $700. This reflects the decrease in the owners' claim to assets as a result of <u>the operation of the business</u>. In this case, the operation of the business is paying rent.

February 7 – Pay Wages to Employees

On February 7, Gray Co. pays $1,000 to its workers for their first week of work.

🖑 Click **Pay Wages**

Because cash is paid out, the Cash account is credited to reduce the balance in the Cash account. The $1,000 decrease in cash causes Gray Co.'s total assets to decrease by $1,000; thus somebody's claim to assets must also decrease. It is the owners' claim to assets that decreases as a result of paying wages; thus a $1,000 debit to the ~~Retained Earnings~~ **Wages Expense** account.

🖑 Click **Post to Ledger**

Observe the effect on the Cash account and the ~~Retained Earnings~~ **Wages Expense** account.

February 10 – Sale of Inventory to a Customer on Credit

On February 10, 2017, Gray Co. makes a sale of inventory to a customer. The inventory is sold to the customer at a selling price of $4,500. The inventory that is sold to the customer cost Gray Co. $2,000.

This sale is very similar to the February 1 sale—with one important difference. This customer does not currently have the cash to pay for the purchase. The customer indicates that she will be able to pay a portion of the purchase price near the end of February and the remainder of the purchase price around the middle of March. Gray Co. decides to make the sale to the customer based on the customer's promise to pay in the near future. This is called making a sale on credit—or extending credit to a customer. For Gray Co., the customer's promise to pay in the future is an asset because it gives Gray Co. the right to receive cash at some future date. This asset (the right to receive cash in the future) is called an **Accounts Receivable**.

Let's see how this sale transaction would be recorded in the General Journal.

🖰 Click **Make 2nd Sale**

The first two line items of the entry in the General Journal record the customer giving Gray Co. her promise to pay in the future for the purchase. The $4,500 debit to the Accounts Receivable account records the increase in Gray Co.'s account receivable asset. This $4,500 increase in the Accounts Receivable account causes Gray Co.'s total assets to increase by $4,500; thus somebody's claim to assets must also increase. It is the owners' claim to assets that increases as a result of this part of the sale transaction; thus a $4,500 credit to the ~~Retained Earnings~~ **Sales Revenue** account.

The last two line items of the entry in the General Journal record Gray Co. giving the inventory item to the customer. The $2,000 credit to inventory reduces the Inventory account, and the $2,000 debit to the ~~Retained Earnings~~ **Cost of Goods Sold** account reduces the owners' claim to assets.

Let's now post this sale entry to the General Ledger accounts.

🖰 Click **Post to Ledger**

  ▷ Observe that the Accounts Receivable account increases by $4,500 and the Inventory account decreases by $2,000. The net effect on total assets is an increase of $2,500. This increase in total assets is the result of selling an inventory item that cost Gray Co. $2,000 to a customer for $4,500.

  ▷ Observe that the ~~Retained Earnings~~ **Sales Revenue** account is credited for $4,500 and the ~~Retained Earnings~~ **Cost of Goods Sold** account is debited for $2,000. The net effect in these two accounts is a $2,500 increase in the owners' claim to assets as a result of the operation of the business.

February 11 – Purchase Inventory

On February 11, 2017, Gray Co. purchases additional inventory. The inventory costs $7,500 and is paid for with cash.

🖰 Click **Buy Inventory**

The debit to inventory increases the Inventory account. The credit to cash decreases the Cash account.

🖰 Click **Post to Ledger**

Look at the Inventory account and the Cash account to see the effect of posting this entry. This transaction does <u>not</u> affect any of the newly introduced revenue and expense accounts.

February 26 – Pay Wages to Employees

On February 26, Gray Co. pays $900 cash to its workers for their work during the last three weeks of February. Before you click the blue Pay Wages button and without looking at the wages payment entry on February 7, see if you know what the February 26 wages payment entry will be.

🖱 Click **Pay Wages**

Did you get the entry correct?

🖱 Click **Post to Ledger**

Observe the effect on the General Ledger accounts.

February 27 – Collect Cash from a Customer

On February 10, Gray Co. made a $4,500 sale to a customer and, at that time, did not receive cash from the customer. Instead of getting cash from the customer, Gray Co. received from the customer a promise to pay cash to Gray Co. sometime in the future. Look at the February 10 entry and observe that the customer's promise to pay was put into the Accounts Receivable account.

On February 27, this customer comes to Gray Co.'s store and pays $1,500 of the $4,500 she owes.

🖱 Click **Collect A/R**

Because the customer gives Gray Co. $1,500 cash, the Cash account is increased, debited, for $1,500. As a result of receiving the $1,500 cash from the customer, Gray Co.'s right to receive cash from the customer in the future has been decreased by $1,500; thus the Accounts Receivable account is decreased, credited, for $1,500.

🖱 Click **Post to Ledger**

Look at the Cash account and the Accounts Receivable account to see the effect of posting this entry. Observe that this transaction does not affect any of the newly introduced revenue and expense accounts.

February 28 – Record the Interest Due on the Bank Loan

On January 5, Gray Co. went to the bank and got a loan for $8,000. You recorded that loan in Gray Co.'s accounts when you made January's entries. As an incentive for Gray Co. to make the loan, the bank did not charge Gray Co. any interest for the month of January; thus the total amount of the bank's claim to Gray Co.'s assets at the end of January was $8,000, which was the balance in the Note Payable account.

Interest on the bank loan started on February 1. At the end of February, Gray Co. owes the bank one month of interest. On February 28, Gray Co. calls the bank to find out how much interest it owes. The bank indicates that the interest on the loan for the month of February is $40, but that Gray Co. can wait until the end of March to actually pay February's interest. While no cash is paid to the bank at the end of February for February's interest, Gray Co. does need to make an entry for the interest owed to the bank. Observe that Gray Co. records the interest due on the bank loan even though no cash was paid to the bank—this is consistent with the accrual basis of accounting (introduced in Chapter 2 on Pg 21).

🖑 Click **Adjusting**

The $40 credit to the Interest Payable account records the bank's claim to Gray Co.'s assets that is the result of the interest on the loan. Observe the following:

> ▷ This entry increases the bank's claim to Gray Co.'s assets.

> ▷ Total assets do not change as a result of this entry.

As a result, somebody's claim to assets must decrease. It is the owners' claim to assets that must be decreased; thus the $40 debit to the ~~Retained Earnings~~ **Interest Expense** account.

🖑 Click **Post to Ledger**

Look at the Interest Payable account and the ~~Retained Earnings~~ **Interest Expense** account to see the effect of posting this entry.

This type of entry is called an <u>adjusting</u> entry. The entry is not the result of a transaction, but rather the result of the passage of time causing interest to be due to the bank. Adjusting entries are important because they "tune-up" the balances in the accounts prior to the preparation of financial statements. Chapters 7 and 8 will be devoted entirely to adjusting entries.

Prepare a Pre-Closing Trial Balance

You have recorded all of Gray Co.'s February transactions and adjusted the Interest Payable account for the February interest owed to the bank. Before preparing the Financial Statements, you need to make sure Gray's accounting system is in balance.

🖑 Click **Prepare Pre-Closing Trial Balance**

Notice that the Trial Balance being prepared is now called the <u>Pre-Closing</u> Trial Balance. Pre-Closing has been added to the name to designate that the Trial Balance is being prepared before the closing of the revenue and expense accounts. In the next chapter, you will learn how to close the revenue and expense accounts. You will then prepare a second Trial Balance called the <u>Post-Closing</u> Trial Balance.

Observe that <u>all</u> of the accounts in Gray's General Ledger, including the new revenue and expense accounts, are included in the Pre-Closing Trial Balance. Also observe that the amount shown on the Pre-Closing Trial Balance for Retained Earnings is the Current Balance, which is equal to the Beginning Balance. The Current Balance is equal to the Beginning Balance because there were no entries made to the Retained Earnings account during the month. There were no entries made to Retained Earnings because you are now using revenue and expense accounts.

⇨ PREPARING THE INCOME STATEMENT

Turn back to the *What Caused the February Change in Retained Earnings* report on Pg 35. Notice that the ending balances in the newly introduced revenue and expense accounts are the same amounts needed to produce the report. You can see that the revenue and expense accounts make it easy for Gray Co. to prepare its monthly *What Caused the Change in Retained Earnings* report. While the report title, *What Caused the Change in Retained Earnings,* describes the purpose of the report, it is not the title companies use for this financial report. **Income Statement** is the title companies use for this financial statement.

Let's now use the ending balances in the revenue and expense accounts to prepare Gray Co.'s Income Statement.

🖰 Click **Prepare the Income Statement**

Observe the following about Gray Co.'s February Income Statement:

▷ The heading tells the reader that the information given in the report is for a period of time— that period of time is <u>for the Period Feb. 1 to Feb. 28, 2017</u>.

▷ <u>All</u> of the ending balances in the revenue and expense accounts are used to prepare the report.

▷ <u>All</u> of the data needed to produce the report are contained in the revenue and expense accounts ending balances.

▷ The Gross Profit line item does not come directly from a revenue account or expense account ending balance. Gross Profit is a calculated sub-total:
> **Gross Profit** = **Sales Revenue** less **Cost of Goods Sold**.

▷ The Total Expenses line item does not come directly from a revenue account or expense account ending balance. Total Expenses is a calculated sub-total:
> **Total Expenses** = **Wages Expense** + **Rent Expense** + **Interest Expense**.

▷ The Net Income line item does not come directly from a revenue account or expense account ending balance. Net Income is a calculated amount:
> **Net Income** = **Gross Profit** less **Total Expenses**.

▷ The Net Income amount shows that during the month of February the owners' claim to the assets increased by $3,860 as a result of <u>the operation of the business</u>.

Prepare the Balance Sheet

As you learned in previous chapters, the Balance Sheet is prepared from the <u>ending balances</u> in the asset, liability, and owners' equity accounts. Look at Gray Co.'s accounts and observe that:

▷ All of the asset accounts contain ending balances.

▷ All of the liability accounts contain ending balances.

▷ The Common Stock account contains an ending balance.

▷ The Retained Earnings account only contains a <u>current balance</u>, which is equal to the beginning balance.

The reason the Retained Earnings account does not have an ending balance is because all of February's entries, which could have been put into the Retained Earnings account, were put into the newly introduced revenue and expense accounts. However, the ending balance in Retained Earnings can be easily calculated.

🖰 Click **Calculate Feb. 28 Retained Earnings**

Observe that the Feb. 28 Retained Earnings ending balance of $3,860 is calculated by adding February's Net Income to the Retained Earnings current balance. This calculation results in the correct ending balance for Retained Earnings because Net Income is calculated using the ending balances from <u>all</u> of the revenue and expense accounts.

Now that you have determined the ending balance for Retained Earnings, you are ready to prepare Gray Co.'s Balance Sheet.

🖰 Click **Prepare the Balance Sheet**

Notice that the amounts on the February Balance Sheet are exactly the same amounts that were shown on the February Balance Sheet in Chapter 3. The only change in this chapter is that you had to calculate the ending balance for Retained Earnings. You had to calculate the Retained Earnings ending balance; because all of February's entries, which you made to the Retained Earnings account in Chapter 3, were put in the newly introduced revenue and expense accounts.

⇨ **Additional Observations and Summary of New Concepts**

▷ Two new types of accounts were introduced in this chapter—revenue accounts and expense accounts.

▷ Revenue accounts and expense accounts are used to make the preparation of the Income Statement easier.

▷ The entries that are put into the revenue accounts and the expense accounts are entries that could be put directly into the Retained Earnings account if it was not necessary to prepare an Income Statement.

▷ The credit entries that could have been put directly into the Retained Earnings account are put into revenue accounts; thus revenue accounts track increases in the owners' claim to assets as a result of <u>the operation of the business</u>.

▷ The debit entries that could have been put directly into the Retained Earnings account are put into expense accounts; thus expense accounts track decreases in the owners' claim to assets as a result of <u>the operation of the business</u>.

▷ When a credit is placed into a revenue account, the revenue account is said to be increased. At the end of the accounting cycle the credit balance in a revenue account will be moved to the Retained Earnings account; thus a credit to a revenue account will ultimately increase Retained Earnings.

▷ When a debit is placed into an expense account, the expense account is said to be increased. At the end of the accounting cycle the debit balance in an expense account will be moved to the Retained Earnings account; thus a debit to an expense account will ultimately decrease Retained Earnings.

▷ The Income Statement is prepared using <u>all</u> of the ending balances from the revenue and expense accounts; thus Net Income, as shown on the Income Statement, is:

The sum of <u>all</u> of the revenue accounts

less

The sum of <u>all</u> of the expense accounts.

▷ If the sum of all of the revenue accounts less the sum of all of the expense accounts results in a negative number, the bottom number on the Income Statement will be negative and will be titled <u>Net Loss</u> rather than Net Income. A Net Loss indicates that the owners' claim to assets has been decreased as a result of <u>the operation of the business</u>.

In the next chapter, you will complete Gray Co.'s Accounting Cycle by moving the balances in the revenue and expense accounts to the Retained Earnings account.

Chapter 4 Homework

Problem 4-1   OverPriced Jeans, Inc. Revenue and Expense Accounts

This problem is for the month of February for OverPriced Jeans (OPJ). You will be using the new Revenue and Expense accounts that you learned about in this chapter to record OPJ's February transactions. Remove and use the forms on Pgs 203 to 206 to complete this problem. Notice that the beginning balances have been put into the General Ledger accounts. These beginning account balances were the January ending account balances from Problem 2-1.

Requirement 1
(*If you previously completed Problem 3-1, these are the same February transactions utilized in that problem.*)

February's transactions and adjusting entry information are shown below. For each item make the required entry in the General Journal.
(See the General Ledger on Pg 205 for the accounts in OPJ's accounting system.)

Feb 01   Take $4,000 cash out of Big Bank to pay for February's warehouse rent.

Feb 04   Sale of inventory to a customer – selling price $62,000 – cost of inventory sold $16,000 – customer paid cash which was deposited in Big Bank.

Feb 07   Take $10,000 cash out of Little Bank to pay employees for wages they have earned.

Feb 15   Sale of inventory to a customer – selling price $88,000 – cost of inventory sold $22,000 – customer will pay in the future.

Feb 18   Sale of inventory to a customer – selling price $110,000 – cost of inventory sold $28,000 – customer pays $40,000 cash which is deposited in Little Bank – customer will pay for the remaining amount of the sale in 30 days.

Feb 22   Purchase additional inventory – pay $17,000 cash out of Big Bank for the inventory.

Feb 27   Take $23,000 cash out of Little Bank to pay employees for wages they have earned.

Feb 28   Adjust the Interest Payable-Big Bank account to record the $600 of interest owed to Big Bank for February – interest will be paid in June.

Feb 28   Adjust the Interest Payable-Little Bank account to record the $450 of interest owed to Little Bank for February – interest will be paid in March.

Requirement 2
Post the entries from the General Journal to the General Ledger accounts.

Requirement 3
Except for Retained Earnings, compute an ending balance for each General Ledger account. For Retained Earnings, place the current balance in the account.

Requirement 4
Prepare a Pre-Closing Trial Balance.

Requirement 5
Prepare an Income Statement for the period February 1 to February 28, 2017.

Requirement 6

Calculate the Retained Earnings balance needed for the February 28 Balance Sheet.

Requirement 7

Prepare OPJ's Balance Sheet as of February 28, 2017.

Problem 4-2   True / False Questions

If this problem is assigned as a homework turn-in, remove and use the answer sheet on Pg 207 to record and turn-in your answers.

Circle True or False for the following questions:

T   F   **1.**   Revenue accounts will always start each new accounting period with a beginning balance of zero.

T   F   **2.**   Expense accounts will always start each new accounting period with a beginning balance equal to all of the debit entries that were made into the expense account during the previous accounting period.

T   F   **3.**   Credit amounts entered into the Sales Revenue account increase the account balance and will ultimately increase Retained Earnings.

T   F   **4.**   Debit amounts entered into an expense account increase the expense account and will ultimately decrease Retained Earnings.

T   F   **5.**   The Cost of Goods Sold account is an asset account similar to the Inventory account.

T   F   **6.**   Some of the revenue and expense accounts are used to prepare the Income Statement, and some of the revenue and expense accounts appear on the Balance Sheet.

T   F   **7.**   If there was no need to prepare the Income Statement, then there would be no need to have revenue and expense accounts.

T   F   **8.**   A company will have a Net Loss when the sum of all the expense accounts is greater than the sum of all the revenue accounts.

T   F   **9.**   When a sale is made to a customer on credit, there is no entry made to the Sales Revenue account because no cash has been received.

T   F   **10.** The Retained Earnings amount needed for the Balance Sheet can be calculated as follows: the current balance in the Retained Earnings account, plus the sum of the revenue account balances, less the sum of the expense account balances.

Problem 4-3   Gray Co. Revenue and Expense Accounts

This additional problem is located in the **Word** file named Chapter 04 Additional Problem.doc. To print this additional problem, open the file using your Word application.

NOTES

Chapter 5
Closing Revenue and Expense Accounts
Preparing a Post-Closing Trial Balance

In this chapter, you will continue to use the workbook that you used in the last chapter entitled "02-Gray Co".   If this workbook is not open on your computer, do the following:

⇨ Open the workbook **02-Gray Co** in the **Solid Footing 10e** folder

⇨ Enable Macros

🖰 Click the **Feb Close** tab.

You should see **Screen 5 A** in the upper left corner of the screen.

In Chapter 4, you took Gray Co. from its first sale to a customer to the preparation of the month-end Balance Sheet. In this chapter, you will complete Gray Co.'s Accounting Cycle for the month of February.

⇨ CLOSING GRAY CO.'s REVENUE AND EXPENSE ACCOUNTS

As discussed in Chapters 3 and 4, entries are made to the revenue and expense accounts to enable a company to easily prepare an Income Statement. The current ending balances in the revenue and expense accounts have been used to produce Gray Co.'s February Income Statement. To prepare for March's transactions, the ending balances in the revenue and expense accounts need to be moved to the Retained Earnings account. As a result of this move, the balances in the revenue and expense accounts will be reset to zero. This process is called the closing process, and the entries made during this process are called closing entries.

Look at the Feb Close screen on your computer. All of the General Ledger accounts and the Pre-Closing Trial Balance are exactly as they were on the February screen after you completed Chapter 4.

The first closing entry will close the Sales Revenue account. The process used to close this account is listed below.

Closing Process for the Sales Revenue Account

1. Look at the Sales Revenue account in the General Ledger to determine its ending credit balance.

2. In the General Journal, debit the Sales Revenue account for an amount equal to its ending balance.

3. In the General Journal, credit the Retained Earnings account for the amount needed to balance the General Journal entry.

4. Post the entry to the General Ledger accounts.

🖰 Click **Close Revenues**

Notice the entry in the General Journal is the entry that results from Steps 2 and 3 in the closing process listed on the previous page.

🖰 Click **Post to Ledger**

Observe the following:

▷ The debit to the Sales Revenue account causes the balance to go to zero. This balance is labeled After Close Bal because it is the balance after the closing entry has been posted.

▷ The effect of this closing entry is to transfer the credit balance that was in the Sales Revenue account into the Retained Earnings account.

The second closing entry will close all of the expense accounts. The process used to close the expense accounts is listed below.

Closing Process for the Expense Accounts
1. Look at the expense accounts in the General Ledger to determine the ending debit balance in each of the accounts.
2. In the General Journal, <u>credit</u> each of the expense accounts for an amount equal to its ending balance.
3. In the General Journal, <u>debit</u> the Retained Earnings account for the amount needed to balance the General Journal entry. This is an amount equal to the sum of all the credit entries made to the expense accounts.
4. Post the entry to the General Ledger accounts.

🖰 Click **Close Expenses**

Notice that the entry in the General Journal is the entry that results from Steps 2 and 3 above.

🖰 Click **Post to Ledger**

Observe the following:

▷ The credit to each of the expense accounts causes each expense account's balance to go to zero. These balances are labeled After Close Bal because they are the balances after the closing entry has been posted.

▷ The effect of this closing entry is to transfer the sum of all the expense account balances into the Retained Earnings account.

▷ All of the expense accounts were closed in one entry. You could have made a closing entry for each of the expense accounts, but normally all of the expense accounts are closed in one entry because it is more efficient.

⇨ PREPARING THE POST-CLOSING TRIAL BALANCE

Now that all of the revenue and expense accounts have been closed into the Retained Earnings account, you can prepare a Post-Closing Trial Balance.

🖱 Click **Prepare Post-Closing Trial Balance**

This Trial Balance is called a <u>Post-Closing</u> Trial Balance because it shows all of the General Ledger account balances after the closing entries have been made. The purpose of the Post-Closing Trial Balance is to determine that the General Ledger is in balance and ready to start a new Accounting Cycle.

Notice the following:

▷ The asset account balances, the liability account balances, and the Common Stock account balance are the same on both the Pre-Closing Trial Balance and the Post-Closing Trial Balance. None of these accounts will ever be affected by closing entries.

▷ The Retained Earnings account was increased as a result of the closing entries. This will be true when the total of the revenue account(s) is greater than the total of the expense accounts.

▷ All of the revenue and expense accounts have zero balances on the Post-Closing Trial Balance.

▷ The **$3,860** Ending Balance in the Retained Earnings account is the same amount that was calculated for the Balance Sheet on the February screen.

Because the revenue and expense accounts are closed at the end of every accounting period, they are often referred to as <u>temporary accounts</u>. Because the asset accounts, liability accounts, Common Stock account, and Retained Earnings account are never closed, they are called <u>permanent accounts</u>.

Now that the closing entries have been made and the Post-Closing Trial Balance prepared, Gray Co.'s February Accounting Cycle is complete.

On the next page is a listing of all of the steps in the Accounting Cycle. You have completed all of these steps by working through the February screen and the Feb Close screen.

Steps in the Accounting Cycle

Step 1   For each business transaction that occurs during the accounting period, determine the effect of the transaction on the General Ledger accounts.

Step 2   Make an entry in the General Journal for each transaction and post the entry to the General Ledger accounts.

Step 3   At the end of the accounting period, before preparing the financial statements, determine if any of the General Ledger account balances need to be adjusted. Enter any required adjusting entries into the General Journal and post the adjusting entries to the General Ledger accounts.

Step 4   Prepare a Pre-Closing Trial Balance to determine that the accounts in the General Ledger are in balance.

Step 5   Prepare an Income Statement from the ending balances in the General Ledger revenue and expense accounts.

Step 6   Calculate the ending balance of the Retained Earnings account that is needed for the preparation of the Balance Sheet.

Step 7   Prepare the Balance Sheet from the ending balances in the General Ledger asset accounts, liability accounts, Common Stock account, and the calculated ending balance for the Retained Earnings account.

Step 8   Prepare and enter the revenue and expense closing entries into the General Journal, and post the closing entries to the General Ledger accounts.

Step 9   Prepare a Post-Closing Trial Balance to determine that the accounts in the General Ledger are in balance and ready to start a new Accounting Cycle.

In the next chapter, you will take Gray Co. through its entire Accounting Cycle for the March accounting period.

Chapter 5 Homework

Problem 5-1   OverPriced Jeans, Inc. Closing Entries for February

In this problem you will be closing OPJ's Revenue and Expense accounts for the month of February 2017. Remove and use the forms on Pgs 209 to 211 to complete this problem.

Requirement 1

Based on the General Ledger account balances given on Pg 211 prepare OPJ's February closing entries. Place the closing entries in the General Journal on Pg 209.

Requirement 2

Post the closing entries to the General Ledger accounts.

Requirement 3

Compute an Ending Balance for the Retained Earnings account and put that balance in the account.

Compute the After Close Balances for the Revenue and Expense accounts and put those balances in the accounts.

Requirement 4

Prepare a Post-Closing Trial Balance.

Requirement 5

If you have your solution to Problem **4-1** available, compare:

▷   The Ending Balance in OPJ's Retained Earnings account on Pg 211, to

▷   The Retained Earnings amount in OPJ's Balance Sheet on Pg 206 of Problem **4-1**.

Problem 5-2   True / False Questions

If this problem is assigned as a homework turn-in, remove and use the answer sheet on Pg 212 to record and turn-in your answers.

Circle **T**rue or **F**alse for the following questions:

T   F   **1.** As a result of the closing process, all General Ledger accounts will be reset to zero.

T   F   **2.** The After Close Balance for both revenue and expense accounts should always be a zero balance.

T   F   **3.** During the closing process for expense accounts, the Retained Earnings account is debited, which decreases Retained Earnings.

T   F   **4.** During the closing process for revenue accounts, the Retained Earnings account is credited, which increases Retained Earnings.

T   F   **5.** If the sum of the Ending Balance(s) in the revenue account(s) is greater than the sum of the Ending Balances in the expense accounts, then Retained Earnings will increase as a result of the closing entries.

T   F   **6.** The temporary accounts should always have a zero balance on the Post-Closing Trial Balance.

T   F   **7.** The Post-Closing Trial Balance should be prepared after the Income Statement is prepared but before the Balance Sheet is prepared.

T   F   **8.** Adjusting entries should be entered into the General Journal and posted to the General Ledger accounts after preparing a Pre-Closing Trial Balance.

T   F   **9.** The asset account balances, liability account balances, and the Common Stock account balance will always be the same on both the Pre-Closing Trial Balance and the Post-Closing Trial Balance.

T   F   **10.** The Retained Earnings amount on the Post-Closing Trial Balance will always be greater than the Retained Earnings amount on the Pre-Closing Trial Balance.

Problem 5-3   Gray Co. Closing Entries for February

This additional problem is located in the **Word** file named <u>Chapter 05 Additional Problem.doc</u>. To print this additional problem, open the file using your Word application.

Chapter 6
The Accounting Cycle

In this chapter, you will continue to use the workbook that you used in the last chapter entitled "02-Gray Co".   If this workbook is not open on your computer, do the following:

⇨ Open the workbook **02-Gray Co** in the **Solid Footing 10e** folder

⇨ Enable Macros

🖰 Click the **March** tab.

You should see **Screen 6 A** in the upper left corner of the screen.

There is one new account on this screen, **Accounts Payable**. The Accounts Payable account will be used when Gray Co. purchases inventory from its vendors, but does not pay cash to the vendors at the time of the purchases. There will be more discussion of this new account later in this chapter.

Before you begin the month of March, observe the following on the March screen:

▷ The beginning balances in the permanent accounts (assets, liabilities, Common Stock, and Retained Earnings) are the same as the February ending balances that were shown on the Feb Close screen.

▷ The beginning balance in the new account, Accounts Payable, is zero.

▷ The beginning balances in the temporary accounts (revenue and expenses) are all zero. These temporary accounts have zero balances because they were all closed into the Retained Earnings account at the end of Gray Co.'s February Accounting Cycle.

⇨ SELF-TEST OF ALL CONCEPTS LEARNED TO THIS POINT

This chapter provides an opportunity for you to review all of the concepts learned to this point and to perform a self-test of your level of knowledge. As you work through this chapter, be sure to fill-in all of the journal entries, trial balances, and financial statements before clicking the related button in the software.

After you click the button in the software, check your answer against the answer shown on the computer screen. Highlight in your book any errors you make and then return to those highlighted areas after you complete this chapter. Before moving on to Chapter 7, be sure you have mastered those highlighted concepts.

⇨ COMPLETING THE NINE STEPS IN THE ACCOUNTING CYCLE

The nine steps in the Accounting Cycle were summarized at the end of the last chapter. In this chapter, you will take Gray Co. through its March Accounting Cycle, by completing each of the nine Accounting Cycle steps.

Step 1	For each business transaction that occurs during the accounting period, determine the effect of the transaction on the General Ledger accounts.
Step 2	Make an entry in the General Journal for each transaction and post the entry to the General Ledger accounts.

You will complete these first two steps in the Accounting Cycle by recording Gray Co.'s March transactions.

⇨ GRAY CO.'s MARCH TRANSACTIONS

To test your knowledge, you should do the following for each of Gray Co.'s March transactions:

 ▷ Read the description of the transaction.

 ▷ Record the entry for the transaction on the General Journal form presented just below the description of the transaction.

 ▷ Click the button for the transaction and compare your journal entry to the entry in the General Journal shown on the screen.

March 1 – Pay Rent for the Month of March

On March 1, the landlord stops by the store to collect the rent for the month of March. Gray Co. pays the landlord $700 cash for the March rent.

Record below the rent payment entry.

General Journal			
Date	**Account**	**Debit**	**Credit**
Mar 01			
	Paid Rent for March		

✍ Click **Pay Rent**

✓ Compare your journal entry to the General Journal entry on the screen.

✍ Click **Post to Ledger**

March 10 – Sale of Inventory to a Customer for Cash and on Account

On March 10, 2017, Gray Co. makes a sale of inventory to a customer. The inventory is sold to the customer at a selling price of $16,000. The inventory sold to the customer costs Gray Co. $7,000. The customer pays Gray Co. $5,000 cash at the time of the sale and promises to pay the remaining $11,000 in the near future.

Record below the sale entry.

General Journal			
Date	Account	Debit	Credit
Mar 10			
	Sale for cash and on account		

🖰 Click **Make a Sale**

✓ Compare your journal entry to the General Journal entry on the screen.

Observe that in this sale transaction, Gray Co. receives two assets from the customer. The first asset it receives from the customer is $5,000 cash. The second asset it receives from the customer is the customer's promise to pay Gray Co. $11,000 in the future. The $5,000 debit to Cash records the cash Gray Co. receives from the customer. The $11,000 debit to Accounts Receivable records the customer's promise to pay Gray Co. in the future. The $16,000 credit to Sales Revenue records the owners' claim to assets that increases as a result of receiving the two assets from the customer.

🖰 Click **Post to Ledger**

March 12 – Collect Cash from a Customer

Last month, on February 10, Gray Co. made a $4,500 sale to a customer on credit. On February 27, this customer paid Gray Co. $1,500 of the $4,500 she owed, leaving $3,000 to be paid in March. On March 12, this customer comes to Gray Co.'s store and pays the remaining $3,000.

Record below the collection of $3,000.

General Journal			
Date	Account	Debit	Credit
Mar 12			
	Collect cash from customer on account		

🖰 Click **Collect A/R**

✓ Compare your journal entry to the General Journal entry on the screen.

🖰 Click **Post to Ledger**

March 14 – Purchase Inventory

On March 14, 2017, Gray Co. purchases additional inventory. The cost of the inventory is $8,000. The vendor, from whom Gray Co. purchases the inventory, does not require Gray Co. to pay for the inventory at the time of purchase; thus Gray Co. purchases the inventory on credit. Gray Co. will pay the vendor for a portion of this purchase at the end of March—the remaining amount will be paid to the vendor in April.

As a result of this purchase, Gray Co.'s Inventory account will increase by $8,000. Gray Co. does not pay cash for this inventory at the time of purchase; thus no asset will be decreased. This $8,000 increase in inventory causes Gray Co.'s total assets to increase by $8,000; thus somebody's claim to assets must also increase. It is the vendor's claim to assets that increases as a result of this transaction. Vendors' claims to assets are put in the **Accounts Payable** account.

Record below the purchase of inventory on account.

General Journal			
Date	**Account**	**Debit**	**Credit**
Mar 14			
	Purchase inventory on account		

🖰 Click **Buy Inventory**

✓ Compare your journal entry to the General Journal entry on the screen.

🖰 Click **Post to Ledger**

March 15 – Pay Wages to Employees

On March 15, Gray Co. pays $1,200 to its workers for their work during the first two weeks of March.

Record below the payment of wages.

General Journal			
Date	**Account**	**Debit**	**Credit**
Mar 15			
	Paid wages to workers		

🖱 Click **Pay Wages**

✓ Compare your journal entry to the General Journal entry on the screen.

🖱 Click **Post to Ledger**

March 28 – Make a Payment on Accounts Payable

On March 14, Gray Co. purchased $8,000 of inventory from a vendor, but did not pay cash to the vendor at the time of the purchase. The current $8,000 balance in the Accounts Payable account is the vendor's claim to Gray Co.'s assets. On March 28, Gray Co. pays the vendor $2,500 cash to pay off a portion of this Accounts Payable liability.

Record below the payment to the vendor.

General Journal			
Date	**Account**	**Debit**	**Credit**
Mar 28			
	Make payment on account		

🖱 Click **Make a Payment**

✓ Compare your journal entry to the General Journal entry on the screen.

🖱 Click **Post to Ledger**

This is the first time you have recorded an entry that reduces one of Gray Co.'s liability accounts. As previously discussed, the liability accounts track the claims to assets of the non-owners of the business. The above entry decreases Cash, which results in a reduction of total assets. The entry also decreases Accounts Payable, which is the vendors' claims to assets.

March 30 – Interest Payment to the Bank

Last month, on February 28, there was an adjusting entry made to the Interest Payable account for $40. This adjusting entry was made to record the interest Gray Co. owed to the bank for the month of February. The February interest did not have to be paid to the bank until the end of March.

On March 30, Gray Co. calls the bank to find out how much interest it owes for the month of March. The bank indicates that the interest on the loan for the month of March is $45. On that same day, March 30, Gray Co. pays the bank $85 cash for the February and March interest.

It is easier to understand the recording of the $85 interest payment to the bank, if the recording is broken into two journal entries.

Entry #1

General Journal			
Date	**Account**	**Debit**	**Credit**
Mar 30	Interest Payable	40	
	Cash		40
	Pay the Interest Payable liability		

Entry #1 records the $40 payment of the Interest Payable liability. This entry reduces Gray Co.'s total assets and reduces the bank's claim to assets. Recall from Chapter 4, that Interest Expense for February was previously recorded by the February month-end adjusting entry.

Entry #2

General Journal			
Date	**Account**	**Debit**	**Credit**
Mar 30	Interest Expense	45	
	Cash		45
	Pay March interest		

Entry #2 records the $45 payment of the March interest owed to the bank. This entry reduces Gray Co.'s total assets by $45 and increases the Interest Expense account by $45. As previously discussed, an increase in an expense account reduces owners' claim to assets.

Below, use just one journal entry to record the $85 interest payment to the bank. Your one journal entry should be a combination of *Entry #1* and *Entry #2* shown above.

General Journal			
Date	**Account**	**Debit**	**Credit**
Mar 30			
	Pay February & March interest to the bank		

🖱 Click **Pay Interest**

✓ Compare your journal entry to the General Journal entry on the screen.

🖱 Click **Post to Ledger**

As discussed above, the $85 interest payment to the bank could be recorded in one journal entry or in two journal entries. Both the one-entry method and the two-entry method are correct. Both methods result in the correct amounts being posted to the Interest Payable account, the Interest Expense account, and the Cash account.

March 31 – Pay Wages to Employees

On March 31, Gray Co. pays $850 to its workers for their work during the last two weeks of March.

Record below the payment of wages.

General Journal			
Date	**Account**	**Debit**	**Credit**
Mar 31			
	Paid wages to workers		

🖱 Click **Pay Wages**

✓ Compare your journal entry to the General Journal entry on the screen.

🖱 Click **Post to Ledger**

Gray Co.'s March 31 wage payment is the last transaction for the month of March.

You have completed Step 1 and Step 2 in the Accounting Cycle process.

You will now complete Step 3 through Step 9 in the Accounting Cycle. Each of these remaining steps will be displayed in a box. Below each box will be a discussion of the action you need to perform to complete the step.

Step 3	At the end of the accounting period, before preparing the financial statements, determine if any of the General Ledger account balances need to be adjusted. Enter any required adjusting entries into the General Journal and post the adjusting entries to the General Ledger accounts.

You review the General Ledger accounts and determine that no adjusting entries are required at the end of March. (Chapters 7 and 8 will cover the topic of adjusting entries.)

> **Step 4** Prepare a Pre-Closing Trial Balance to determine that the accounts in the General Ledger are in balance.

On the form below, prepare Gray Co.'s Pre-Closing Trial Balance.

Pre-Closing Trial Balance		
Account Name	Debit	Credit
Cash		
Accounts Receivable		
Inventory		
Equipment		
Accounts Payable		
Note Payable		
Interest Payable		
Common Stock		
Retained Earnings		
Sales Revenue		
Cost of Goods Sold		
Wages Expense		
Rent Expense		
Interest Expense		
Total		

🖰 Click **Prepare Pre-Closing Trial Balance**

✓ Compare your Pre-Closing Trial Balance to the Pre-Closing Trial Balance on the screen.

> **Step 5** Prepare an Income Statement from the ending balances in the General Ledger revenue and expense accounts.

On the form at the top of the next page, prepare Gray Co.'s Income Statement for March.

```
┌─────────────────────────────────────────────────────────┐
│                    Gray Co., Inc.                         │
│                  Income Statement                         │
│          for the Period March 1 to March 31, 2017         │
├─────────────────────────────────────────────────────────┤
│                                                           │
│        Sales Revenue          $  _____          │
│                                                           │
│        Cost of Goods Sold        _____          │
│                                                           │
│          Gross Profit            _____          │
│                                                           │
│        Expenses:                                          │
│          Wage Expense            _____          │
│                                                           │
│          Rent Expense            _____          │
│                                                           │
│          Interest Expense        _____          │
│                                                           │
│          Total Expenses          _____          │
│                                                           │
│               Net Income      $  _____          │
│                                                           │
└─────────────────────────────────────────────────────────┘
```

🖰 Click **Prepare the Income Statement**

✓ Compare your Income Statement to the Income Statement on the screen.

Step 6	Calculate the ending balance of the Retained Earnings account that is needed for the preparation of the Balance Sheet.

On the form below, calculate the Retained Earnings balance as of the end of March.

```
┌─────────────────────────────────────────────────────────┐
│                    Calculation of                        │
│                 Retained Earnings as of                   │
│               March 31 for the Balance Sheet             │
├─────────────────────────────────────────────────────────┤
│                                                           │
│    Retained Earnings Current Balance     _____    │
│                                                           │
│    Plus March Net Income                 _____    │
│                                                           │
│    Retained Earnings as of                                │
│    March 31 for the Balance Sheet        _____    │
│                                                           │
└─────────────────────────────────────────────────────────┘
```

🖱 Click **Calculate Mar. 31 Retained Earnings**

✓ Compare your calculation on the previous page to the Calculation of Retained Earnings as of Mar. 31 for the Balance Sheet on the screen.

Step 7	Prepare the Balance Sheet from the ending balances in the General Ledger asset accounts, liability accounts, Common Stock account, and the calculated ending balance for the Retained Earnings account.

On the form below, prepare Gray Co.'s Balance Sheet as of March 31.

Gray Co., Inc.
Balance Sheet
as of March 31, 2017

Assets:

Cash $ _____

Accounts Receivable _____

Inventory _____

Equipment _____

Total Assets $ _____

Liabilities:

Accounts Payable $ _____

Note Payable _____

Interest Payable _____

Total Liabilities _____

Equity:

Common Stock _____

Retained Earnings _____

Total Equity _____

Total Liabilities and Equity $ _____

🖱 Click **Prepare the Balance Sheet**

✓ Compare your Balance Sheet to the Balance Sheet on the screen.

Step 8	Prepare and enter the revenue and expense closing entries into the General Journal, and post the closing entries to the General Ledger accounts.

Gray Co.'s closing entries for March are shown on the March 2017 Closing screen.

🖱 Click the **Mar Close** tab, to move to the March 2017 Closing screen.

You should see **Screen 6 B** in the upper left corner of the screen.

Record below the entry to close the Sales Revenue account.

General Journal			
Date	**Account**	**Debit**	**Credit**
Mar 31			
	Close Sales Revenue account		

🖱 Click **Close Revenues**

✓ Compare your journal entry to the General Journal entry on the screen.

🖱 Click **Post to Ledger**

Record below the entry to close the expense accounts.

General Journal			
Date	**Account**	**Debit**	**Credit**
Mar 31			
	Close Expense accounts		

🖱 Click **Close Expenses**

✓ Compare your journal entry to the General Journal entry on the screen.

🖱 Click **Post to Ledger**

> **Step 9**   Prepare a Post-Closing Trial Balance to determine that the accounts in the General Ledger are in balance and ready to start a new Accounting Cycle.

On the form below, prepare Gray Co.'s Post-Closing Trial Balance.

Post-Closing Trial Balance		
Account Name	Debit	Credit
Cash		
Accounts Receivable		
Inventory		
Equipment		
Accounts Payable		
Note Payable		
Interest Payable		
Common Stock		
Retained Earnings		
Sales Revenue		
Cost of Goods Sold		
Wages Expense		
Rent Expense		
Interest Expense		
Total		

🖱 Click **Prepare Post-Closing Trial Balance**

✓ Compare your Post-Closing Trial Balance to the Post-Closing Trial Balance on the screen.

You have taken Gray Co. through the entire March Accounting Cycle by completing each of the nine Accounting Cycle steps.

Before completing the Mini-Project on the next page, be sure to review any areas where you made a mistake while reading Chapter 6. The **Chapter 6 – OPJ Mini-Project** will give you an opportunity to test yourself again over all of the concepts you have learned to this point in Solid Footing.

Chapter 6 – OPJ Mini-Project

The OPJ Mini-Project for OverPriced Jeans March Accounting Period

Included with your Solid Footing software is a workbook that contains the Chapter 6 – OPJ Mini-Project. This Mini-Project will take you through the month of March for OverPriced Jeans, and will cover all of the topics you have learned in the first six chapters of Solid Footing. Your instructor will give you directions on how to complete and submit your OPJ Mini-Project.

While working on your project:

    ▷ Never do a **Cut** operation.

    ▷ If a page contains a <u>CAUTION</u> box, follow the directions in that box.

Starting the OPJ Mini-Project

To start the OPJ Mini-Project do the following:

1. **Complete the Blue OPJ Mini-Project Registration Slip**

        ▷ Remove and complete the blue OPJ Mini-Project Registration Slip. The Registration Slip is on the last page in this book (Pg 251). Turn in your completed Registration Slip to your instructor. Be sure to leave the Accounting Cycle Project Registration Slip in your Solid Footing book.

2. **Open the OPJ Mini-Project Workbook**
    The OPJ Mini-Project is in a workbook entitled "06-OPJ Mini-Project 10e". To open this workbook, do the following:

        ▷ Open the workbook **06-OPJ Mini-Project 10e** in the **Solid Footing 10e** folder

        ▷ Enable Macros

3. **Activate Your Project**

        ▷ Enter your <u>Software ID Code</u>   Your code is located on the Permanent Record Slip, which is the last page in this book.

        ▷ Enter your <u>First Name</u>

        ▷ Enter your <u>Last Name</u>, and press the <u>Enter key</u>

        ▷ Click the Activate Project button

        ▷ Be sure that your name is correct before clicking **Yes** to the question "Is your name correct?". Once your name is entered into your project, it cannot be changed.

        ▷ Complete the yellow information boxes that are located in the top right of the page.

4. **Save Your Activated Project**

        ▷ Save your project using your <u>Last Name</u> and your <u>First Name</u> as the first part of the file name. The file name should be in the form: LastName**FirstName**-OPJ

        ▷ To save your Activated Project, follow the directions in the box entitled:
    SAVING YOUR PROJECT – Immediately after Activation

(OPJ Mini-Project directions continued on the next page)

Working On and Completing the OPJ Mini-Project

▷ To complete your project, follow the **Instructions** on the Directions tab of the project.

▷ Save your project often.

▷ You can complete a portion of your project – stop working on it – then continue working on it at a later time. Before you stop working on your project, be sure it has been saved. When you return to your project, be sure the workbook you open is the workbook that you named using your LastName**FirstName**-OPJ

Additional Information About Your Project

How Your Project will be Graded
Your project will be graded by your instructor using the OPJ Mini-Project grading software. The grading software will not grade all of the information you entered into your project.

Your instructor may choose to grade additional items in your project that are not graded by the grading software.

Submitting Your Project

Your instructor will provide you with directions for submitting your completed project.

(End of OPJ Mini-Project directions)

Chapter 7
Introduction to Adjusting Entries
Property, Plant, & Equipment – Prepaid Assets – Accrued Liabilities

In the first chapter of this book, you learned the basics of double-entry accounting by working with the Cash Bucket Accounting System to track the status of your Cash Bucket. In Chapters 2 through 6, you greatly expanded your accounting knowledge by working with a merchandising company called Gray Co.

In this chapter, you will be introduced to a new company, Lenny's Lawn Service, Inc. Lenny's earns its revenue by providing a service to customers; thus Lenny's is a service company. The accounting knowledge that you developed by working with Gray Co., Inc. will also apply to Lenny's.

The main difference you will notice as you work with Lenny's Lawn Service is that Lenny's does not have inventory. Gray Co. purchased inventory and earned revenue by selling that inventory to customers. Lenny's earns revenue by providing a service; thus Lenny's does not have inventory.

Lenny Smith started Lenny's Lawn Service, Inc. on January 1, 2016. Lenny Smith runs his new business from his farm house in Tampa, Florida. Lenny's provides lawn service to condominium developments. Lenny's has completed its first year in business. During its first year in business, Lenny's:

> ▷ Sold common stock to stockholders to get the money to start the business.

> ▷ Purchased various types of lawn mowing equipment.

> ▷ Hired employees to perform the lawn mowing service.

> ▷ Signed a contract with a property management company to mow the lawns at four condominium developments.

> ▷ Rented a truck and a trailer to transport the lawn mowing equipment.

We will begin the accounting for Lenny's Lawn Service, Inc. at the start of Lenny's second year in business, January 1, 2017.

⇨ INTRODUCTION TO ADJUSTING ENTRIES

In this chapter, you will be using Lenny's Lawn Service, Inc. to expand your knowledge of adjusting entries. When working with Gray Co. you made one adjusting entry. (The February 28 entry, for interest due to Gray Co.'s bank, was an adjusting entry.) You will be learning about many different types of adjusting entries in this chapter and in the next chapter.

Adjusting entries are needed to tune-up the balances in the Asset accounts and the Liability accounts. Adjusting entries are made just before financial statements are prepared.

The nine steps in the Accounting Cycle are repeated below so that you can see where adjusting entries fit into the Accounting Cycle.

Steps in the Accounting Cycle
Step 1	For each business transaction that occurs during the accounting period, determine the effect of the transaction on the General Ledger accounts.
Step 2	Make an entry in the General Journal for each transaction and post the entry to the General Ledger accounts.
➔ **Step 3**	**At the end of the accounting period, before preparing the financial statements, determine if any of the General Ledger account balances need to be adjusted. Enter any required adjusting entries into the General Journal and post the adjusting entries to the General Ledger accounts.**
Step 4	Prepare a Pre-Closing Trial Balance to determine that the accounts in the General Ledger are in balance.
Step 5	Prepare an Income Statement from the ending balances in the General Ledger revenue and expense accounts.
Step 6	Calculate the ending balance of the Retained Earnings account that is needed for the preparation of the Balance Sheet.
Step 7	Prepare the Balance Sheet from the ending balances in the General Ledger asset accounts, liability accounts, Common Stock account, and the calculated ending balance for the Retained Earnings account.
Step 8	Prepare and enter the revenue and expense closing entries into the General Journal, and post the closing entries to the General Ledger accounts.
Step 9	Prepare a Post-Closing Trial Balance to determine that the accounts in the General Ledger are in balance and ready to start a new Accounting Cycle.

Lenny's accounting period is a month; thus Lenny's completes the nine steps in the Accounting Cycle each month. For most of the time each month, Lenny's is doing Steps 1 and 2 in the Accounting Cycle. From the first day in the month, to the last business day in the month, Lenny's records its transactions as directed by Steps 1 and 2 in the Accounting Cycle.

It is not until the end of the last day in the month that Lenny's will complete Step 3 through Step 9 in the Accounting Cycle. **Step 3** in the Accounting Cycle is the adjusting entry step; thus preparing adjusting entries is the start of the month-end process.

After recording all the transactions for the month, most of the asset and liability accounts in the General Ledger contain correct balances. But some of the accounts do not contain correct balances; thus the need for adjusting entries.

January depreciation will be the first adjusting entry you will do for Lenny's; but first, January's transactions need to be entered into the accounting system.

⇨ LENNY's JANUARY TRANSACTIONS

In this chapter, you will be using the workbook entitled "03-Lenny's Lawn Service". To open this workbook, do the following:

> ⇨ Open the workbook **03-Lenny's Lawn Service** in the **Solid Footing 10e** folder

> ⇨ Enable Macros

🖱 Click the **January** tab (if the January tab is not selected).

You should see **Screen 7 A** in the upper left corner of the screen.

This screen contains several new accounts that will be explained when they are used to record Lenny's transactions and adjusting entries.

Observe the beginning balances in the Asset, Liability, and Owners' Equity accounts. These balances are the result of Lenny's first year of operations. As previously indicated, we will pickup the accounting for Lenny's Lawn Service, Inc. on January 1, 2017, the start of its second year in business.

Because the main focus of this chapter is on adjusting entries, all of Lenny's January 2017 transactions will be entered into the General Journal and will be posted to the General Ledger by clicking just one button.

🖱 Click **Enter January Transactions into the Journal and Post to the Ledger**

The following is a brief discussion of each transaction:

Jan 01	Lenny's rents a truck and a trailer to transport its lawn mowing equipment. The rent is $500 per month. This entry records the payment of the January rent for the equipment.
Jan 03	Gasoline and various lawn mower maintenance parts are purchased each month. This entry records the purchase of these items for the month of January. The gasoline and maintenance parts will be consumed during the month of January.
Jan 20	Near the end of each month, Lenny's invoices the property management company for the mowing services performed by Lenny's during that month. On January 20, the property management company pays the $22,500 it owes Lenny's for the December 2016 mowing services.
Jan 29	Lenny's provided $26,000 of mowing services for the month of January. This entry records the invoice sent to the property management company for January's services. Notice the following:

> ▷ The revenue account is called Service Revenue because the revenue is the result of providing a service.

> ▷ There is <u>no</u> entry to an Inventory account or a Cost of Goods Sold account. Lenny's does not sell inventory to its customers. Revenue is earned by providing a service to its customers.

Jan 31	This entry records the payment of January's wages to Lenny's employees.

Now that all of January's transactions have been entered, it is time to prepare adjusting entries, Step 3 in the Accounting Cycle. By reviewing the ending account balances, you determine that the only adjusting entry required at the end of January is for depreciation. The following is a discussion about depreciation and the required depreciation adjusting entry.

⇨ PROPERTY, PLANT, & EQUIPMENT and THE DEPRECIATION ADJUSTING ENTRY

The Accumulated Depreciation account is one of the accounts that will require an adjusting entry at the end of each accounting period. Before discussing the Accumulated Depreciation account, let's first discuss the long-term asset accounts that are related to Accumulated Depreciation.

Companies buy many types of long-term assets. Long-term assets are assets a company will keep and use for more than one year. Most long-term assets purchased by a company are of the Property, Plant, & Equipment type. Lenny's lawn mowing equipment is an example of a Property, Plant, & Equipment asset. Property, Plant, & Equipment assets are also called Fixed Assets.

Observe on the screen that Lenny's has a $48,000 balance in its **Equipment** account. This equipment was purchased over a year ago, on January 2, 2016, when Lenny's started in business. At that time, Lenny's estimated:

▷ The lawn mowing equipment would last for four years (48 months).

▷ At the end of the four years, the equipment would have no future value and would be scrapped.

Therefore, for each month that Lenny's uses the lawn mowing equipment, $1/48^{th}$ of the equipment's service life is used up. If the balance in the Equipment account is reduced by $1/48^{th}$ of its original cost each month; then by the end of four years, the balance in the Equipment account will be zero.

The calculation of the monthly reduction amount is:

$$\frac{\text{Equipment Cost}}{\text{Months of Useful Life}} = \text{Monthly reduction in Equipment account}$$

$$\frac{\$48,000}{48 \text{ months}} = \$1,000 \text{ per month}$$

The $1,000 is called the monthly depreciation. **Depreciation** is the process of allocating the cost of Property, Plant, & Equipment to the accounting periods in which these assets are used.

There are many different ways to calculate the amount of depreciation. The above method is called the straight-line depreciation method because the amount of depreciation is the same each accounting period. Only the straight-line depreciation method will be used in this book.

Each month, the $1,000 could be entered as a credit into the Equipment account to reduce the balance in that account. But rather than putting the $1,000 credit directly into the Equipment account, the credit will be put into an account that is related to the Equipment account. The account where the credit will be placed is the **Accumulated Depreciation** account. By putting the $1,000 credit into the Accumulated Depreciation account, rather than directly into the Equipment account, Lenny's will easily be able to see the original cost of the lawn mowing equipment by looking at the Equipment account. By looking at the Accumulated Depreciation account, Lenny's will be able to see how much of the original cost has been written off by the monthly depreciation entries.

Observe on the screen that the balance in the Equipment account is a $48,000 debit; thus you can easily see that the amount paid for the lawn mowing equipment was $48,000. Also observe on the screen that the balance in the Accumulated Depreciation account is a $12,000 credit; thus Lenny's knows that $12,000 of the cost of the equipment has been written off by prior depreciation entries.

The Accumulated Depreciation account will always have a credit balance. The Accumulated Depreciation account is a negative asset account. This type of asset account is called a contra-asset account. Its credit balance partially offsets the debit balance in the Equipment account.

Let's make Lenny's depreciation adjusting entry for January 2017.

 Click **Depreciation**

The $1,000 credit to the Accumulated Depreciation account is what you would expect based on the previous discussion of depreciation. This credit to the contra-asset account, Accumulated Depreciation, causes Lenny's total assets to be reduced; thus there must be a reduction to somebody's claim to assets. It is the owners' claim to assets that must be reduced. The $1,000 debit to the Depreciation Expense account reduces the owners' claim to assets.

 Click **Post to Ledger**

Observe the $1,000 debit in the Depreciation Expense account. The Depreciation Expense account is located under the Retained Earnings account along with all of the other expense accounts. This is the case because the Depreciation Expense account is just another expense account. Just like all other expense accounts, the Depreciation Expense account will appear on the Income Statement and will be closed into the Retained Earnings account at the end of each accounting period.

Observe the $1,000 credit to the Accumulated Depreciation account. This credit changes the balance in the Accumulated Depreciation account from a beginning balance of $12,000 credit to an ending balance of $13,000 credit. By looking at the ending balance in the Accumulated Depreciation account, you can see that a total of $13,000 of the cost of the lawn mowing equipment has been written-off as of the end of January 2017. The $13,000 ending balance is what you would expect; since $1,000 is the monthly depreciation for the mowing equipment and the mowing equipment has been used for 13 months.

Lenny's January Income Statement and Balance Sheet

Let's prepare the Income Statement for January and see how the Depreciation Expense account appears on the Income Statement. To save space, Step 4 in the Accounting Cycle, *Prepare a Pre-Closing Trial Balance*, is not shown on the screen. Preparing the Income Statement is Step 5 in the Accounting Cycle.

 Click **Prepare the Income Statement**

Observe the following related to the Depreciation Expense account:

> ▷ Depreciation Expense is shown in the Expenses section of the Income Statement—it is just another expense.

> ▷ Depreciation Expense increases Total Expenses.

> ▷ Depreciation Expense decreases Net Income.

To save space, Step 6 in the Accounting Cycle, *Calculate the ending balance of the Retained Earnings account that is needed for the preparation of the Balance Sheet*, is not shown on the screen. The ending Retained Earnings balance needed for the Balance Sheet is:

Current balance in Retained Earnings	$17,000
Plus January Net Income	7,075
Ending balance in Retained Earnings	$24,075

Now let's prepare the Balance Sheet and see how the Accumulated Depreciation account appears on the Balance Sheet. Preparing the Balance Sheet is Step 7 in the Accounting Cycle.

🖱 Click **Prepare the Balance Sheet**

Observe the following related to the Accumulated Depreciation account:

> ▷ Accumulated Depreciation is shown in the Assets section of the Balance Sheet.

> ▷ Accumulated Depreciation is shown as a negative amount on the Balance Sheet, which is consistent with its credit account balance.

> ▷ Accumulated Depreciation is shown just under Equipment, which is the asset it is "contra" to.

> ▷ Accumulated Depreciation reduces Total Assets.

To finish January's Accounting Cycle, Lenny's would complete Step 8 – *Prepare and enter the revenue and expense closing entries*, and Step 9 – *Prepare a Post-Closing Trial Balance*. These two steps will not be shown in this chapter. These steps are the same as previously shown for Gray Co.

⇨ ERRORS – NOT MAKING THE DEPRECIATION ENTRY

What would be the effect on the financial statements if Lenny's had failed to make the depreciation adjusting entry at the end of January?

🖱 Click **Show the Errors**

By comparing Lenny's correct **Income Statement for the Month of January** to the **Income Statement with Errors**, you can see the following would be the effects if Lenny's failed to make the January depreciation adjusting entry:

> ▷ Depreciation Expense would be understated by $1,000.

> ▷ Total Expenses would be understated by $1,000.

> ▷ Net Income would be overstated by $1,000.

By comparing Lenny's correct **Balance Sheet as of January 31** to the **Balance Sheet with Errors**, you can see the following would be the effects if Lenny's failed to make the January depreciation adjusting entry:

> ▷ Accumulated Depreciation would be understated by $1,000.

> ▷ Total Assets would be overstated by $1,000.

> ▷ Retained Earnings would be overstated by $1,000.

> ▷ Total Equity would be overstated by $1,000.

> ▷ Total Liabilities and Equity would be overstated by $1,000.

As demonstrated by the above lists of errors, adjusting entries have a significant impact on the amounts shown on the financial statements.

Observe that even though some of the line items on the **Balance Sheet with Errors** are not correct, that Balance Sheet does balance. The "with Errors" Balance Sheet balances because the Total Assets amount is overstated by $1,000 and the Total Liabilities and Equity amount is also overstated by $1,000. This demonstrates that just because a Balance Sheet balances, it does not guarantee that all line items on that Balance Sheet are correct.

⇨ LENNY's FEBRUARY TRANSACTIONS

You will now take Lenny's Lawn Service through its February accounting period.

🖑 Click the **February** tab.

You should see **Screen 7 B** in the upper left corner of the screen.

Last month, on January 3, Lenny's purchased the supplies it needed for the month of January. These supplies consisted of gasoline and various maintenance parts for the lawn mowers. The cost of these supplies was $925, and the supplies were consumed during the month of January. Near the end of January, the vendor of these supplies made a special offer to Lenny's. The vendor offered to give Lenny's a 20% discount and to provide to Lenny's a free gasoline storage tank. To take advantage of this special offer, Lenny's would be required to purchase, all at one time, a minimum of $11,000 of gasoline and maintenance parts.

Lenny's decides to take advantage of the vendor's offer. On February 1, Lenny's purchases $11,000 of supplies.

🖑 Click **Buy Supplies**

Observe that the debit is to the **Supplies** account. The Supplies account is an asset account.

In prior months when Lenny's purchased supplies, the Supplies Expense account was debited. The reason the debit went to the Supplies Expense account was because the supplies would be consumed in that month.

The reason the Supplies asset account is debited for this $11,000 purchase is because this large amount of supplies will last Lenny's beyond the current accounting period. This purchase will benefit not only the month of February (the current accounting period), but will also benefit Lenny's future accounting periods.

Let's now post the supplies entry to the General Ledger accounts.

🖑 Click **Post to Ledger**

Observe that this entry increases the Supplies asset account and decreases the Cash account. Lenny's total assets do not change because of this transaction.

Let's now enter the rest of Lenny's February transactions.

🖑 Click **Enter Other February Transactions into Journal and Post to the Ledger**

The following is a brief discussion of February's other transactions:

Feb 01   Lenny's pays the $500 monthly truck and trailer rental.

Feb 20   The property management company pays to Lenny's the $26,000 owed for the January 2017 mowing services.

Feb 28   Lenny's bills the property management company for $24,250 of mowing services for the month of February.

Feb 28   February's wages are paid to Lenny's employees.

All of February's transactions have been entered. By reviewing the ending account balances, you determine that the balances in two accounts need to be adjusted at the end of February. One account that needs to be adjusted is Accumulated Depreciation. The other account that requires an adjusting entry is the Supplies asset account.

⇨ FEBRUARY's DEPRECIATION ADJUSTING ENTRY

The adjusting entry for February's depreciation follows the same logic as the January depreciation adjusting entry.

🖰 Click **Depreciation**

Observe that the February depreciation adjusting entry is the same as the January adjusting entry for depreciation.

🖰 Click **Post to Ledger**

Observe the $1,000 credit to the Accumulated Depreciation account. This credit changes the balance in the Accumulated Depreciation account from a beginning balance of $13,000 credit to an ending balance of $14,000 credit.

⇨ FEBRUARY's SUPPLIES ADJUSTING ENTRY

At the end of February, a major portion of the $11,000 of supplies, which Lenny's purchased on February 1, are still on-hand. Lenny's counts the maintenance parts that remain in stock and determines the quantity of gasoline in the storage tank. Using the original purchase cost of these remaining items, Lenny's determines that $10,125 of supplies are in stock as of February 28.

To determine the required adjusting entry to the Supplies asset account, the following three questions need to be answered:

Three Questions for Determining the Supplies Adjusting Entry
1. What is the current balance in the Supplies account?
2. What should be the balance in the Supplies account?
3. What adjustment is required to the Supplies account to adjust it from its current balance to its should be balance?

The answers to the above three questions are:

1. By looking at the Supplies account, you can see that the current balance is $11,000 debit.

2. Based on the month-end counting of the supplies on-hand, the balance in the Supplies account should be $10,125 debit.

3. There needs to be an $875 credit entry made to the Supplies account to adjust its current $11,000 debit balance to its $10,125 should be debit balance.

🖱 Click **Supplies Adj.**

Observe the $875 credit to the Supplies account. That is the amount of the required adjustment to the Supplies account determined by the three question process. This credit to the Supplies account records the reduction of the Supplies asset.

Observe the $875 debit to the Supplies Expense account. This is consistent with other entries you have made when an asset was consumed in the operation of the business. For example: when the asset cash was consumed to pay rent, the Rent Expense account was debited; when the asset cash was consumed to pay wages, the Wages Expense account was debited. In this entry, the asset Supplies is consumed; thus the Supplies Expense account is debited.

🖱 Click **Post to Ledger**

Notice the ending balance of $10,125 debit in the Supplies asset account. This is the dollar amount of the supplies Lenny's has on-hand as of February 28. These supplies will be used to support the operation of Lenny's business in future months; thus the supplies are an asset.

The Supplies asset account is an example of a general category of assets called Prepaid Assets. Other assets in the Prepaid Asset category are: Prepaid Rent, Prepaid Insurance, and Prepaid Maintenance. There will be more discussion of the Prepaid Asset category in Chapter 9.

Lenny's February Income Statement and Balance Sheet

Let's prepare the Income Statement for February and see how the Supplies Expense account appears on the Income Statement. To save space, Step 4 in the Accounting Cycle, *Prepare a Pre-Closing Trial Balance*, is not shown on the screen. Preparing the Income Statement is Step 5 in the Accounting Cycle.

🖱 Click **Prepare the Income Statement**

Observe that the account balance from the Supplies Expense account is shown in the Expense section of the Income Statement, just like all the other expense account balances.

Just like on the January screen, Step 6 in the Accounting Cycle is not shown. The ending Retained Earnings balance needed for the Balance Sheet is:

Current balance in Retained Earnings	$24,075
Plus February Net Income	6,775
Ending balance in Retained Earnings	$30,850

Let's prepare the Balance Sheet and see how the Supplies account appears on the Balance Sheet. Preparing the Balance Sheet is Step 7 in the Accounting Cycle.

🖱 Click **Prepare the Balance Sheet**

Observe that the account balance from the Supplies account is shown in the Assets section of the Balance Sheet, just like all the other asset account balances.

To finish February's Accounting Cycle, Lenny's would complete Step 8 – *Prepare and enter the revenue and expense closing entries,* and Step 9 – *Prepare a Post-Closing Trial Balance.* These two steps will not be shown in this chapter. These steps are the same as previously shown for Gray Co.

⇨ ERRORS – NOT MAKING THE SUPPLIES ADJUSTING ENTRY

What would be the effect on the financial statements if Lenny's had failed to make the supplies adjusting entry at the end of February?

🖰 Click **Show the Errors**

By comparing Lenny's correct **Income Statement for the Month of February** to the **Income Statement with Errors**, you can see the following would be the effects if Lenny's failed to make the February supplies adjusting entry:

> ▷ Supplies Expense would be understated by $875.

> ▷ Total Expenses would be understated by $875.

> ▷ Net Income would be overstated by $875.

By comparing Lenny's correct **Balance Sheet as of February 28** to the **Balance Sheet with Errors**, you can see the following would be the effects if Lenny's failed to make the February supplies adjusting entry:

> ▷ Supplies would be overstated by $875.

> ▷ Total Assets would be overstated by $875.

> ▷ Retained Earnings would be overstated by $875.

> ▷ Total Equity would be overstated by $875.

> ▷ Total Liabilities and Equity would be overstated by $875.

Just as in January, when you looked at what the effect would have been if the depreciation adjusting entry had not been made, the above lists of errors demonstrates the significant impact adjusting entries have on the financial statements.

Observe that, just like in January, even though some of the line items on the **Balance Sheet with Errors** are not correct, that Balance Sheet does balance. The "with Errors" Balance Sheet balances because the Total Assets amount is overstated by $875 and the Total Liabilities and Equity amount is also overstated by $875. Again, this demonstrates that just because a Balance Sheet balances, it does not guarantee that all line items on that Balance Sheet are correct.

⇨ LENNY's MARCH TRANSACTIONS

You will now take Lenny's Lawn Service through its March accounting period.

🖰 Click the **March** tab.

You should see **Screen 7 C** in the upper left corner of the screen.

During the month of March, Lenny's completed its normal monthly transactions.

🖰 Click **Enter March Transactions into Journal and Post to the Ledger**

The following is a discussion of the March transactions:

Mar 01   Lenny's pays the $500 monthly truck and trailer rental.

Mar 20   The property management company pays the $24,250 owed to Lenny's for the February 2017 mowing services.

Mar 29   This entry records the payment of wages to Lenny's employees for the first 29 days of March. Normally the employees are paid their wages for the full month of work on the last day of the month. In March, the employees were paid on March 29 for the first 29 days of March work. On March 30 & 31, all of the employees will be working on an out-of-town mowing job. As a result of being out of town, the employees will not be able to pick-up their paychecks on March 31. During the first week in April, Lenny's will pay the employees for the work performed on these last two days of March.

Mar 31   Lenny's bills the property management company for $30,250 of mowing services for the month of March.

All of March's transactions have been entered. By reviewing the ending account balances, you determine that the balances in three accounts need to be adjusted. The following three accounts need to be adjusted.

▷ Accumulated Depreciation account

▷ Supplies asset account

▷ Wages Payable account

⇨ MARCH's DEPRECIATION ADJUSTING ENTRY

The adjusting entry for March's depreciation follows the same logic as the January and February depreciation adjusting entry.

🖰 Click **Depreciation**

🖰 Click the **Post to Ledger**

Observe the depreciation entry and the effect that entry has on the Accumulated Depreciation and Depreciation Expense accounts.

⇨ MARCH's SUPPLIES ADJUSTING ENTRY

At the end of the month of March, Lenny's counts the maintenance parts that remain in stock and determines the quantity of gasoline in the storage tank. Using the original purchase cost of these remaining items, Lenny's determines that $9,000 of supplies are in stock as of March 31.

"T" Account Analysis for Asset and Liability Accounts		
Account Name →	**Supplies** (asset account)	
	Debit	**Credit**
(1)　What is the <u>current</u> balance?		
(3)　What adjustment is required to adjust from the <u>current</u> balance to the <u>should be</u> balance?		
(2)　What <u>should be</u> the balance?		

⇨　Enter the amounts in the above "T" account analysis based on the following process:

　　1.　Look on the screen at the current balance in the Supplies asset account. Write that amount in the "T" account analysis for step (**1**).

　　2.　The amount of supplies in stock as of March 31 was determined to be $9,000. Write that amount in the "T" account analysis for step (**2**).

　　3.　Determine the Debit or Credit amount that is required to adjust the Supplies account from its <u>current</u> balance to its <u>should be</u> balance. Write that amount in the "T" account analysis for step (**3**).

The amount for step (**3**) in the "T" account analysis is the required adjustment to the Supplies asset account. The other portion of the supplies adjusting entry will be to the Supplies Expense account.

Record below the March supplies adjusting journal entry.

General Journal			
Date	Account	Debit	Credit
Mar 31			
	Adjust supplies to March 31 on-hand balance		

🖑 Click **Supplies Adj.**

🖑 Click **Post to Ledger**

Look on the screen at the supplies adjusting entry in the General Journal and at the posting of that entry to the Supplies account in the General Ledger. Based on your "T" account analysis, did you prepare the correct supplies adjusting entry?

⇨ MARCH's WAGES PAYABLE ADJUSTING ENTRY and the MATCHING PRINCIPLE

As previously indicated, on March 29, Lenny's paid its employees for the work the employees performed during the first 29 days of March.

Lenny's employees worked on March 30 & 31. The employees will be paid for these two days of work during the first week in April. On March 31, Lenny's calculates that the employees earned $1,825 for these last two days of March. This will be the amount the employees will receive in the first week of April.

While Lenny's will not actually pay the $1,825 of wages until April, Lenny's does owe those wages to the employees as of March 31. As of March 31, a $1,825 **Wages Payable** liability should be recorded in Lenny's General Ledger accounts. This is another example of Lenny's applying the accrual basis of accounting (for additional discussion see the heading **Accrual Basis** on Pg 21).

A portion of the revenue, which was billed to the property management company on March 31, was for the out-of-town mowing job done on March 30 & 31. The revenue from the March 30 & 31 mowing job will be included in the March Income Statement; thus the cost of the wages incurred to produce that revenue should also be included in the March Income Statement. When the wages payable adjusting entry is recorded, Lenny's will be including the $1,825 of wages in the March Wages Expense account balance, and thus in the March Income Statement. This matching of revenues and expenses in the same accounting period is referred to as the **Matching Principle**.

"T" Account Analysis for Asset and Liability Accounts		
Account Name →	*Wages Payable*	
	Debit	**Credit**
(1) What is the <u>current</u> balance?		0
(3) What adjustment is required to adjust from the <u>current</u> balance to the <u>should be</u> balance?		1,825
(2) What <u>should be</u> the balance?		1,825

Observe the amounts in the above "T" account analysis and notice how this analysis is prepared based on the following process:

1. Look on the screen at the current balance in the Wages Payable account. That amount is put in the "T" account analysis for step (**1**).

2. The amount of wages owed to the employees, as of March 31, is determined to be $1,825. That amount is put in the "T" account analysis for step (**2**).

3. Determine the Debit or Credit amount that is required to adjust the Wages Payable account from its <u>current</u> balance to its <u>should be</u> balance. An $1,825 credit amount is put in the "T" account analysis for step (**3**). This is the amount required to take the Wages Payable account from a <u>current</u> balance of $0 credit to a <u>should be</u> balance of $1,825 credit.

The amount for step (**3**) in the "T" account analysis is the required adjustment to the Wages Payable account. The other portion of the wages payable adjusting entry will be to the Wages Expense account.

Record below the March wages payable adjusting journal entry.

General Journal			
Date	Account	Debit	Credit
Mar 31			
	Adjust for March 30 & 31 Unpaid Wages		

🖰 Click **Wages Adj.**

🖰 Click **Post to Ledger**

Look on the screen at the wages payable entry in the General Journal. Also look at the posting of that entry to both the Wages Payable and the Wages Expense accounts in the General Ledger. Did you prepare the correct adjusting entry?

Observe the following about this adjusting entry:

▷ The entry does not affect any asset account. The amount of Total Assets is not changed by this adjusting entry.

▷ The entry records the employees' claims to Lenny's assets in a liability account called Wages Payable.

▷ The entry increases the Wages Expense account by $1,825. This properly matches the Wages Expense for March to the Service Revenue for March. This is an example of the **Matching Principle**.

▷ The $1,825 increase in Wages Expense reduces the owners' claim to assets by $1,825; thus the effect of this adjusting entry is to increase the employees' claims to Lenny's assets and reduce the owners' claim.

The Wages Payable account is an example of a general category of liabilities called Accrued Liabilities. Other liability accounts in the Accrued Liability category are:

▷ Interest Payable – The credit balance in this account is the amount of interest we owe on money we have borrowed.

▷ Rent Payable – The credit balance in this account is the amount of rent we owe as a tenant to our landlord.

There will be more discussion of the Accrued Liability category in Chapter 9.

Lenny's March Income Statement and Balance Sheet

Let's prepare the Income Statement for March. To save space, Step 4 in the Accounting Cycle, *Prepare a Pre-Closing Trial Balance*, is not shown on the screen. Preparing the Income Statement is Step 5 in the Accounting Cycle.

🖰 Click **Prepare the Income Statement**

Observe that three of the expense amounts shown on the Income Statement (Supplies Expense, Wages Expense, and Depreciation Expense) were all affected by the March adjusting entries.

As in January and February, Step 6 in the Accounting Cycle is not shown. The ending Retained Earnings balance needed for the Balance Sheet is:

Current balance in Retained Earnings	$30,850
Plus March Net Income	10,600
Ending balance in Retained Earnings	$41,450

Now let's prepare the Balance Sheet and see how the Wages Payable account appears on the Balance Sheet. Preparing the Balance Sheet is Step 7 in the Accounting Cycle.

🖰 Click **Prepare the Balance Sheet**

Observe the employees' claim, Wages Payable, on the Balance Sheet.

To finish March's Accounting Cycle, Lenny's would complete Step 8 – *Prepare and enter the revenue and expense closing entries,* and Step 9 – *Prepare a Post-Closing Trial Balance.* These two steps will not be shown in this chapter. These steps are the same as previously shown for Gray Co.

⇨ ERRORS – NOT MAKING THE WAGES PAYABLE ENTRY

What would be the effect on the financial statements if Lenny's had failed to make the Wages Payable adjusting entry at the end of March?

🖰 Click **Show the Errors**

By comparing Lenny's correct **Income Statement for the Month of March** to the **Income Statement with Errors**, you can see the following would be the effects if Lenny's failed to make the March Wages Payable adjusting entry:

▷ Wages Expense would be understated by $1,825.

▷ Total Expenses would be understated by $1,825.

▷ Net Income would be overstated by $1,825.

By comparing Lenny's correct **Balance Sheet as of March 31** to the **Balance Sheet with Errors**, you can see the following would be the effects if Lenny's failed to make the March Wages Payable adjusting entry:

▷ Wages Payable would be understated by $1,825.

▷ Total Liabilities would be understated by $1,825.

▷ Retained Earnings would be overstated by $1,825.

▷ Total Equity would be overstated by $1,825.

Also by comparing Lenny's correct **Balance Sheet as of March 31** to the **Balance Sheet with Errors**, you can see what would <u>not</u> have been affected if Lenny's failed to make the March Wages Payable adjusting entry:

▷ All asset accounts and Total Assets are the same on both Balance Sheets.

▷ Total Liabilities and Equity would not be affected by the omission of the Wages Payable adjusting entry.

Chapter 7 Homework

Problem 7-1   Purchase and Depreciate a New Delivery Truck

Speedy Delivery Service, Inc. has always rented their delivery truck. Speedy decided to replace the rented delivery truck by purchasing a new truck. The following are the facts for the new truck Speedy just purchased:

Date on which truck was purchased .... March 1, 2017
Purchase price $64,800
Method of payment .... Cash
Estimated life .... 6 years
Estimated value at the end of 6 years $0
Depreciation method .... Straight-Line

The following is a partial list of the accounts in Speedy's General Ledger. These are the only accounts you need for this problem.

▷ Cash
▷ Truck *(asset account)*
▷ Accumulated Depreciation – Truck
▷ Depreciation Expense

Remove and use the forms on Pg 213 to complete this problem.

Requirement 1

Prepare the General Journal entry to record the purchase of the new delivery truck on March 1, 2017.

Requirement 2

Calculate the amount of <u>monthly</u> depreciation for the new truck.

Requirement 3

Prepare the March 31 General Journal adjusting entry to record depreciation for the month.

Requirement 4

What would be the balance in the <u>Accumulated Depreciation–Truck</u> account after the 18th month's depreciation adjusting entry has been made?

Requirement 5

If Speedy had estimated that the life of the truck was 4 years, what would have been the amount of monthly depreciation?

Problem 7-2 Purchase and Depreciate Two Items of Property, Plant, & Equipment

Recently the Ace Manufacturing Company purchased an office building and a new computer system. Below is the information about these two new items of Property, Plant, & Equipment.

The following are the facts for the **office building**:

Date on which the building was purchased .... April 1, 2017
Purchase price $1,800,000
Method of payment .... paid $300,000 cash – signed a note for the remainder of the purchase price
Estimated life .... 50 years
Estimated value at the end of 50 years $0
Depreciation method .... Straight-Line

The following are the facts for the **computer system**:

Date on which computer was purchased .... May 1, 2017
Purchase price $58,800
Method of payment .... Cash
Estimated life .... 7 years
Estimated value at the end of 7 years $0
Depreciation method .... Straight-Line

The following is a partial list of the accounts in Ace's General Ledger. These are the only accounts you need for this problem.

▷ Cash
▷ Building *(asset account)*
▷ Accumulated Depreciation–Building
▷ Computer *(asset account)*
▷ Accumulated Depreciation–Computer
▷ Note Payable
▷ Depreciation Expense

Remove and use the forms on Pgs 215 and 216 to complete this problem.

Requirement 1
Prepare the General Journal entry to record the purchase of the new building on April 1.

Requirement 2
Calculate the amount of <u>monthly</u> depreciation for the new building.

Problem 7-2   (continued)

Requirement 3

Prepare the April 30 General Journal adjusting entry to record depreciation of the office building for the month of April.

Requirement 4

Prepare the General Journal entry to record the purchase of the new computer system on May 1.

Requirement 5

Calculate the amount of monthly depreciation for the new computer system.

Requirement 6

Prepare the May 31 General Journal adjusting entry to record depreciation of the computer system for the month of May.

Requirement 7

Prepare the May 31 General Journal adjusting entry to record depreciation of the office building for the month of May.

Requirement 8

Ace prepares financial statements monthly. Assuming that these are Ace's only two items of Property, Plant, & Equipment, what would be the amount of Depreciation Expense on Ace's May Income Statement?

Problem 7-3   Purchasing Supplies and the Monthly Supplies Adjusting Entry

On July 1, 2017, Martha Jones started Martha's Auto Repair Shop, Inc. On that same day, Martha purchased the following supplies for use in the repair shop:

Item	Unit of Measure	Quantity Purchased	Price per Unit	Extended Total Cost
Shop Towels	Rolls	120	$4	$480
Degreasing Fluid	Quarts	75	$9	$675
Gasket Sealer	Tubes	40	$6	$240
				Total $1,395

On July 1, Martha paid cash for the supplies and set the accounting policy that all supplies would initially be recorded in the Supplies asset account.

At the end of **July**, Martha counted the supplies that were left and prepared the following listing:

Item	Unit of Measure	Quantity Remaining
Shop Towels	Rolls	80
Degreasing Fluid	Quarts	65
Gasket Sealer	Tubes	32

At the end of **August**, Martha counted the supplies that were left and prepared the following listing:

Item	Unit of Measure	Quantity Remaining
Shop Towels	Rolls	55
Degreasing Fluid	Quarts	48
Gasket Sealer	Tubes	22

The following is a partial list of the accounts in Martha's General Ledger. These are the only accounts you need for this problem.

▷ Cash
▷ Supplies
▷ Supplies Expense

Remove and use the forms on Pgs 217 and 218 to complete this problem.

Problem 7-3   (continued)

Requirement 1

Prepare the General Journal entry to record the purchase of the supplies on July 1.

Requirement 2

Calculate the dollar amount of supplies on-hand as of July 31.

Requirement 3

Prepare a "T" account analysis to determine the required July 31 adjustment to the Supplies account.

Requirement 4

Prepare the July 31 General Journal supplies adjusting entry.

Requirement 5

Calculate the dollar amount of supplies on-hand as of August 31.

Requirement 6

Prepare a "T" account analysis to determine the required August 31 adjustment to the Supplies account.

Requirement 7

Prepare the August 31 General Journal supplies adjusting entry.

Requirement 8

What was the total dollar amount of supplies consumed during Martha's first two months of operation?

Problem 7-4   Paying Rent in Advance and the
Monthly Prepaid Rent Adjusting Entry

On June 20, 2017, Amy Smith, owner of Amy's Floral Shop, Inc., signed a contract to rent a retail store. As part of the contract, Amy paid four months of rent in advance. The rental rate is $3,000 per month, thus she paid $12,000 cash in advance when she signed the contract on June 20. Amy will move into the retail store on July 1, 2017, which is the start of her rental period.

The company has the accounting policy that all prepaid assets are initially recorded in asset accounts.

The following is a partial list of the accounts in Amy's General Ledger. These are the only accounts you need for this problem.

> ▷ Cash
> ▷ Prepaid Rent *(asset account)*
> ▷ Rent Expense

Remove and use the forms on Pgs 219 and 220 to complete this problem.

Requirement 1

Prepare the General Journal entry to record the $12,000 payment made when the rental contract was signed on June 20, 2017.

Requirement 2

Fill-in the amounts on the Prepaid Rent timeline. The boxes above the timeline show the amount of Prepaid Rent still remaining at various dates during the four month period. The boxes below the timeline show the amount of Prepaid Rent that expires (is used-up) during each of the four months. *Hint: The amount that expires will be the same each month.*

Requirement 3

Prepare a "T" account analysis to determine the required July 31 adjustment to the Prepaid Rent account.

Requirement 4

Prepare the July 31 General Journal adjusting entry for Prepaid Rent.

Requirement 5

Assuming that all monthly General Journal adjusting entries were correctly made:

> ▷ What would be the amount of Prepaid Rent shown on Amy's Floral Shop, Inc.'s Balance Sheet as of August 31, 2017?
> ▷ What would be the amount of Rent Expense on the Income Statement for the period August 1 to August 31, 2017?

Problem 7-5   Prepaid Insurance and the
Monthly Prepaid Insurance Adjusting Entry

On September 1, 2017, Amy's Floral Shop, Inc. paid cash for the following two insurance policies.

Insurance Policy #1

Type of insurance coverage .... Auto and Truck

Starting date of the insurance coverage .... September 1, 2017

Period of time coverage is for .... 3 months

Total cost of coverage paid in advance $525

Insurance Policy #2

Type of insurance coverage .... Business Liability

Starting date of the insurance coverage .... September 1, 2017

Period of time coverage is for .... 4 months

Total cost of coverage paid in advance $1,400

The company has the accounting policy that all prepaid assets are initially recorded in asset accounts.

The following is a partial list of the accounts in Amy's General Ledger. These are the only accounts you need for this problem.

- ▷ Cash
- ▷ Prepaid Insurance *(asset account)*
- ▷ Insurance Expense

Remove and use the forms on Pgs 221 and 222 to complete this problem.

Requirement 1

Prepare the General Journal entry to record the September 1 cash payment made to purchase the two insurance policies. Note that there is only one General Ledger account for Prepaid Insurance, and that the amount of Prepaid Insurance related to both insurance policies is kept in that one account.

Requirement 2

Fill-in the amounts on the **Auto and Truck** Prepaid Insurance timeline. The boxes above the timeline show the amount of Auto and Truck Prepaid Insurance still remaining at various dates during the three month period. The boxes below the timeline show the amount of Auto and Truck Prepaid Insurance that expires (is used-up) during each of the three months.

Requirement 3

Fill-in the amounts on the **Business Liability** Prepaid Insurance timeline. The boxes above the timeline show the amount of Business Liability Prepaid Insurance still remaining at various dates during the four month period. The boxes below the timeline show the amount of Business Liability Prepaid Insurance that expires (is used-up) during each of the four months.

(Problem 7-5 continued on the next page)

Problem 7-5   (continued)

Requirement 4

Prepare a "T" account analysis to determine the required September 30 adjustment to the Prepaid Insurance account. Note that your "T" account analysis is for the Prepaid Insurance account, which contains the <u>total</u> amount of Prepaid Insurance for <u>both</u> insurance policies.

Requirement 5

Prepare the September 30 General Journal adjusting entry for Prepaid Insurance.

Requirement 6

Assuming that all monthly General Journal adjusting entries were correctly made and that no additional insurance has been purchased:

▷ What would be the amount of Prepaid Insurance shown on Amy's Floral Shop, Inc.'s Balance Sheet as of October 31, 2017?

▷ What would be the amount of Insurance Expense on the Income Statement for the period October 1 to October 31, 2017?

Problem 7-6   Weekly Wage Payment Entries and the Month-End Wages Payable Adjusting Entry

Baker Construction, Inc. pays its employees each Friday for the work they performed that week. Baker's employees only work on Monday through Friday. They do not work on Saturday or Sunday. Baker produces monthly financial statements; thus they prepare adjusting entries at the end of each month.

For the month of June, the last payday was on Friday June 25th. The last day of June was on Wednesday June 30th. The first payday of July was on Friday July 2nd. The following partial calendar shows these days and dates:

Sunday	Monday	Tuesday	Wednesday	Thursday	Friday	Saturday
June **20**	June **21**	June **22**	June **23**	June **24**	June **25**	June **26**
June **27**	June **28**	June **29**	June **30**	*July 1*	*July 2*	*July 3*

The following table shows the amount the employees were paid on Friday June 25th and on Friday July 2nd. The table also shows the data required to calculate the amount the employees earned for the last three workdays of June.

Wages paid on Friday, June 25th $6,200

Wages paid on Friday, July 2nd $5,950

Data for June 28, 29, & 30 – the last three days worked in June:

Number of employees working each day ....10 employees per day

Hours each employee worked per day ....8 hours per day

Hourly wage rate ....$16 per hour

Problem 7-6   (continued)

The following is a partial list of the accounts in Baker's General Ledger. These are the only accounts you need for this problem.

▷ Cash
▷ Wages Payable
▷ Wages Expense

Remove and use the forms on Pg 223 to complete this problem.

Requirement 1

Prepare the General Journal entry to record the wage payment made to the employees on Friday June 25th.

Requirement 2

Calculate the total amount the employees earned for:
Monday June 28th + Tuesday June 29th + Wednesday June 30th.

Requirement 3

Prepare the June 30 General Journal adjusting entry for Wages Payable.

Requirement 4

Prepare the General Journal entry to record the wage payment made to the employees on Friday July 2nd.

Hint: A portion of the wage payment is paying-off the Wages Payable liability that was recorded in the June 30th adjusting entry, and a portion of the wage payment is Wages Expense for the month of July.

Problem 7-7   Take-Out a Loan – Accrue Interest on the Loan – Pay Interest

On April 1, 2017, Baker Construction, Inc. signed a note for a loan from its bank. The following are the terms and other information pertaining to the loan:

Amount of the loan	$100,000
How long the loan is for (the term of the loan)	1 year
Date the loan was made	April 1, 2017
Date of first interest payment to the bank	June 30, 2017
Amount of interest charged by the bank for April	$550
Amount of interest charged by the bank for May	$568
Amount of interest charged by the bank for June	$550

The following is a partial list of the accounts in Baker's General Ledger. These are the only accounts you need for this problem.

- ▷ Cash
- ▷ Note Payable
- ▷ Interest Payable
- ▷ Interest Expense

Remove and use the forms on Pg 225 to complete this problem.

Requirement 1
Prepare the April 1, 2017 General Journal entry to record getting the loan from the bank.

Requirement 2
Prepare the April 30, 2017 General Journal adjusting entry to accrue the interest owed to the bank for the month of April.

Requirement 3
Prepare the May 31, 2017 General Journal adjusting entry to accrue the interest owed to the bank for the month of May.

Requirement 4
Prepare the June 30, 2017 General Journal entry to record the payment of the April, May, and June interest to the bank.

Hint: *For help with how this interest payment should be recorded:*

- ▷ *Look at* <u>*March 30 – Interest Payment to the Bank*</u> *starting on Pg 57 in your Solid Footing Book.*
- ▷ *Look at the March 30 interest payment transaction (Pay Interest button) on the March tab of the 02-Gray Co workbook.*

Problem 7-8   Accrue Rent Payable – Pay Rent the Following Month

On September 1, 2017, Baker Construction, Inc. signed a contract to rent a warehouse. Baker's rent on the warehouse started that same day. On September 1, the landlord did not require Baker to pay the first month's rent. The landlord indicated that she would stop-by on October 5 to collect the $2,000 of rent for the month of September.

The following is a partial list of the accounts in Baker's General Ledger. These are the only accounts you need for this problem.

▷ Cash
▷ Rent Payable *(liability account)*
▷ Rent Expense

Remove and use the forms on Pg 226 to complete this problem.

Requirement 1

Prepare the General Journal entry Baker should make on September 1, 2017. If no entry is required, put "No Entry Required" on the General Journal form.

Requirement 2

Prepare the September 30, 2017 Rent Payable adjusting entry. If no entry is required, put "No Entry Required" on the General Journal form.

Requirement 3

Prepare the General Journal entry Baker should make on October 5, 2017 to record the $2,000 payment of September's rent. If no entry is required, put "No Entry Required" on the General Journal form.

Additional Chapter 7 Adjusting Entry Homework Problems

Located in the **Word** file named Chapter 07 Additional Problems.doc are more adjusting entry homework problems:

▷ Problem 7-9   Lenny's January Accounting Period

▷ Problem 7-10   Lenny's February Accounting Period

▷ Problem 7-11   Lenny's March Accounting Period

To print these additional problems, open the Chapter 07 Additional Problems.doc file using your Word application.

NOTES

Chapter 8
Adjusting Entries Continued
Unearned Revenue Liabilities – Accrued Assets

⇨ LENNY's APRIL TRANSACTIONS
___

In this chapter, you will continue to use the workbook that you used in the last chapter entitled "03-Lenny's Lawn Service".   If this workbook is not open on your computer, do the following:

  ⇨ Open the workbook **03-Lenny's Lawn Service** in the **Solid Footing 10e** folder

  ⇨ Enable Macros

🖰 Click the **April** tab.

You should see **Screen 8 A** in the upper left corner of the screen.

⇨ RECEIVE ADVANCE PAYMENT TRANSACTION
___

On April 1, Lenny's signs a contract to perform lawn services for a new customer. The new customer is a university in the Tampa area. The contract Lenny's signs with the university stipulates that Lenny's will be paid an $8,000 monthly fee for the lawn services. As part of the contract agreement, the university agrees to pay the first four months of services in advance; thus Lenny's receives $32,000 cash from the university on April 1.

🖰 Click **Advance Pmt.**

The $32,000 debit to the Cash account records the increase in cash that results from the advance payment. The credit portion of this entry is to the **Unearned Revenue** liability account. The Unearned Revenue account records the university's $32,000 claim to Lenny's assets. A liability account is increased because Lenny's has a future obligation to perform $32,000 of services for the university, and as of April 1, Lenny's has not earned any of the $32,000.

The Unearned Revenue liability account is just like any other liability account. It records the claim to assets of someone (in this case, the university) who is not an owner of the business. The one thing that does make the Unearned Revenue account different from most other liability accounts is that the Unearned Revenue liability will be "paid-off" by Lenny's providing services to the university—not by Lenny's paying cash to the university.

Let's now post the advance payment entry to the General Ledger accounts.

🖰 Click **Post to Ledger**

Observe that this entry increases the Cash account and increases the Unearned Revenue liability account. This entry does not increase the owners' claim to assets because Lenny's has not performed any of the services; thus none of the $32,000 has been earned as of April 1.

⇨ PAY LAST MONTH's WAGES TRANSACTION

At the end of March, an adjusting entry was recorded for the wages due Lenny's employees for their last two days of work in March. Look on the screen and observe the $1,825 credit balance in the Wages Payable account. This balance is the amount due the employees. On April 3, the employees are paid the $1,825.

🖰 Click **Pay Mar Wages**

🖰 Click **Post to Ledger**

Observe the following about this entry:

▷ The current balance in the Wages Payable liability account is now zero because Lenny's no longer owes the employees for the March wages.

▷ The debit in this entry is to the Wages Payable account.

▷ This entry is different than prior wage payment transactions. Previously when wages were paid, the debit was to the Wage Expense account. The debit to the Wage Expense account, for these two days of work, was made as part of the adjusting entry at the end of March.

Lenny's Normal Monthly Transactions

Let's now enter the rest of Lenny's April transactions.

🖰 Click **Enter Other April Transactions into Journal and Post to the Ledger**

Review these transactions and observe that they are Lenny's normal monthly transactions.

All of April's transactions have been entered. By reviewing the ending account balances, you determine that the balances in three accounts need to be adjusted at the end of April. The three accounts that need to be adjusted are the:

▷ Accumulated Depreciation account

▷ Supplies asset account

▷ Unearned Revenue liability account

⇨ APRIL's DEPRECIATION ADJUSTING ENTRY

The adjusting entry for April's depreciation follows the same logic as the three previous months' depreciation adjusting entries.

🖱 Click **Depreciation**

🖱 Click **Post to Ledger**

Observe the depreciation entry and the effect that entry has on the Accumulated Depreciation and Depreciation Expense accounts.

⇨ APRIL's SUPPLIES ADJUSTING ENTRY

Lenny's determines that $7,600 of supplies remain in stock as of April 30.

Complete the following "T" account analysis for the Supplies account as of the end of April.

"T" Account Analysis for Asset and Liability Accounts		
Account Name →	**Supplies** *(asset account)*	
	Debit	**Credit**
(1) What is the <u>current</u> balance?		
(3) What adjustment is required to adjust from the <u>current</u> balance to the <u>should be</u> balance?		
(2) What <u>should be</u> the balance?		

Record below the April supplies adjusting journal entry.

General Journal			
Date	**Account**	**Debit**	**Credit**
Apr 30			
	Adjust supplies to April 30 on-hand balance		

🖱 Click **Supplies Adj.**

🖱 Click **Post to Ledger**

Based on your "T" account analysis, did you prepare the correct supplies adjusting entry?

⇨ APRIL's UNEARNED REVENUE ADJUSTING ENTRY

On April 1, when Lenny's signed the contract with the university, Lenny's was paid $32,000 in advance for the first four months of services. During the month of April, Lenny's performed the lawn services for the university.

The timeline below shows the period of service covered by the $32,000 Lenny's received on April 1. You can see from the timeline that on April 1, Lenny's owed the university $32,000 of services. The original $32,000 entry into the Unearned Liability account reflected Lenny's $32,000 liability for future services to the university.

The timeline also shows the period of time and the dollar amount of services the university is still due as of the end of April. As of April 30, Lenny's owes the university three months of service. Each month of service has a value of $8,000; thus Lenny's owes the university $24,000 of future services as of April 30. Because the balance in the Unearned Revenue account tracks Lenny's liability for future services to the university, the April 30 balance in the Unearned Revenue account <u>should be</u> $24,000.

Unearned Revenue Timeline

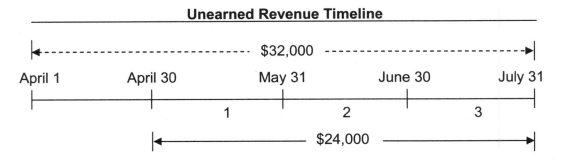

"T" Account Analysis for Asset and Liability Accounts		
Account Name →	**Unearned Revenue**	
	Debit	**Credit**
(1) What is the <u>current</u> balance?		32,000
(3) What adjustment is required to adjust from the <u>current</u> balance to the <u>should be</u> balance?	8,000	
(2) What <u>should be</u> the balance?		24,000

Observe the amounts in the "T" account analysis and how this analysis was prepared based on the following process:

1. Look on the screen at the current balance in the Unearned Revenue account. That amount is put into the "T" account analysis for Step (**1**).

2. The <u>should be</u> balance in the Unearned Revenue account is determined from the timeline analysis. From the timeline analysis, you can determine that the <u>should be</u> balance in the Unearned Revenue account is $24,000; thus $24,000 is put in the "T" account analysis for Step (**2**).

3. Determine the Debit or Credit amount that is required to adjust the Unearned Revenue liability account from its <u>current</u> balance to its <u>should be</u> balance. The $8,000 debit amount is put in the "T" account analysis for Step (**3**); because this is the amount required to take the Unearned Revenue liability account from a <u>current</u> balance of $32,000 credit to a <u>should be</u> balance of $24,000 credit.

The amount for Step (**3**) in the "T" account analysis is the required adjustment to the Unearned Revenue liability account. The other portion of the Unearned Revenue adjusting entry will be to the Service Revenue account.

Record below the April Unearned Revenue adjusting journal entry.

General Journal			
Date	**Account**	**Debit**	**Credit**
Apr 30			
	Adjust Unearned Revenue to April 30 amount		

🖰 Click **Unearned Adj.**

🖰 Click **Post to Ledger**

Look on the screen at the Unearned Revenue adjusting entry in the General Journal and at the posting of that entry to both the Unearned Revenue and the Service Revenue accounts in the General Ledger. Did you prepare the correct adjusting entry?

Observe the following about this adjusting entry:

▷ The entry does not affect any asset account. The amount of Total Assets is not changed by this adjusting entry.

▷ The entry reduces the credit balance in the Unearned Revenue liability account; thus reducing the university's claims to Lenny's assets.

▷ The entry increases the Service Revenue account by $8,000. This properly reflects the $8,000 Lenny's earned by providing the April lawn services to the university.

▷ The $8,000 increase in Service Revenue increases the owners' claim to assets by $8,000; thus the effect of this adjusting entry is to increase the owners' claim to assets and reduce the university's claim to assets.

Other examples of transactions that result in Unearned Revenue liabilities are:

> ▷ A landlord receives cash in advance for rent.

> ▷ A magazine publisher receives cash in advance for magazine subscriptions.

> ▷ A sports team receives cash in advance for season tickets.

There will be more discussion of Unearned Revenues in Chapter 9.

Lenny's April Income Statement and Balance Sheet

Let's prepare the Income Statement for April. To save space, Step 4 in the Accounting Cycle, *Prepare a Pre-Closing Trial Balance*, is not shown on the screen. Preparing the Income Statement is Step 5 in the Accounting Cycle.

✍ Click **Prepare the Income Statement**

Look at the Service Revenue account in the General Ledger and notice that the $36,250 Ending Balance is the result of the $28,250 monthly billing to the property management company plus $8,000 from the Unearned Revenue adjusting journal entry. Because the Service Revenue line on the Income Statement comes from the Ending Balance in the Service Revenue account, you can see that the Unearned Revenue adjusting journal entry had a significant impact on Lenny's April Income Statement.

As in the three previous months, Step 6 in the Accounting Cycle is not shown. The ending Retained Earnings balance needed for the Balance Sheet is:

Current balance in Retained Earnings	$41,450
Plus April Net Income	13,100
Ending balance in Retained Earnings	$54,550

Now let's prepare the Balance Sheet and see how the Unearned Revenue account appears on the Balance Sheet. Preparing the Balance Sheet is Step 7 in the Accounting Cycle.

✍ Click **Prepare the Balance Sheet**

Observe the university's claim, Unearned Rev, on the Balance Sheet. As previously discussed, the Unearned Revenue account is just another liability account. Also notice that Wages Payable is zero on the April Balance Sheet.

To finish April's Accounting Cycle, Lenny's would complete Step 8 – *Prepare and enter the revenue and expense closing entries,* and Step 9 – *Prepare a Post-Closing Trial Balance.* These two steps will not be shown in this chapter. These steps are the same as previously shown for Gray Co.

⇨ ERRORS – NOT MAKING THE UNEARNED REVENUE ENTRY

What would be the effect on the financial statements if Lenny's had failed to make the Unearned Revenue adjusting entry at the end of April?

🖱 Click **Show the Errors**

By comparing Lenny's correct **Income Statement for the Month of April** to the **Income Statement with Errors**, you can see the following would be the effects if Lenny's failed to make the April Unearned Revenue adjusting entry:

> ▷ Service Revenue would be understated by $8,000.

> ▷ Total Expenses would not be affected and would be correct.

> ▷ Net Income would be understated by $8,000.

By comparing Lenny's correct **Balance Sheet as of April 30** to the **Balance Sheet with Errors**, you can see the following would be the effects if Lenny's failed to make the April Unearned Revenue adjusting entry:

> ▷ Unearned Revenue would be overstated by $8,000.

> ▷ Total Liabilities would be overstated by $8,000.

> ▷ Retained Earnings would be understated by $8,000.

> ▷ Total Equity would be understated by $8,000.

Also by comparing Lenny's correct **Balance Sheet as of April 30** to the **Balance Sheet with Errors**, you can see what would <u>not</u> have been affected if Lenny's failed to make the April Unearned Revenue adjusting entry:

> ▷ All asset accounts and Total Assets are the same on both Balance Sheets.

> ▷ Total Liabilities and Equity would not be affected by the omission of the April Unearned Revenue adjusting entry.

From the above analysis, you can see that the Unearned Revenue adjusting entry has a significant impact on both April's Income Statement and April's Balance Sheet.

As noted above, <u>Total Assets</u> and <u>Total Liabilities and Equity</u> are the same on both the correct **Balance Sheet as of April 30** and the **Balance Sheet with Errors**, even though some of the line items on the **Balance Sheet with Errors** are not correct. As noted in Chapter 7, just because a Balance Sheet balances, it does not guarantee that all line items on that Balance Sheet are correct. Now we see that just because <u>Total Assets</u> and <u>Total Liabilities and Equity</u> are correct on a Balance Sheet, it does not guarantee that all line items on that Balance Sheet are correct.

⇨ LENNY's MAY TRANSACTIONS

You will now take Lenny's Lawn Service through its May accounting period.

🖱 Click the **May** tab.

You should see **Screen 8 B** in the upper left corner of the screen.

During the month of May, Lenny's completed its normal monthly transactions.

🖱 Click **Enter May Transactions into Journal and Post to the Ledger**

Review these transactions and observe that they are Lenny's normal monthly transactions.

All of May's transactions have been entered. By reviewing the ending account balances, you determine that the balances in four accounts need to be adjusted at the end of May. The four accounts that need to be adjusted are the:

  ▷ Accumulated Depreciation account

  ▷ Supplies account

  ▷ Unearned Revenue account

  ▷ Accounts Receivable account

⇨ MAY's DEPRECIATION ADJUSTING ENTRY

The adjusting entry for May's depreciation follows the same logic as the four previous months' depreciation adjusting entries.

🖱 Click **Depreciation**

🖱 Click **Post to Ledger**

Observe the depreciation entry and the effect that entry has on the Accumulated Depreciation and Depreciation Expense accounts.

⇨ MAY's SUPPLIES ADJUSTING ENTRY

Lenny's determines that $5,875 of supplies remain in stock as of May 31.

On the following page, complete the "T" account analysis for the Supplies account as of the end of May.

"T" Account Analysis for Asset and Liability Accounts		
Account Name →	*Supplies* (asset account)	
	Debit	Credit
(1) What is the <u>current</u> balance?		
(3) What adjustment is required to adjust from the <u>current</u> balance to the <u>should be</u> balance?		
(2) What <u>should be</u> the balance?		

Record below the May supplies adjusting journal entry.

General Journal			
Date	Account	Debit	Credit
May 31			
	Adjust supplies to May 31 on-hand balance		

🖰 Click **Supplies Adj.**

🖰 Click **Post to Ledger**

Based on your "T" account analysis, did you prepare the correct supplies adjusting entry?

⇨ MAY's UNEARNED REVENUE ADJUSTING ENTRY

On April 1, Lenny's signed a contract with the university and was paid $32,000 in advance for the first four months of services. During the month of May, Lenny's performed the lawn services for the university.

The timeline below shows the period of service covered by the $32,000 Lenny's received on April 1. The timeline also shows the period of time and the dollar amount of services the university is still due as of the end of May. As of May 31, Lenny's owes the university two months of service. Each month of service has a value of $8,000; thus Lenny's owes the university $16,000 of future services as of May 31. This $16,000 amount is the <u>should be</u> balance in the Unearned Revenue liability account as of May 31.

Unearned Revenue Timeline

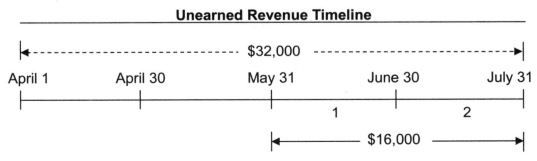

Complete the following "T" account analysis for the Unearned Revenue account as of the end of May.

"T" Account Analysis for Asset and Liability Accounts		
Account Name →	**Unearned Revenue**	
	Debit	**Credit**
(1) What is the <u>current</u> balance?		
(3) What adjustment is required to adjust from the <u>current</u> balance to the <u>should be</u> balance?		
(2) What <u>should be</u> the balance?		

Record below the May Unearned Revenue adjusting journal entry.

General Journal			
Date	**Account**	**Debit**	**Credit**
May 31			
	Adjust Unearned Revenue to May 31 amount		

🖰 Click **Unearned Adj.**

🖰 Click **Post to Ledger**

Based on your "T" account analysis, did you prepare the correct Unearned Revenue adjusting entry?

⇨ MAY's ACCOUNTS RECEIVABLE ADJUSTING ENTRY

Early on the morning of May 31, Lenny's receives a call from a local golf course. The golf course is hosting a golf tournament starting the following day, and an overnight fire has destroyed several of the golf course's large mowing machines. The golf course wants to contract with Lenny's for mowing service. Lenny's meets with the manager of the golf course and is shown how much area needs to be mowed. Lenny's quotes the manager of the golf course a price of $3,500, and the manager accepts that price.

Lenny's mowing crew works at the golf course on May 31, from 9:00 A.M. in the morning until 11:30 P.M. in the evening and completes mowing the area covered by the $3,500 price. Given that it is 11:30 P.M. on May 31 when Lenny's completes the mowing job, there is no time to invoice the golf course prior to the end of May.

The following facts relate to this mowing job:

> ▷ Lenny's earned the $3,500 prior to the end of May; because the mowing job was complete prior to midnight on May 31.

> ▷ Lenny's has the right to receive the $3,500 from the golf course as of the end of May.

> ▷ Lenny's current balance in Accounts Receivable does **not** include the $3,500 due from the golf course; because there was no time to invoice the golf course prior to the end of the day on May 31.

> ▷ An adjusting entry needs to be made to Accounts Receivable to include this $3,500 in the ending Accounts Receivable account balance.

You could go through the three step "T" account analysis process to determine what the required adjusting entry is to Accounts Receivable. But in some cases, and this is one of them, the required adjustment is obvious. Accounts Receivable needs to be increased by $3,500.

Record below the May Accounts Receivable adjusting journal entry for the unbilled work at the golf course.

	General Journal			
Date	**Account**		**Debit**	**Credit**
May 31				
	Adjust A/R for unbilled golf course job			

🖰 Click **A/R Adj.**

🖰 Click **Post to Ledger**

Did you prepare the correct Accounts Receivable adjusting entry?

After making this adjusting entry, the Accounts Receivable account balance of $32,500 is the result of the $29,000 of regular monthly invoicing plus the $3,500 Accrued Asset amount from the adjusting entry. Other examples of accruing an asset are:

> ▷ Accruing interest that is owed to us by someone that has borrowed money from us. The amount of interest owed to us would be the debit balance in an Interest Receivable account.

> ▷ Accruing rent owed to us by a tenant when we are the landlord. The amount of rent owed to us would be the debit balance in a Rent Receivable account.

There will be more discussion of the Accrued Asset category in Chapter 9.

Lenny's May Income Statement and Balance Sheet

Let's prepare the Income Statement for May. To save space, Step 4 in the Accounting Cycle, *Prepare a Pre-Closing Trial Balance*, is not shown on the screen. Preparing the Income Statement is Step 5 in the Accounting Cycle.

🖰 Click **Prepare the Income Statement**

Look at the Service Revenue account in the General Ledger and the Service Revenue amount shown on the Income Statement. Observe that the $40,500 Ending Balance in the Service Revenue account is the result of the $29,000 monthly billing to the property management company, plus $8,000 from the Unearned Revenue adjusting journal entry, plus $3,500 from the Accounts Receivable adjusting entry.

As in the four previous months, Step 6 in the Accounting Cycle is not shown. The ending Retained Earnings balance needed for the Balance Sheet is:

Current balance in Retained Earnings	$54,550
Plus May Net Income	14,775
Ending balance in Retained Earnings	$69,325

Now let's prepare the Balance Sheet – Step 7 in the Accounting Cycle.

🖱 Click **Prepare the Balance Sheet**

Observe that Accounts Receivable is $32,500 on the Balance Sheet. As previously stated, that amount is the $29,000 due from the property management company plus the $3,500 due from the golf course.

To finish May's Accounting Cycle, Lenny's would complete Step 8 – *Prepare and enter the revenue and expense closing entries,* and Step 9 – *Prepare a Post-Closing Trial Balance.* These two steps will not be shown in this chapter. These steps are the same as previously shown for Gray Co.

⇨ ERRORS – NOT MAKING THE A/R ADJUSTING ENTRY

What would be the effect on the financial statements if Lenny's had failed to make the Accounts Receivable adjusting entry at the end of May?

🖱 Click **Show the Errors**

By comparing Lenny's correct **Income Statement for the Month of May** to the **Income Statement with Errors**, you can see the following would be the effects if Lenny's failed to make the May Accounts Receivable adjusting entry:

▷ Service Revenue would be understated by $3,500.

▷ Total Expenses would not be affected and would be correct.

▷ Net Income would be understated by $3,500.

By comparing Lenny's correct **Balance Sheet as of May 31** to the **Balance Sheet with Errors**, you can see the following would be the effects if Lenny's failed to make the May Accounts Receivable adjusting entry:

▷ Accounts Receivable would be understated by $3,500.

▷ Total Assets would be understated by $3,500.

▷ Retained Earnings would be understated by $3,500.

▷ Total Equity would be understated by $3,500.

▷ Total Liabilities and Equity would be understated by $3,500.

From the above analysis, you can see that the Accounts Receivable adjusting entry has a significant impact on both May's Income Statement and May's Balance Sheet.

Chapter 8 Homework

Problem 8-1   Collecting Rent In Advance and the Monthly Adjusting Entry

Apex Properties, Inc. owns two warehouse buildings that it rents to other businesses. The two buildings are very desirable properties and this enables Apex to require that renters pay rent in advance. The following is data for each building:

Building #1 – Located at 111 Warehouse Way

Rental rate .... $3,000 per month

Number of months of rent collected in advance ...... 3 months

Dates when rent is collected in advance .... January 1, April 1, July 1, October 1

Building #2 – Located at 444 Storage Street

Rental rate .... $4,000 per month

Number of months of rent collected in advance ...... 3 months

Dates when rent is collected in advance .... January 1, April 1, July 1, October 1

Apex has the accounting policy that rent collected in advance be initially recorded in a liability account.

The balance in the Unearned Rent Revenue account as of December 31, 2016 was $0.

On January 1, 2017, Apex collected cash for the 3 month advance payment of rent for both buildings. The cash collected is detailed below:

Building #1 – for Jan., Feb. & March – 3 months cash collected...... (3 x $3,000) ..... $ 9,000

Building #2 – for Jan., Feb. & March – 3 months cash collected...... (3 x $4,000) $12,000

Total cash collected on January 1, 2017 $21,000

The following is a partial list of the accounts in Apex's General Ledger. These are the only accounts you need for this problem.

▷ Cash
▷ Unearned Rent Revenue *(liability account)*
▷ Rent Revenue *(revenue account)*

Remove and use the forms on Pgs 227 and 228 to complete this problem.

Requirement 1

Prepare the January 1, 2017 General Journal entry to record the receipt of the $21,000 cash for 3 months advance payment of rent for both buildings.

Problem 8-1   (continued)

Requirement 2

Prepare a "T" account analysis to determine the required January 31, 2017 adjustment to the Unearned Rent Revenue account.

Hint: The <u>should be</u> balance amount has been put in the "T" account analysis form.

Requirement 3

Prepare the January 31, 2017 General Journal adjusting entry for Unearned Rent Revenue.

Requirement 4

Prepare a "T" account analysis to determine the required February 28, 2017 adjustment to the Unearned Rent Revenue account.

Requirement 5

Prepare the February 28, 2017 General Journal adjusting entry for Unearned Rent Revenue.

Requirement 6

▷ What would be the amount of Unearned Rent Revenue (*a liability*) shown on Apex Properties, Inc.'s Balance Sheet as of February 28, 2017?

▷ What would be the amount of Rent Revenue on the Income Statement for the period February 1 to February 28, 2017?

Problem 8-2   Collect Cash for Season Tickets and the Monthly Adjusting Entry

Sports Enterprise, Inc. (SEI) owns a semi-pro football team. SEI sells three types of season ticket packages.

▷ Package **#1** is for <u>all</u> 10 home games.

▷ Package **#2** is for the <u>first</u> 5 home games.

▷ Package **#3** is for the <u>last</u> 5 home games.

All season tickets are sold in September.

The following table shows the 2017 season ticket sales by season ticket package.

Package	Total Season Ticket Sales
#1 – <u>all</u> 10 Games	$250,000
#2 – <u>first</u> 5 Games	$30,000
#3 – <u>last</u> 5 Games	$75,000
Total	**$355,000**

The following table shows the:

  ▷ Number of home games by month included in each season ticket package.
  ▷ The % each month's games are of the package's total games.

	Package #1		Package #2		Package #3	
	Games Included in the Package by Month		**Games** Included in the Package by Month		**Games** Included in the Package by Month	
October	2	20%	2	40%	0	0%
November	4	40%	3	60%	1	20%
December	4	40%	0	0%	4	80%
Total	10	100%	5	100%	5	100%

SEI has the accounting policy that season ticket sales be initially recorded in a liability account.

The following is a partial list of the accounts in SEI's General Ledger. These are the only accounts you need for this problem.

  ▷ Cash
  ▷ Unearned Ticket Revenue *(liability account)*
  ▷ Ticket Revenue *(revenue account)*

Remove and use the forms on Pgs 229 and 230 to complete this problem.

Requirement 1
  Prepare the General Journal entry to record the total season ticket sales. As noted on the previous page, all season ticket sales are made in the month of September. Date your General Journal entry September 30, 2017.

Requirement 2
  Prepare a "T" account analysis to determine the required October 31, 2017 adjustment to the Unearned Ticket Revenue account. See the calculation under the "T" account analysis form on Pg 229 for how the <u>should be</u> Unearned Ticket Revenue balance is calculated.

Requirement 3
  Prepare the October 31, 2017 General Journal adjusting entry for Unearned Ticket Revenue.

Requirement 4
  Prepare a "T" account analysis to determine the required November 30, 2017 adjustment to the Unearned Ticket Revenue account.

Requirement 5
  Prepare the November 30, 2017 General Journal adjusting entry for Unearned Ticket Revenue.

Requirement 6
  ▷ What would be the amount of Unearned Ticket Revenue shown on SEI's Balance Sheet as of November 30, 2017?

  ▷ For the home games during November 2017, SEI's total "day-of-the-game" ticket sales were $650,000. What would be the total amount of Ticket Revenue on SEI's Income Statement for the period November 1 to November 30, 2017?

Problem 8-3   Loan Money – Accrue Monthly Interest – Collect Interest

On July 1, 2017, MegaMoney, Inc. loaned money to ShortOfCash company (SOC). MegaMoney had SOC sign a note for the loan. The following are the terms and other information pertaining to the loan:

Amount of the loan	$750,000
How long the loan is for (the term of the loan)	1 year
Date the loan was made	July 1, 2017
Date when interest will first be received by MegaMoney	September 30, 2017
Amount of interest earned by MegaMoney for July	$3,825
Amount of interest earned by MegaMoney for August	$3,825
Amount of interest earned by MegaMoney for September	$3,710

The following is a partial list of the accounts in MegaMoney's General Ledger. These are the only accounts you need for this problem.

> ▷ Cash
> ▷ Note Receivable (*see below for a definition of this account*)
> ▷ Interest Receivable (*see below for a definition of this account*)
> ▷ Interest Revenue (*revenue account*)

Note Receivable account – An asset account that tracks the amount owed to the entity (MegaMoney) by another company (SOC). This asset results from the entity making a loan to the other company and the other company signing a Note. The normal balance is a debit.

Interest Receivable account – An asset account that tracks the amount of interest owed to the entity (MegaMoney) by another company (SOC). The normal balance is a debit.

Remove and use the forms on Pg 231 to complete this problem.

Note: You are recording the transactions in <u>MegaMoney's</u> accounting system.

Requirement 1
Prepare the July 1, 2017 General Journal entry to record the loan MegaMoney made to SOC.

Hint: MegaMoney gave out the asset Cash. MegaMoney got in the asset Note Receivable.

Requirement 2
Prepare the July 31, 2017 General Journal adjusting entry to increase the Interest Receivable account by the amount of interest MegaMoney earned on the Note Receivable for July.

Requirement 3
Prepare the August 31, 2017 General Journal adjusting entry to increase the Interest Receivable account by the amount of interest MegaMoney earned on the Note Receivable for August.

Requirement 4
Prepare the September 30, 2017 General Journal entry to record the receipt of cash by MegaMoney from SOC for the July, August, and September interest.

Hint: The account names have been put in the General Journal.

Problem 8-4   Accrue Monthly Rent Receivable – Collect Rent

Office Rental, Inc. owns an office building that it rents to Watson Company. The building is in a location that is not very desirable. To provide an incentive for Watson to rent the building, Office Rental, Inc. collects rent at the <u>end</u> of each 6 months. The following is data for the office building:

Office Building – Located at 123 ItsADump Drive

Rental rate .... $450 per month

Date when the 6 months of rent for January to June is collected ...... June 30

Date when the 6 months of rent for July to December is collected .... December 31

The office building located at 123 ItsADump Drive is the only rental property owned by Office Rental, Inc.

After making the April 30, 2017 Rent Receivable adjusting entry, the balance in Office Rental Inc.'s Rent Receivable account is $1,800. This balance represents 4 month's (Jan., Feb., Mar., Apr.) of rent due from Watson.

The following is a partial list of the accounts in Office Rental Inc.'s General Ledger. These are the only accounts you need for this problem.

> ▷ Cash
> ▷ Rent Receivable *(asset account)*
> ▷ Rent Revenue *(revenue account)*

Remove and use the forms on Pg 232 to complete this problem.

Requirement 1

Prepare the May 31, 2017 General Journal adjusting entry to accrue May's Rent Receivable.

Requirement 2

> ▷ What would be the amount of Rent Receivable shown on Office Rental Inc.'s Balance Sheet as of May 31, 2017?

> ▷ What would be the amount of Rent Revenue on Office Rental Inc.'s Income Statement for the period May 1 to May 31, 2017?

Requirement 3

Prepare the June 30, 2017 General Journal entry to record the receipt of cash by Office Rental, Inc. from Watson for the 6 months of rent from January to June.

Hint: The account names have been put in the General Journal.

Additional Chapter 8 Adjusting Entry Homework Problems

Located in the **Word** file named <u>Chapter 08 Additional Problems.doc</u> are more adjusting entry homework problems:

           ▷   Problem 8-5   Lenny's April Accounting Period

           ▷   Problem 8-6   Lenny's May Accounting Period

To print these additional problems, open the <u>Chapter 08 Additional Problems.doc</u> file using your Word application.

Chapter 9

Categories of Accounts that Require Adjusting Entries
Summary of Timing Issues Related to the Account Categories

Accounts that require adjusting entries can be grouped into five different categories. Accountants often refer to these categories when describing adjusting entries. In Chapters 7 and 8, when you made Lenny's adjusting entries, you utilized accounts in each of these five categories. Now, let's take a look at each of the five categories.

⇨ PROPERTY, PLANT, & EQUIPMENT

The first category of accounts to be discussed is Long-Term Assets. Most of the Long-Term Assets purchased by a company are Property, Plant, & Equipment assets; thus this discussion will focus on Property, Plant, & Equipment. Property, Plant, & Equipment assets are also called **Fixed Assets**. The balances in these asset accounts result when:

1. An item of Property, Plant, or Equipment is purchased in the current accounting period.

   and

2. The item purchased will benefit one or more future accounting periods.

Refer back to the discussion of Lenny's lawn mowing equipment starting on Pg 70. The $48,000 of mowing equipment is an example of Property, Plant, & Equipment. Look at Lenny's January screen to see an example of an Equipment account and the related Accumulated Depreciation contra-asset account.

An adjusting entry is required each accounting period to record the depreciation related to a company's Property, Plant, & Equipment. At the end of the January accounting period, you made an adjusting entry to Lenny's Accumulated Depreciation contra-asset account. This entry recorded the allocation of 1/48th of the mowing equipment's cost to the January accounting period. You made similar adjusting entries to the Accumulated Depreciation account in February, March, April, and May.

⇨ PREPAID ASSETS

The second category of accounts to be discussed is Prepaid Assets.

Prepaid Assets are also called Deferred Expenses. Do not be confused by this "also-called-name" containing the word Expenses. Prepaid Assets (Deferred Expenses) **are** assets.

The balances in these asset accounts result when:

1. An item or service is purchased in the current accounting period.

   and

2. The item or service is not totally consumed in the current accounting period.

   and

3. The item or service will benefit one or more future accounting periods.

Refer back to Lenny's February purchase of supplies starting on Pg 74, and look at Lenny's February screen to see an example of a Prepaid Asset. The $11,000 of supplies, which Lenny's purchased on February 1, is an example of a Prepaid Asset. They are a Prepaid Asset because:

1. The supplies were purchased in the <u>current</u> accounting period, February.

2. The supplies were not totally consumed in the February accounting period.

3. The supplies will benefit <u>future</u> accounting periods, in Lenny's case: March, April, May, etc.

An adjusting entry is required as Prepaid Assets are consumed. At the end of the February accounting period, you made an adjusting entry to Lenny's Supplies account. This entry adjusted the Supplies account to reflect the actual supplies still on-hand on February 28. You made similar adjusting entries to the Supplies account in March, April, and May.

Other examples of Prepaid Assets are:

▷ Prepaid Rent   (We pay more than one month rent in advance to our landlord.)

▷ Prepaid Insurance   (We purchase insurance coverage lasting more than one month.)

▷ Prepaid Maintenance (We purchase a maintenance contract that will provide coverage for more than one month.)

⇨ ACCRUED LIABILITIES

The third category of accounts to be discussed is Accrued Liabilities.

Accrued Liabilities are also called Accrued Expenses. Do not be confused by this "also-called-name" containing the word <u>Expenses</u>. Accrued Liabilities (Accrued Expenses) **are** liabilities.

The balances in these liability accounts result when:

1. A company, such as Lenny's, utilizes the services of another company or person during the <u>current</u> accounting period.

          and

2. The company, such as Lenny's, will not pay for these services until some <u>future</u> accounting period.

Refer back to the discussion, starting on Pg 80, related to the two days of wages Lenny's owes its employees at the end of March. Also, look at Lenny's March screen. The Wages Payable account, utilized to record the two days of wages due to the employees, is an example of an Accrued Liability. Lenny's Wages Payable account is an Accrued Liability because:

1. Two days of employee services were utilized in the <u>current</u> accounting period, March.

2. Lenny's will not pay the employees for these two days of services until some <u>future</u> accounting period, April.

The March 31 adjusting entry records Lenny's liability to its employees in the Accrued Liability account, Wages Payable.

Other examples of Accrued Liabilities are:

▷ Interest Payable   (As a borrower, we owe interest to our bank.)

▷ Rent Payable   (As a renter, we owe rent to our landlord.)

⇨ UNEARNED REVENUE LIABILITIES

The fourth category of accounts to be discussed is Unearned Revenue liabilities.

Unearned Revenue liabilities are also called Deferred Revenues. Do not be confused by this "also-called-name" containing the word <u>Revenues</u>. Unearned Revenues (Deferred Revenues) **are** liabilities.

The balances in these liability accounts result when:

1. Cash is received from a customer in the <u>current</u> accounting period.

    and

2. Goods or services are not being delivered to the customer at the same time the cash is received from the customer.

    and

3. Goods or services will be delivered to the customer sometime in the <u>future</u>; thus "paying-off" the Unearned Revenue liability.

Refer back to the discussion on Pg 95 concerning the advance payment Lenny's received from the university, and look at Lenny's April screen. The $32,000 Lenny's received from the university on April 1 is an example of an Unearned Revenue. This is an Unearned Revenue because:

1. Cash is received from the university in the <u>current</u> accounting period.

2. When Lenny's receives the $32,000 cash, the mowing service has not yet been performed.

3. The mowing service will be performed in the <u>future</u>; thus "paying-off" the Unearned Revenue liability.

An adjusting entry is required as the Unearned Revenue is earned. Refer back to Pg 98, and look at Lenny's April screen to see the adjusting entry to the Unearned Revenue account. In May, you also made an adjusting entry to the Unearned Revenue account.

Other examples of Unearned Revenue liabilities are:

▷ Unearned Rent Revenue   (As a landlord, we receive an advance payment from our renter for more than one month of rent.)

▷ Unearned Subscription Revenue (As a publisher, we receive an advance payment from our subscribers for more than the current issue of our magazine.)

▷ Unearned Ticket Revenue   (As a sports team owner, we receive an advance payment from our fans for season tickets.)

⇨ ACCRUED ASSETS

The fifth category of accounts to be discussed is Accrued Assets.

Accrued Assets are also called Accrued Revenues. Do not be confused by this "also-called-name" containing the word <u>Revenues</u>. Accrued Assets (Accrued Revenues) **are** assets.

The balances in these asset accounts result when:

1. Goods or services are delivered to the customer in the <u>current</u> accounting period.

   and

2. Payment for the goods or services will be received from the customer in a <u>future</u> accounting period.

Refer back to the discussion on Pg 104 concerning the mowing job at the golf course, and look at Lenny's May screen to see an example of an Accrued Asset. The $3,500 adjustment to the Accounts Receivable account on May 31 is an example of an Accrued Asset. This is an Accrued Asset because:

1. The mowing service was delivered to the golf course in the <u>current</u> accounting period, May.

2. The cash will not be received from the golf course until a <u>future</u> accounting period, July.

Other examples of Accrued Assets are:

▷ Interest Receivable (As a lender, a person or company owes us interest on a loan we made to them.)

▷ Rent Receivable   (As a landlord, a tenant owes us rent for one or more months.)

For the five categories of accounts utilized in adjusting entries, the following table summarizes:

▷ The timing of when cash flows.

▷ The timing of when the adjusting entries are made.

▷ The timing of when revenues and expenses are recognized.

Summary of Timing Issues Related to Adjusting Entries				
Account Category	**Account Category Also Called**	**Examples**	**When Does Cash Flow?**	**When is the Adjusting Entry Made? When is Revenue or Expense Recognized?**
Property, Plant, & Equipment	Fixed Assets	• Equipment • Buildings • Trucks	Cash flows out: • Before the adjusting entry is made. • Before the expense is recognized.	The adjusting entry is made: • After cash flows out. The expense is recognized: • After cash flows out.
Prepaid Assets	Deferred Expenses	• Supplies • Prepaid Rent • Prepaid Insurance	Cash flows out: • Before the adjusting entry is made. • Before the expense is recognized.	The adjusting entry is made: • After cash flows out. The expense is recognized: • After cash flows out.
Accrued Liabilities	Accrued Expenses	• Wages Payable • Interest Payable	Cash flows out: • After the adjusting entry has been made. • After the expense has been recognized.	The adjusting entry is made: • Before cash flows out. The expense is recognized: • Before cash flows out.
Unearned Revenue Liabilities	Deferred Revenues	• Receive Cash for Rent in Advance • Receive Cash for Season Tickets in Advance	Cash flows in: • Before the adjusting entry is made. • Before the revenue is recognized.	The adjusting entry is made: • After cash flows in. The revenue is recognized: • After cash flows in.
Accrued Assets	Accrued Revenues	• Interest Owed to us on a Note Receivable • Rent Owed to us by a Tenant	Cash flows in: • After the adjusting entry has been made. • After the revenue has been recognized.	The adjusting entry is made: • Before cash flows in. The revenue is recognized: • Before cash flows in.

```
┌─────────────────────────────────────────────────────────────┐
│                   Chapter 9 Homework                          │
└─────────────────────────────────────────────────────────────┘
```

Problem 9-1   True / False Questions
Timing Issues Related to Adjusting Entries

If this problem is assigned as a homework turn-in, remove and use the answer sheet on Pg 233 to record and turn-in your answers.

For each item in the **Account** column, determine if the entries in the **other three columns** are correct. If all three entries are correct, then circle **T**rue. If one or more of the entries are not correct, then circle **F**alse.

True or False		Account	Account Category	When Does Cash Flow?	When is Revenue or Expense Recognized?
T F	1.	Prepaid Maintenance	Prepaid Asset	Before expense recognition	Expense is recognized after cash flows out
T F	2.	Interest Receivable	Accrued Asset	Before revenue recognition	Revenue is recognized after cash flows in
T F	3.	Equipment	Property, Plant & Equipment	Before expense recognition	Expense is recognized after cash flows out
T F	4.	Rent Payable	Accrued Liability	Before expense recognition	Expense is recognized after cash flows out
T F	5.	Unearned Rent Revenue	Unearned Revenue	Before revenue recognition	Revenue is recognized after cash flows in
T F	6.	Buildings	Property, Plant & Equipment	After expense recognition	Expense is recognized before cash flows out
T F	7.	Prepaid Rent	Prepaid Asset	Before expense recognition	Expense is recognized after cash flows out
T F	8.	Interest Payable	Unearned Revenue	After expense recognition	Expense is recognized before cash flows out
T F	9.	Unearned Ticket Revenue	Unearned Revenue	Before revenue recognition	Revenue is recognized after cash flows in
T F	10.	Rent Receivable	Accrued Asset	After revenue recognition	Revenue is recognized before cash flows in
T F	11.	Prepaid Insurance	Prepaid Asset	Before expense recognition	Expense is recognized after cash flows out
T F	12.	Unearned Subscription Revenue	Prepaid Asset	Before revenue recognition	Revenue is recognized after cash flows in

Chapter 10

Dividends
and
A Review of the Nine Steps in the Accounting Cycle

In this chapter, you will continue to use the workbook that you used in Chapter 8 entitled "03-Lenny's Lawn Service".   If this workbook is not open on your computer, do the following:

⇨ Open the workbook **03-Lenny's Lawn Service** in the **Solid Footing 10e** folder

⇨ Enable Macros

🖱 Click the **June** tab.

You should see **Screen 10 A** in the upper left corner of the screen.

⇨ LENNY's DECLARES AND PAYS A DIVIDEND

Dividends Payable is the one new account on the June screen. The Dividends Payable account will be used when a dividend is declared, and when that dividend is paid to the owners of Lenny's Lawn Service, Inc. You will gain an understanding of what a dividend is as you record Lenny's dividend.

There are three dates associated with the payment of a dividend:

1. **Date of Declaration**   On this date, the Board of Directors declares the dividend.

2. **Date of Record**   The individuals who own the stock of the corporation on this date will receive the dividend.

3. **Date of Payment**   On this date, the dividend will be paid.

On June 1, 2017, Lenny's Board of Directors meets and declares that Lenny's will pay a dividend to its stockholders. Each share of Lenny's Common Stock will be paid a dividend of $3.50 per share. There are currently 10,000 shares of Lenny's Common Stock held by Lenny's shareholders. Thus, the total dividend to be paid will be $35,000 (10,000 shares x $3.50 per share). The following are the facts related to this dividend:

▷ Dividend per Share $3.50

▷ Total Dividend Amount $35,000

▷ Date of Declaration .... June 1, 2017

▷ Date of Record .... June 10, 2017

▷ Date of Payment .... June 30, 2017

The ultimate effect of Lenny's paying this dividend will be a $35,000 reduction in the Cash account balance and a $35,000 reduction in the Retained Earnings account balance. As you will see below, there will be two entries made in Lenny's accounting system related to this dividend.

On June 1 (Date of Declaration), Lenny's makes the first entry in its accounting system related to this dividend. This is the entry to record the declaration of the dividend.

🖰 Click **Dividend Decl.**

🖰 Click **Post to Ledger**

Look at the effect of this entry on the Dividends Payable account and the effect of this entry on the Retained Earnings account in Lenny's General Ledger. As will be discussed below, the purpose of this entry is to transfer $35,000 of the owners' claim to assets from Owners' Equity to Liabilities.

The credit to the Dividends Payable liability account will be discussed first. On June 1 (Date of Declaration), Lenny's Board of Directors declares that a $35,000 dividend will be paid; thus on June 1, Lenny's has a legal obligation to pay the dividend to the stockholders. The actual cash payment of the dividend will not take place until June 30 (Date of Payment), but on June 1, Lenny's does have a legal obligation to pay the dividend. The credit to the Dividends Payable account records this legal obligation. The Dividends Payable account is a claim to assets account, just like any other liability account.

Now let's look at the debit to the Retained Earnings account. When Lenny's transfers $35,000 of the owners' claim to assets into the Dividends Payable liability account, there must be a related $35,000 reduction in an Owners' Equity account. As you first learned in Chapters 2 and 3, there are two permanent Owners' Equity accounts that track owners' claim to assets—the Common Stock account and the Retained Earnings account.

The following definitions of these two accounts are repeated from Chapter 3.

Common Stock Account – Retained Earnings Account
▷ When the owners' claim to the assets results from <u>the owners putting money into the business</u>, the claim is put in the **Common Stock** account.
▷ When the owners' claim to the assets results from <u>the operation of the business</u>, the claim is put in the **Retained Earnings** account.

When Lenny's pays a dividend to its owners, the owners receive some of the assets that have resulted from the profitable operation of the lawn mowing business. By looking at the definition of Retained Earnings in the above box, you can see that the Retained Earnings account is the owners' claim account that relates to the operation of the business. Thus, when a dividend is declared, the Retained Earnings account is the Owners' Equity account that is debited.

With the addition of the dividend declaration entry, there are now three entries that are made directly into the Retained Earnings account:

> ▷ Closing entry for Revenue account(s)
> ▷ Closing entry for Expense accounts
> ▷ Dividend declaration entry

As you take Lenny's through the rest of its June Accounting Cycle you will record the payment of the dividend.

⇨ LENNY's JUNE ACCOUNTING CYCLE

You will now take Lenny's through the rest of its June accounting period. The steps in the Accounting Cycle will be presented in the boxes. Because you are now an Accounting Cycle expert, there will be very little discussion after each step.

Step 1	For each business transaction that occurs during the accounting period, determine the effect of the transaction on the General Ledger accounts.
Step 2	Make an entry in the General Journal for each transaction and post the entry to the General Ledger accounts.

You have already recorded Lenny's June 1 dividend declaration entry. The declaration of the dividend was Lenny's first transaction in June. Do the following to record Lenny's normal monthly transactions for June.

🖱 Click **Enter Other June Transactions into Journal and Post to the Ledger**

Observe that during June, Lenny's did not get paid for the golf course mowing job that was completed on the last day of May; thus the $33,500 balance in the Accounts Receivable account represents the $3,500 still owed by the golf course for the May mowing job, plus the $30,000 billed to the property management company for June's services.

There is one more transaction to record for the month—the payment of the dividend. The cash is paid to the stockholders on June 30, the Date of Payment for the dividend.

🖱 Click **Dividend Pmt.**

🖱 Click **Post to Ledger**

Observe the following related to the dividend:

▷ The balance in the Dividends Payable account is now zero.

▷ The paying of the dividend is recorded like any other payment of a liability—a credit to cash and a debit to the liability account.

▷ There is <u>no</u> entry made to the Retained Earnings account when the dividend is paid.

▷ The <u>net</u> effect of the June 1 dividend declaration entry <u>and</u> the June 30 dividend payment entry is:

- A $35,000 debit to the Retained Earnings account, and
- A $35,000 credit to the Cash account.

▷ There was no entry made on June 10, the Date of Record for this dividend. All that is determined on the Date of Record is who will get the dividend when it is paid. This does not require any entry into the accounting system.

> **Step 3**   At the end of the accounting period, before preparing the financial statements, determine if any of the General Ledger account balances need to be adjusted. Enter any required adjusting entries into the General Journal and post the adjusting entries to the General Ledger accounts.

Before preparing Lenny's June financial statements, there are three accounts that need to be adjusted. The adjustments to the Accumulated Depreciation account and to the Unearned Revenue account are based on information given in Chapters 7 and 8. The adjustment to the Supplies account is based on the determination that $4,375 of supplies are on-hand at June 30.

🖱 Click the three black adjustment buttons and the related **Post to Ledger** buttons.

> **Step 4**   Prepare a Pre-Closing Trial Balance to determine that the accounts in the General Ledger are in balance.

🖱 Click **Prepare the Pre-Closing Trial Balance**

Observe that the amount shown on the Pre-Closing Trial Balance for Retained Earnings is the Current Balance in the Retained Earnings account and is **not** the Beginning Balance. This is the first time that the Current Balance in the Retained Earnings account is not the same as the Beginning Balance. This is the case because Retained Earnings was debited for $35,000 when the dividend was declared.

> **Step 5**   Prepare an Income Statement from the ending balances in the General Ledger revenue and expense accounts.

🖱 Click **Prepare the Income Statement**

Observe that the declaration and payment of the June dividend did **not** have any effect on the Income Statement. This is consistent with the description of Step 5 in the box above, which states that the Income Statement is prepared from the ending balances in the revenue and expense accounts. When the dividend was declared, the Retained Earnings account was debited—there was no entry made to any of the expense accounts. While the declaration and payment of a dividend may seem like an expense, the declaration and payment of a dividend is **not** considered an expense and will **never** appear on the Income Statement.

> **Step 6**   Calculate the ending balance of the Retained Earnings account that is needed for the preparation of the Balance Sheet.

On the form at the top of the following page, calculate the Retained Earnings balance as of the end of June that is needed for the preparation of the Balance Sheet.

```
┌─────────────────────────────────────────────────────┐
│                  Calculation of                       │
│                Retained Earnings as of                │
│             June 30 for the Balance Sheet             │
├─────────────────────────────────────────────────────┤
│                                                       │
│   Retained Earnings Current Balance    _____    │
│                                                       │
│   Plus June Net Income                 _____    │
│                                                       │
│   Retained Earnings as of                             │
│   June 30 for the Balance Sheet        _____    │
│                                                       │
└─────────────────────────────────────────────────────┘
```

🖑 Click **Calculate June 30 Retained Earnings**

Did you calculate the June 30 Retained Earnings balance correctly?

┌──┐
│ **Step 7**   Prepare the Balance Sheet from the ending balances in the General │
│   Ledger asset accounts, liability accounts, Common Stock account, │
│   and the calculated ending balance for the Retained Earnings │
│   account. │
└──┘

🖑 Click **Prepare the Balance Sheet**

Observe that the two liability accounts with zero balances, Wages Payable and Dividends Payable, are not shown on the Balance Sheet. Accounts with zero balances will be listed on the Pre-Closing Trial Balance and the Post-Closing Trial Balance, but will not normally be shown on the formal financial statements.

┌──┐
│ **Step 8**   Prepare and enter the revenue and expense closing entries into the │
│   General Journal, and post the closing entries to the General Ledger │
│   accounts. │
└──┘

Lenny's closing entries for June are shown on the June 2017 Closing screen.

🖑 Click the **June Close** tab, to move to the June 2017 Closing screen.

You should see **Screen 10 B** in the upper left corner of the screen.

🖑 Click **Close Revenues**

🖑 Click **Post to Ledger**

🖰 Click **Close Expenses**

🖰 Click **Post to Ledger**

These closing entries are the same as the closing entries you prepared in previous chapters.

Observe that the title <u>Current Balance</u> in the Retained Earnings account changes to <u>Ending Balance</u> once the closing entries have been posted to the General Ledger.

<table>
<tr><td>Step 9</td><td>Prepare a Post-Closing Trial Balance to determine that the accounts in the General Ledger are in balance and ready to start a new Accounting Cycle.</td></tr>
</table>

🖰 Click **Prepare Post-Closing Trial Balance**

Observe that the Ending Balance in the Retained Earnings account is the amount that is shown on the Post-Closing Trial Balance.

This concludes Chapter 10.

⇨ **Appendix – USING A DIVIDENDS ACCOUNT**

In Chapter 10 you learned the most common way that companies account for the declaration and payment of a dividend. There is another method that some companies use to record the declaration and payment of a dividend. This alternative method involves the use of an additional General Ledger account called the **Dividends** account. If you are interested in learning this alternative method, or if your instructor requires that you learn this method, then continue reading this appendix. **You do not need to read this appendix for the purpose of completing the Chapter 10 homework or the Accounting Cycle Project.** The Chapter 10 homework and the Accounting Cycle Project do **not** use the Dividends account that is explained in this appendix.

Let's again look at Lenny's June dividend entries, but this time Lenny's will use a Dividends account to record the declaration of the dividend. In the entry below, note how the ~~Retained Earnings~~ account that was used in Chapter 10 is replaced by the new **Dividends** account.

On June 1, 2017, Lenny's Board of Directors declares the dividend. The total dividend that will be paid on June 30, 2017, is $35,000. If a Dividends account is used, then the entry on the Date of Declaration would be as follows:

<table>
<tr><td colspan="4" align="center">General Journal</td></tr>
<tr><td>Date</td><td>Account</td><td>Debit</td><td>Credit</td></tr>
<tr><td>June 01</td><td>Dividends ~~Retained Earnings~~</td><td>35,000</td><td></td></tr>
<tr><td></td><td>   Dividends Payable</td><td></td><td>35,000</td></tr>
<tr><td></td><td>Declare Dividends</td><td></td><td></td></tr>
</table>

Observe that the debit is to the new Dividends account—not to the ~~Retained Earnings~~ account. As you will see on the next page, ultimately the Retained Earnings account will be debited, but first the debit is placed in the Dividends account. The Dividends account is a <u>temporary</u> account that will be closed into the Retained Earnings account as part of the period-end closing process.

On June 30, 2017, the dividends are paid to Lenny's stockholders. The journal entry on the Date of Payment is exactly the same as the Date of Payment entry that was discussed in Chapter 10.

General Journal			
Date	**Account**	**Debit**	**Credit**
June 30	Dividends Payable	35,000	
	Cash		35,000
	Pay Dividends		

The <u>net</u> effect of the June 1 dividend declaration entry and the June 30 dividend payment entry is a $35,000 debit to the ~~Retained Earnings~~ Dividends account, and a $35,000 credit to the Cash account.

When preparing the **Pre-Closing Trial Balance**, the Dividends account is listed on the Pre-Closing Trial Balance and the amount listed is the $35,000 debit balance.

The preparation and presentation of the **Income Statement** is exactly the same as was shown in Chapter 10. The Dividends account **is** a temporary account, but it is **not** an expense account and does **not** appear on the Income Statement.

The **Calculation of Retained Earnings as of June 30 for the Balance Sheet** contains an additional line item when the Dividends account is used. The following is the calculation:

Retained Earnings Current Balance	$69,325
Plus June Net Income	13,800
Less Dividends declared	**(35,000)**
Retained Earnings as of June 30 for Bal. Sheet	$48,125

The preparation and presentation of the **Balance Sheet** is exactly the same as was shown in Chapter 10. The Dividends account is not shown on the Balance Sheet. As shown above, the balance in the Dividends account, $35,000, is used to calculate the Retained Earnings amount for the Balance Sheet.

The Dividends account is a temporary account. Thus, when a Dividends account is used, there is an additional closing entry that is part of Step 8—Closing Entries in the Accounting Cycle. The entry to close the Dividends account into the Retained Earnings account is as follows:

General Journal			
Date	**Account**	**Debit**	**Credit**
June 30	Retained Earnings	35,000	
	Dividends		35,000
	Close the Dividends account		

After posting this entry, the balance in the Dividends account will be zero. This is what you would expect the balance to be in a temporary account after it is closed. The debit, which was originally put into the Dividends account on the Date of Declaration, has now been moved to the Retained Earnings account as a result of this closing entry. After this closing entry, the Ending Balance in the Retained Earnings account will be $48,125—the same Ending Balance that was in the Retained Earnings account after the closing entries were made in Chapter 10.

This concludes this appendix.

Chapter 10 Homework

Problem 10-1   Recording Dividends

On August 15, 2017, EasyMoney, Inc.'s Board of Directors meets and declares that EasyMoney will pay a dividend to its stockholders. Each share of EasyMoney's Common Stock will be paid a dividend of $1.25 per share. There are currently 100,000 shares of EasyMoney's Common Stock held by EasyMoney's shareholders.

The following are the facts related to this dividend:

- ▷ Dividend per Share $1.25
- ▷ Date of Declaration .... August 15, 2017
- ▷ Date of Record .... September 5, 2017
- ▷ Date of Payment .... September 20, 2017

The following is a partial list of the accounts in EasyMoney, Inc.'s General Ledger. These are the only accounts you need for this problem.

- ▷ Cash
- ▷ Dividends Payable
- ▷ Retained Earnings

As of August 1, 2017, the Beginning Balance in the Dividends Payable account is $0 and the Beginning Balance in the Retained Earnings account is $625,000.

Remove and use the forms on Pgs 235 and 236 to complete this problem.

Requirement 1

A. Record the entry that EasyMoney should make in the General Journal on August 15, 2017 to record the declaration of the dividend.

B. After making and posting the August 15 entry, what are the Current Balances in the:

- ▷ Dividends Payable account?
- ▷ Retained Earnings account?

Requirement 2

A. EasyMoney's Accounting Cycle is one month long. EasyMoney's Net Income for the month of August is $52,000. Prepare the Calculation of Retained Earnings as of August 31 for the Balance Sheet.

B. What would be the amount of Dividends Payable on EasyMoney's August 31 Balance Sheet?

Requirement 3

A. Record the entry that EasyMoney should make in the General Journal on September 20, 2017 to record the payment of the dividend.

B. After making and posting the September 20 entry, what is the Current Balance in the:

- ▷ Dividends Payable account?

Problem 10-2   Summary of Accounts Introduced in Solid Footing

This Summary of Accounts and Self-Test is located in the workbook entitled <u>10-Review of Accounts and Self Test</u>. To work with the Summary of Accounts and Self-Test, do the following:

⇨ Open the workbook **10-Review of Accounts and Self Test** in the **Solid Footing 10e** folder

⇨ Enable Macros

The first tab in this workbook, **Study Guide Accounts by Type**, is a listing of all of the accounts you have been introduced to in the first ten chapters of Solid Footing. Study this listing and then take the Self-Test.

The second tab, **Self Test**, is a listing of the same accounts but they are <u>not</u> grouped by account type. The accounts are listed in alphabetical order. To test your knowledge of each of the accounts, select the correct entry for each of the cells in the 4 columns associated with the account. To select the correct entry:

▷ Click into the cell.

▷ Click on the drop-down button at the end of the cell.

▷ Click on the correct entry for that cell.

After you have filled-in the cells for all of the accounts, then click the **Grade Your Test** button to see your grade.

Any account that contains an incorrect or blank answer will have a red "**X**" in the right most column. All incorrect answers will be shown in red. Fix any incorrect or blank answers, and then again click the **Grade Your Test** button. If your fixed answers are correct, the fixed answers will turn from red to black and the red "**X**" in the right most column will be removed.

NOTES

Accounting Cycle Project

Included with your Solid Footing software is a workbook that contains the **A**ccounting **C**ycle **P**roject. This project will take you through the month of July for Lenny's Lawn Service, and will cover all of the topics you have learned in the first ten chapters of Solid Footing. Your instructor will give you directions on how to complete and submit your project.

While working on your project:

> ▷ Never do a **Cut** operation.

> ▷ If a page contains a CAUTION box, follow the directions in that box.

Starting the Accounting Cycle Project

To start the ACP do the following:

1. Complete the Blue Accounting Cycle Project Registration Slip

> ▷ Remove and complete the blue Accounting Cycle Project Registration Slip. The Registration Slip is on the last page in this book (Pg 251). Turn in your completed Accounting Cycle Project Registration Slip to your instructor.

2. Open the Accounting Cycle Project Workbook

The Accounting Cycle Project is in a workbook entitled "20-Accounting Cycle Project 10e". To open this workbook, do the following:

> ▷ Open the workbook **20-Accounting Cycle Project 10e** in the **Solid Footing 10e** folder

> ▷ Enable Macros

3. Activate Your Project

> ▷ Enter your Software ID Code   Your code is located on the Permanent Record Slip, which is the last page in this book.

> ▷ Enter your First Name

> ▷ Enter your Last Name, and press the Enter key

> ▷ Click the Activate Project button

> ▷ Be sure that your name is correct before clicking **Yes** to the question "Is your name correct?". Once your name is entered into your project, it cannot be changed.

> ▷ Complete the yellow information boxes that are located in the top right of the page.

4. Save Your Activated Project

> ▷ Save your project using your Last Name and your First Name as the first part of the file name. The file name should be in the form: LastName**FirstName**-ACP

> ▷ To save your Activated Project, follow the directions in the box entitled:

> **SAVING YOUR PROJECT – Immediately after Activation**

(ACP directions continued on the next page)

Working On and Completing the ACP

▷ To complete your project, follow the **Instructions** on the Directions tab of the project.

▷ Save your project often.

▷ You can complete a portion of your project – stop working on it – then continue working on it at a later time. Before you stop working on your project, be sure it has been saved. When you return to your project, be sure the workbook you open is the workbook that you named using your LastName**FirstName**-ACP

Additional Information About Your Project

How Your Project will be Graded
Your project will be graded by your instructor using the Accounting Cycle Project grading software. The grading software will not grade all of the information you entered into your project.

Your instructor may choose to grade additional items in your project that are not graded by the grading software.

Submitting Your Project

Your instructor will provide you with directions for submitting your completed project.

(End of ACP directions)

Chapter 11

Introduction to the Statement of Cash Flows

Through the first ten chapters of Solid Footing you learned about three of the four primary financial statements:

> ▷ Balance Sheet
> ▷ Income Statement
> ▷ Statement of Stockholders' Equity

As you have learned—these three financial statements are prepared on an accrual basis.

The **Statement of Cash Flows** is the fourth primary financial statement. The Statement of Cash Flows is prepared on a cash basis. When a financial statement is prepared on a cash basis, only transactions resulting from cash inflows or cash outflows are included in the financial statement. In this chapter, you will learn how to prepare and read/understand the Statement of Cash Flows—a cash basis financial statement.

The Statement of Cash Flows:

> ▷ Focuses on the Cash account.
> ▷ Shows the **S**ources of cash (cash inflows) during the period.
> ▷ Shows the **U**ses of cash (cash outflows) during the period.
> ▷ Categorizes the sources and uses of cash into three types of activities:
>> • Operating Activities
>> • Investing Activities
>> • Financing Activities
> ▷ Shows:
>> • The amount of cash at the beginning of the accounting period.
>> • The increase or decrease in cash during the accounting period.
>> • The amount of cash at the end of the accounting period.

While the basic concepts of the Statement of Cash Flows are simple, the preparation of this financial statement can be complex. The preparation is complex because the accounting system is not set-up to gather the information required to prepare the Statement of Cash Flows. As you have seen, the Cash account in the General Ledger keeps track of the entity's cash balance. The Cash account does **not** keep track of what causes the increases and decreases in cash. If you look at the Cash account in the General Ledger, all you see is:

> ▷ The Beginning Balance
> ▷ The Debit entry amounts (cash inflows)
> ▷ The Credit entry amounts (cash outflows)
> ▷ The Ending Balance

By just looking at a Debit entry amount in the Cash account, you cannot determine what was the **S**ource of that cash inflow. By just looking at a Credit entry amount in the Cash account, you cannot determine what was the **U**se that caused that cash outflow.

As counter-intuitive as it may seem, to determine the **S**ources of cash (the causes of cash inflows) and the **U**ses of cash (the causes of cash outflows), you will calculate and use the change from the beginning balance to the ending balance in:

> ▷ All of the Asset accounts—except for the Cash account
>
> ▷ All of the Liability accounts
>
> ▷ All of the Owners' Equity accounts

In this chapter, you will learn a worksheet approach for preparing this new financial statement. By learning this worksheet approach, you will not only develop a step-by-step method for preparing the Statement of Cash Flows, but you will gain an understanding of how to read and use the information in a Statement of Cash Flows.

You will be using a new company, Connie's Consulting, Inc. (*CCI*), to master the Statement of Cash Flows. Lenny Smith, the owner of Lenny's Lawn Service, has a sister Connie. After seeing the success of her brother's business, Connie decides to leave her job in a large corporation and start Connie's Consulting, Inc. You will use the first four months of operation of *CCI* to learn how to prepare and read the Statement of Cash Flows.

Open the workbook entitled "04-Connie's Consulting" by doing the following:

> ⇨ Open the workbook **04-Connie's Consulting** in the **Solid Footing 10e** folder
>
> ⇨ Enable Macros

The June tab at the bottom of the workbook should be the selected tab.

🖰 Click the **June** tab (if the June tab is not selected).

You should see **Screen 11 A** in the upper left corner of the screen.

Connie formed her corporation on June 15, 2017. You will account for *CCI*'s first month of operation to learn the following about the Statement of Cash Flows:

> ▷ The worksheet process used to prepare the statement.
>
> ▷ The general form of the statement.
>
> ▷ The type of cash flow activities that are shown in the **Investing** section of the statement.
>
> ▷ The type of cash flow activities that are shown in the **Financing** section of the statement.

⇨ CONNIE STARTS HER CORPORATION – Month of June

June 15 – Issue Common Stock

To finance the start-up of the corporation, *CCI* sells 5,000 shares of $1 par value[1] Common Stock for $10 per share. Connie purchases 51% of the stock, and the remainder is sold to other investors.

🖰 Click **Issue Stock**

Notice that in this workbook when you click a transaction button the entry is made in the General Journal and immediately posted to the General Ledger.

The amount of cash received from issuing the Common Stock is $50,000 (5,000 shares x $10 selling price per share); thus the Cash account is debited (increased) for $50,000.

The Common Stock has a $1 par value; thus the Common Stock account is credited (increased) for $5,000 (5,000 shares x $1 par value per share). The Pd-in Cap in Excess[2] account is credited (increased) for the $45,000 remainder ($50,000 - $5,000).

The Statement of Cash Flows reports on the cash inflows and cash outflows of an entity and what causes those cash flows; thus the effect of each transaction on the Cash account and how to identify the activity that causes the cash flow will be emphasized.

Before this transaction the Cash account had a $0 balance. After this transaction the Cash account has a $50,000 balance. That is a cash inflow of $50,000.

By looking at the Cash account in the General Ledger, you can see the $50,000 cash inflow, but you cannot determine the **S**ource of the cash inflow. By looking at the other accounts in the General Ledger, you can determine the **S**ource of the cash inflow. The **S**ource of the cash inflow can be found in the change of the two Owners' Equity accounts.

The changes in the two equity accounts are:
> **Common Stock** account increased by .... $ 5,000
> **Pd-in Cap in Excess** account increased by 45,000
>
> **S**ource of cash inflow—Issuance of common stock $50,000

As indicated above, *CCI* issued the Common Stock to finance the start-up of the new corporation. As you will see when you prepare the Statement of Cash Flows, this issuance of Common Stock will be shown in the Financing Activities section of the statement.

[1,2]*Some states require that Common Stock be assigned a Par Value; thus Par Value is a legal concept. The Par Value that is assigned to a share of Common Stock in no way indicates the real value of the Common Stock. For legal reasons, Par Value is normally set at a very low amount such as $1 per share. As can be seen in the journal entry to record CCI's issuance of Common Stock, the amount that is credited to the Common Stock account is the number of shares issued times the Par Value per share. The rest of the actual selling price of the stock is credited to another owners' equity account called Paid-in Capital in Excess of Par Value (to save screen space, this account will be called Pd-in Cap in Excess).*

June 30 – Borrow on a Long-Term Note from the Bank

During the second half of June, Connie determines the equipment that *CCI* will need for the consulting office, and she finds a parcel of land that will be a perfect site for the construction of a small office building in the future. The combined cost of the equipment and the parcel of land is $85,000. The balance in the Cash account from the issuance of Common Stock is only $50,000; thus *CCI* needs additional financing to be able to make these two purchases.

Connie contacts a local bank and arranges for *CCI* to obtain a 5 year $40,000 bank loan. *CCI* signs a long-term note with the bank.

🖰 Click **Issue Note**

The amount of cash received from the bank is $40,000; thus the Cash account is debited (increased) for $40,000, and the Note Payable Long-Term account is credited (increased) for $40,000.

Before this transaction the Cash account had a $50,000 balance. After this transaction the Cash account has a $90,000 balance. That is a cash inflow of $40,000.

The **S**ource of this cash inflow can be found in the change of the **Note Payable Long-Term** account in the General Ledger. This account changed from a $0 balance to a $40,000 balance. This increase of $40,000 in the Note Payable Long-Term account is the **S**ource of the $40,000 cash inflow.

CCI borrowed long-term from the bank to get additional financing for the start-up of the business. As you will see when you prepare the Statement of Cash Flows, borrowing on a long-term note will be shown in the Financing Activities section of the statement.

June 30 – Buy Land

On June 30, *CCI* buys the parcel of land that will be used in the future as the site of the corporation's office building.

🖰 Click **Buy Land**

The amount of cash paid for the land is $30,000; thus the Land account is debited (increased) for $30,000, and the Cash account is credited (decreased) for $30,000.

Before this transaction the Cash account had a $90,000 balance. After this transaction the Cash account has a $60,000 balance. That is a cash outflow of $30,000.

The cause of this cash outflow can be found in the change of the **Land** account. The Land account changed from a $0 balance to a $30,000 balance. This increase of $30,000 in the Land account identifies the $30,000 **U**se of cash.

Using the terminology of the Statement of Cash Flows, when *CCI* bought the parcel of land, the corporation invested some of its cash in a long-term asset. As you will see when you prepare the Statement of Cash Flows, the purchase of Land, a long-term asset, will be shown in the Investing Activities section of the statement.

June 30 – Buy Equipment

On June 30, *CCI* buys and pays cash for the equipment that will be used in the consulting offices. The equipment will be delivered to the offices that *CCI* will rent on July 1.

🖱 Click **Buy Equipment**

The amount of cash paid for the equipment is $55,000; thus the Equipment account is debited (increased) for $55,000, and the Cash account is credited (decreased) for $55,000.

Before this transaction the Cash account had a $60,000 balance. After this transaction the Cash account has a $5,000 balance. That is a cash outflow of $55,000.

The cause of this cash outflow can be found in the change of the **Equipment** account. The Equipment account changed from a $0 balance to a $55,000 balance. This increase of $55,000 in the Equipment account identifies the $55,000 **U**se of cash.

Again, using the terminology of the Statement of Cash Flows, when *CCI* bought the equipment, the corporation invested some of its cash in a long-term asset. As you will see when you prepare the Statement of Cash Flows, the purchase of Equipment, a long-term asset, will be shown in the Investing Activities section of the statement.

⇨ PREPARE JUNE's BALANCE SHEET

During the month of June, *CCI* had no transactions that involved revenue or expense accounts; thus *CCI* will not prepare an Income Statement for the month of June. *CCI* will prepare a Balance Sheet and a Statement of Cash Flows.

🖱 Click **Prepare the June 30 Balance Sheet**

All of the Asset account ending balances, the Liability account ending balances, and the Owners' Equity account ending balances are used to prepare the June 30, 2017 Balance Sheet.

Shown next to the June 30, 2017 Balance Sheet is the May 31, 2017 Balance Sheet. Because *CCI* started in business in June, the May 31, 2017 Balance Sheet is all zeros.

Is it Always this Simple?

Are you thinking that the cash flow effects of the four June transactions are simple and obvious? During your introduction to the Statement of Cash Flows, it is important to develop the ability to evaluate the changes in the accounts (except cash) to determine the Sources and Uses of cash.

Next, you will begin applying a worksheet approach to preparing the Statement of Cash Flows. As you prepare the worksheet, keep-in-mind that while this first month is simple, the preparation of the Statement of Cash Flows will get significantly more complex as the number and complexity of the transactions and the accounts increase. To see an example of a more complex Cash Flow Worksheet and the resulting Statement of Cash Flows:

🖱 Click the **September** tab on the bottom of your workbook.

The activity for September may appear complex to you now, but if you learn and understand the worksheet approach as it is applied to *CCI*'s early less complex months, you will be able to easily handle the ever increasing complexity of *CCI*'s later months.

🖰 Click the **June** tab on the bottom of your workbook.

⇨ PREPARE JUNE's STATEMENT OF CASH FLOWS

You will now prepare *CCI*'s June Statement of Cash Flows using the Cash Flow Worksheet.

Step 1	Copy the Beginning and Ending Balance Sheets to the Worksheet

The preparation of the Statement of Cash Flows is based on the analysis of the changes in the Balance Sheet accounts from the End of the prior accounting period to the End of the current accounting period. To start the preparation of your worksheet, you will copy last period's and this period's Balance Sheets to your worksheet.

◄► Scroll to position the May 31, 2017 Balance Sheet at the left edge of your screen.

🖰 Click **Copy the 5/31 and 6/30 Balance Sheets to the Cash Flow Worksheet**

This is simply a copy process that puts the two Balance Sheets on your worksheet. Notice that the Balance Sheet subtotals such as: Total Current Assets, Total Liabilities, and Total Equity are not needed on your worksheet. Amounts for TOTAL ASSETS and TOTAL LIAB. & EQUITY are calculated on the worksheet to check that the Balance Sheet line item amounts were copied correctly. These two totals are not used in any other part of the worksheet.

Step 2	Calculate the Change in Cash

🖰 Click **Calculate the Increase (Decrease) in Cash**

This calculation shows that cash increased by $5,000 from the end of the last accounting period to the end of the current accounting period. This is the same change amount that you will see by comparing the Beg Balance and the Ending Balance in the Cash account in the General Ledger.

◄► Scroll so that you can see the Cash account in the General Ledger

Observe that the Cash account changed from a Beg Balance of $0 to an Ending Balance of $5,000, an increase of $5,000. As you can see, when you calculate the change from last period's Balance Sheet amount to this period's Balance Sheet amount—it is the same as calculating the change from the Beg Balance in the General Ledger account to the Ending Balance in the General Ledger account.

Step 3	Calculate the Change in All of the Balance Sheet Line Items (except cash)
	Assign an **S** or a **U** to the Changes

◄► Scroll to position the Cash Flow Worksheet at the left edge of your screen.

🖱 Click **For All Items (except cash) Calculate the Absolute Value**

The amount of the change for each of the Balance Sheet line items (except cash), is calculated. The change amount for each of the line items is put on the worksheet as an absolute value, which means that the change amounts will not have a sign (+ or -).

The change amount for each of the Balance Sheet line items is then assigned either a(n):

▷ **S** if the change in the Balance Sheet line item is associated with a **S**ource of cash—a cash inflow.

▷ **U** if the change in the Balance Sheet line item is associated with a **U**se of cash—a cash outflow.

You will now examine the change in each of the Balance Sheet line items.

Equipment
Equipment changed from a $0 balance last period to a $55,000 balance this period, a change of $55,000. The balance increased and is assigned a **U**.

Do the following to help you understand why this change is assigned a **U**.

◄► Scroll so that you can see the General Journal and the General Ledger.

Look at the Jun 30 *Purchase equipment* entry in the General Journal. Also, in the General Ledger, look at the Jun 30 $55,000 entries in the Cash account and the Equipment account. As you can observe, there is a **U**se of cash (a cash outflow) associated with the increase in the Equipment account.

◄► Scroll to position the Cash Flow Worksheet at the left edge of your screen.

There will be many more explanations of when to assign an **S** and when to assign a **U** to changes in **Asset** line items (except cash), but it might be helpful at this time to list the following rules that will **always** apply to changes in **Asset** line items (except cash).

Asset Line Items (except cash) – Rules for Assigning an **S** or a **U** to the Change
▷ If an **Asset** line item **Decreases** from Last period to This period, then the change is associated with a **S**ource of cash. The change is assigned an **S**.
▷ If an **Asset** line item **Increases** from Last period to This period, then the change is associated with a **U**se of cash. The change is assigned a **U**.

Land

Land changed from a $0 balance last period to a $30,000 balance this period, a change of $30,000. The balance increased and is assigned a **U**.

The assignment of a **U** to the change in Land follows the rules for Asset line item changes, and it follows the same logic as the Equipment line item change.

Note Payable Long-Term

Note Payable Long-Term changed by $40,000 and is assigned an **S**. Do the following to help you understand why this change is assigned an **S**:

◄► Scroll so that you can see the General Journal and the General Ledger.

Look at the Jun 30 *Borrow on a long-term note from the bank* entry in the General Journal. Also in the General Ledger, look at the Jun 30 $40,000 entries in the Cash account and the Note Payable Long-Term account. As you can observe, there is a cash inflow associated with the increase in the Note Payable Long-Term account; thus the increase in the Note Payable Long-Term account is a **S**ource of cash.

◄► Scroll to position the Cash Flow Worksheet at the left edge of your screen.

Common Stock and Pd-in Cap in Excess

The changes in these two line items will be discussed together because the changes resulted from the same transaction—the issuance of Common Stock for $50,000 cash. Common Stock changed by $5,000, and Pd-in Cap in Excess changed by $45,000. Both amounts are assigned an **S**. (The arrows next to the $5,000 and $45,000 will be discussed in Step 5.)

Do the following to help you understand why each of these changes is assigned an **S**.

◄► Scroll so that you can see the General Journal and the General Ledger.

Look at the Jun 15 *Issue common stock* entry in the General Journal. Also, in the General Ledger, look at the Jun 15 entries in the Cash account, the Common Stock account, and the Pd-in Cap in Excess account. As you can observe, there is a cash inflow associated with the increases in the Common Stock and Pd-in Cap in Excess accounts; thus the increases in the Common Stock and Pd-in Cap in Excess accounts are a **S**ource of cash.

There will be many more explanations of when to assign an **S** and when to assign a **U** to changes in Liability and Owners' Equity line items, but it might be helpful at this time to list the following rules that will **always** apply to changes in Liability and Owners' Equity line items.

Liability and **Owners' Equity** Line Items – Rules for Assigning an **S** or a **U** to the Change

▷ If a Liability or an Owners' Equity line item **Increases** from <u>Last</u> period to <u>This</u> period, then the change is associated with a **S**ource of cash. The change is assigned an **S**.

▷ If a Liability or an Owners' Equity line item **Decreases** from <u>Last</u> period to <u>This</u> period, then the change is associated with a **U**se of cash. The change is assigned a **U**.

Step 4	Total the **S**'s & **U**'s – Compare the Total to the Change in Cash

◄► Scroll to position the Cash Flow Worksheet at the left edge of your screen.

The <u>Source of Cash – Use of Cash</u> column is completed by doing the following:

    ▷ adding-up the **S**'s

    ▷ adding-up the **U**'s

    ▷ calculate the net **S** amount or the net **U** amount as follows:

        • if the total **S**'s are greater than the total **U**'s, subtract the total **U** number from the total **S** number and assign an **S** to this net amount, or

        • if the total **U**'s are greater than the total **S**'s, subtract the total **S** number from the total **U** number and assign a **U** to this net amount

🖰 Click **Add-up all of the "S"s**

The **S**ources of cash and the **U**ses of cash were identified correctly because:

    ▷ The $5,000 total at the bottom of the <u>Source of Cash – Use of Cash</u> column matches the $5,000 amount at the bottom of the <u>Incr (Decr) Cash</u> column, and

    ▷ The net effect at the bottom of the <u>Source of Cash – Use of Cash</u> column is a net **S**ource of cash—that is, more cash inflows than cash outflows. A net **S** is consistent with an increase in cash.

If cash had decreased during the period, then the net effect at the bottom of the <u>Source of Cash – Use of Cash</u> column would have been a net **U**se of cash. A net **U** would indicate that there were more cash outflows than cash inflows, which would be consistent with a decrease in cash.

Step 5	Combine – Break-Apart Amounts in the <u>Source of Cash – Use of Cash</u> Column

The **S**ources of cash and the **U**ses of cash that are required to prepare the Statement of Cash Flows have now been identified in the <u>Source of Cash – Use of Cash</u> column. Before completing the Cash Flow Worksheet, you need to determine if any of the amounts in this column need to be combined or broken-apart. It is easier to understand when amounts need to be combined or broken-apart by seeing specific examples. The <u>Combine – Break-Apart</u> area on the Cash Flow Worksheet will be used often as you work through *CCI*'s four months of operations.

Let's look at each item in the <u>Source of Cash – Use of Cash</u> column to determine if any amounts need to be combined or broken-apart:

    ▷ <u>Equipment</u> **U** $55,000 – This amount relates to the $55,000 purchase of equipment. This amount does not need to be combined or broken-apart because it correctly states the amount of cash **U**sed to purchase equipment.

    ▷ <u>Land</u> **U** $30,000 – This amount relates to the $30,000 purchase of land. This amount does not need to be combined or broken-apart because it correctly states the amount of cash **U**sed to purchase land.

    ▷ <u>Note Payable Long-Term</u> **S** $40,000 – This amount relates to the $40,000 borrowed from the bank. This amount does not need to be combined or broken-apart because it correctly states the amount of cash inflow from the bank loan—the **S**ource of cash.

> Common Stock **S** $5,000 – This amount relates to part of the $50,000 cash received from the issuance of Common Stock. This amount **does** need to be combined with the Pd-in Cap in Excess amount to correctly state the total amount of cash inflow from the issuance of Common Stock.

> Pd-in Cap in Excess **S** $45,000 – This amount relates to part of the $50,000 cash received from the issuance of Common Stock. This amount **does** need to be combined with the Common Stock amount to correctly state the total amount of cash inflow from the issuance of Common Stock.

✎ Click **Combine Common Stock "S" + Pd-in Cap in Excess "S"**

The Common Stock **S** $5,000 is combined with the Pd-in Cap in Excess **S** $45,000. The resulting **S** $50,000 correctly states the total amount of cash inflow from the issuance of the Common Stock—the **S**ource of cash.

As previously stated, in future months there will be many more examples of using the Combine – Break-Apart area.

Step 6 Move the **S**ources of Cash and the **U**ses of Cash to One of the Activities Columns

---

As indicated at the beginning of this chapter, the Statement of Cash Flows categorizes the **S**ources and **U**ses of cash into three activities:

> Operating Activities
> Investing Activities
> Financing Activities

The following is a brief description of these three activities.

Operating Activities

Operating activities are cash inflows and outflows that result from transactions affecting Net Income. These are transactions that affect Revenue accounts and Expense accounts. During the month of June, *CCI* did not have any cash flows from operating activities because they did not have any Revenue transactions or Expense transactions. *CCI* will have cash flows from operating activities starting in the month of July.

Investing Activities

Investing activities are cash inflows and outflows that result from the purchase or the sale of long-lived productive assets (primarily fixed assets). *CCI*'s purchase of equipment and purchase of land are examples of investing activities. Investing activities also include investments made in the securities of other companies (*CCI* will not invest in such securities).

Financing Activities

Financing activities are cash inflows and cash outflows that result from:

> Transactions with owners.
> Borrowing on notes, bonds, mortgages, etc. from creditors.

CCI's issuance of Common Stock and borrowing from the bank on a long-term note are examples of financing activities.

The following is a listing of financing activities:

> ▷ Issuing stock to stockholders – cash inflow from owners
> ▷ Paying dividends to stockholders – cash outflow to owners
> ▷ Buying back stock from stockholders – cash outflow to owners
> ▷ Borrowing by issuing notes, bonds, or mortgages – cash inflow from creditors
> ▷ Paying-back notes, bonds, or mortgages – cash outflow to creditors

The Cash Flow Worksheet has a column for Operating Activities, a column for Investing Activities, and a column for Financing Activities. Notice that there is a fourth activities column, <u>NonCash Activities</u>, on the worksheet. The NonCash Activities column will be used and explained in *CCI*'s month of September.

To complete the Cash Flow Worksheet, each of the **S**ources of cash and each of the **U**ses of cash will be put into one of these activities columns.

◄► Scroll to position the <u>NonCash Activities</u> column at the **right** edge of your screen.

✓🖰 Click **Move Equipment to an Activity Column**

Cash flow related to the purchase of long-lived productive assets is categorized as an Investing Activity; thus the **U** $55,000 related to the change in the Equipment line item is moved to the Investing Activities column.

✓🖰 Click **Move Land to an Activity Column**

Like equipment, land is a long-lived productive asset; thus the **U** $30,000 related to the change in the Land line item is moved to the Investing Activities column.

✓🖰 Click **Move Note Payable to an Activity Column**

Cash flow related to borrowing by issuing a note is categorized as a Financing Activity; thus the **S** $40,000 related to the change in the Note Payable Long-Term line item is moved to the Financing Activities column.

✓🖰 Click **Move Common Stock to an Activity Column**

Cash flow related to issuing stock to stockholders is categorized as a Financing Activity; thus the combined **S** $50,000 related to the changes in the Common Stock and Pd-in Cap in Excess line items is moved to the Financing Activities column.

You now have *CCI*'s June cash flows categorized by activity. To make sure that the amounts were moved correctly, each Activities Column is totaled and the totals are netted together.

✓🖰 Click **Add-up all of the "S"s**

This final totaling process proves that our Cash Flow Worksheet still nets to **S** $5,000, which supports and explains the $5,000 increase in cash during the period.

The Cash Flow Worksheet is now complete. Next you will prepare *CCI*'s June Statement of Cash Flows.

Step 7	Use the Activities Columns Amounts to Prepare the Statement of Cash Flows

---

Before preparing the Statement of Cash Flows, let's briefly discuss the two alternative methods available for preparing the Cash Flows from Operating Activities section of the statement.

Indirect Method
This method is used by 99% of U.S. companies. When the Indirect Method is used, Net Income is the first amount shown in the Cash Flows from Operating Activities section. Adjustments are then made to Net Income, an accrual based amount, to arrive at the amount for Cash Provided by Operating Activities, a cash based amount.

Direct Method
This method is used by only 1% of U.S. companies. This method does not use Net Income as the starting point—but rather shows gross cash receipts less gross cash payments to calculate Cash Provided by Operating Activities.

The Cash Flows from Operating Activities section is the only section in the Statement of Cash Flows that is presented differently depending on the method used. The Cash Flows from Investing Activities section and the Cash Flows from Financing Activities section look exactly the same under both the Indirect Method and the Direct Method.

The **Indirect Method** will be used to prepare *CCI*'s four monthly Statements of Cash Flows. You will start learning the details of the Indirect Method starting with *CCI*'s month of July. After all four months are completed for *CCI* (using the Indirect Method), there will be an example shown of a Statement of Cash Flows using the Direct Method.

◄► Scroll to position the Information for the Line Item column at the left edge of your screen.

All of the amounts needed to prepare *CCI*'s June Statement of Cash Flows are in the Activities Columns of the Cash Flow Worksheet.

Cash Flows from Operating Activities
The Statement of Cash Flows starts with Cash Flows from Operating Activities. By looking at the Operating Activities column on the Cash Flow Worksheet, you can see that *CCI* had no cash flow from Operating Activities in June; thus the Cash Flows from Operating Activities section will show zero cash flow.

🖱 Click **Net Income**

As indicated previously:
> ▷ The Indirect Method is used to prepare *CCI*'s Statement of Cash Flows.
> ▷ When the Indirect Method is used, the Cash Flows from Operating Activities section always starts with Net Income.

Because *CCI* had no Revenue or Expense transactions for June, *CCI*'s Net Income is $0 for the month of June.

🖱 Click **Operating Total**

Cash Provided by Operating Activities for June is $0 because *CCI* had no Revenue or Expense transactions during the month. Starting in July, *CCI* will have cash flow from Operating Activities.

Cash Flows from Investing Activities

The amounts in the <u>Investing Activities</u> column on the Cash Flow Worksheet will now be used to prepare the Cash Flows from Investing Activities section of *CCI*'s Statement of Cash Flows.

🖱 Click **Purchase Equipment**

The **U** $55,000 amount in the <u>Investing Activities</u> column of the Cash Flow Worksheet is put in the Cash Flows from Investing Activities section on the Statement of Cash Flows. Notice that the $55,000 is shown as a negative amount on the Statement of Cash Flows. This is as you would expect because the **U** on the Cash Flow Worksheet indicates a **U**se of cash—a cash outflow. On the Statement of Cash Flows, a negative amount will always be shown with brackets "( )" around the amount.

Each line item amount in the Activities columns on the Cash Flow Worksheet will be used once, and only once, on the Statement of Cash Flows. When an amount in the Cash Flow Worksheet has been used, that amount will be grayed-out on the Worksheet. Notice that the $55,000 is now grayed-out on the Worksheet.

🖱 Click **Purchase Land**

The **U** $30,000 amount in the <u>Investing Activities</u> column of the Cash Flow Worksheet is put in the Cash Flows from Investing Activities section on the Statement of Cash Flows. Notice that the $30,000 is shown as a negative "( )" amount on the statement.

All of the line item amounts in the <u>Investing Activities</u> column of the Cash Flow Worksheet have now been put on the Statement of Cash Flows. The only thing left to do to complete the Cash Flows from Investing Activities section is to add-up the line item amounts.

🖱 Click **Investing Total**

The Cash Flows from Investing Activities section on the Statement of Cash Flows is now complete. Notice that the total line reads **Cash Used by Investing Activities**. The word "Used" indicates that there was an outflow of cash associated with the Investing Activities for the period. Again, notice that a cash outflow is shown as a negative "( )" amount on the statement.

Cash Flows from Financing Activities

The Cash Flows from Financing Activities section of the Statement of Cash Flows will now be prepared using the line item amounts in the <u>Financing Activities</u> column of the Cash Flow Worksheet.

🖱 Click **Issue Note Payable**

Notice that the $40,000 is shown as a positive amount on the Statement of Cash Flows. This is as you would expect because the **S** on the Cash Flow Worksheet indicates a **S**ource of cash—a cash inflow.

🖰 Click **Issue Common Stock**

Again, notice that an **S** amount is shown as a positive amount on the Statement of Cash Flows.

All of the line item amounts in the <u>Financing Activities</u> column of the Cash Flow Worksheet have now been put on the Statement of Cash Flows. The only thing left to do to complete the Cash Flows from Financing Activities section of the Statement of Cash Flows is to add-up the line item amounts.

🖰 Click **Financing Total**

The Cash Flows from Financing Activities section on the Statement of Cash Flows is now complete. Notice that the total line reads **Cash Provided by Financing Activities**. The word "Provided" indicates that there was an inflow of cash associated with the Financing Activities for the period. Again, notice that a cash inflow is shown as a positive amount on the statement.

Completing the Totals at the Bottom of the Statement

The three activities sections (Operating, Investing, and Financing) of *CCI*'s Statement of Cash Flows are now complete. To finish the statement:

 ▷ The totals of the three sections are added-up to determine the Increase (Decrease) in Cash from June 1 to June 30, 2017.

 ▷ The Increase (Decrease) in Cash amount is then added to the Beginning Cash Balance to arrive at the Ending Cash Balance.

🖰 Click **Increase (Decrease) in Cash and Report Totals**

CCI's June Statement of Cash Flows is now complete.

Observe the following on *CCI*'s completed June Statement of Cash Flows:

 ▷ The statement is for June 1 to June 30, 2017—a period of time.

 ▷ The statement shows the cash flows categorized by the three activities, with a total cash flow shown for each activity:

 • Operating Activities
 • Investing Activities
 • Financing Activities

 ▷ **S** amounts on the Cash Flow Worksheet are shown as positive amounts on the Statement of Cash Flows.

 ▷ **U** amounts on the Cash Flow Worksheet are shown as negative "( )" amounts on the Statement of Cash Flows.

 ▷ The total cash flows for the three activities are added together to arrive at the net Increase (Decrease) in cash for the period.

 ▷ The Beginning Cash Balance shown on the bottom of the statement is the cash balance from last period's Balance Sheet.

 ▷ The Ending Cash Balance shown at the bottom of the statement is the cash balance from this period's Balance Sheet.

You now have a basic understanding of the Statement of Cash Flows and the Cash Flow Worksheet tool. The month of July will be used to introduce the Operating Activities section of the statement. The months of August and September will become progressively more complex. If you understand the basic concepts shown to you in the month of June, you will be able to easily handle the more complex situations.

⇨ *CCI* BEGINS OPERATING ACTIVITIES – Month of July

In this section, you will continue to use the workbook that you used in the last section entitled "04-Connie's Consulting". If this workbook is not open on your computer then do the following:

⇨ Open the workbook **04-Connie's Consulting** in the **Solid Footing 10e** folder

⇨ Enable Macros

To select the month that you will be using in this section:

⌐ Click the **July** tab

You should see **Screen 11 B** in the upper left corner of the screen.

CCI's month of July will introduce you to the <u>Cash Flows from Operating Activities</u> section of the Statement of Cash Flows. The Cash Flows from Operating Activities section of the Statement of Cash Flows reports the cash inflows and cash outflows that relate to revenue and expense transactions.

The following is a brief review related to revenues and expenses:

▷ Revenues and expenses are shown on the Income Statement.

▷ Net Income is increased when a Revenue account is increased.

▷ Net Income is decreased when an Expense account is increased.

▷ Revenue and expense accounts are closed into the Retained Earnings account. This results in the Retained Earnings account being increased by Net Income.
(Retained Earnings is decreased if there is a Net Loss. All of *CCI*'s months will result in Net Income, and Net Income will be the assumption in all discussions and examples in this chapter.)

As you analyze *CCI*'s July operating activity transactions, you will focus on the following:

▷ The effect on the Cash account.

▷ The effect on the Revenue account or the Expense account.

▷ The effect on Net Income.

▷ If the effect on cash and the effect on Net Income are the same.

July 1 – Buy Supplies

On July 1, *CCI* purchases $1,100 of supplies that are needed for the operation of the office. *CCI* records the purchase as an expense because all of the supplies will be consumed by July 31, the end of the current accounting period.

⌐ Click **Buy Supplies**

Observe the following about this transaction:

> ▷ **Cash** is **decreased** by $1,100 – a cash outflow.

> ▷ Supplies Expense is increased by $1,100 – this will cause **Net Income** to be **decreased** by $1,100.

> ▷ The effect on Cash and the effect on Net Income are the same—**decreased**.

> ▷ This transaction is an Operating Activity.

July 1 – Pay the Office Rent for July

CCI rents office space in an office building. On July 1, *CCI* pays $2,000 rent to the owner of the building. This payment is for the July rent. *CCI* records the rent payment as an expense because all of the rent will be consumed by July 31, the end of the current accounting period.

🖱 Click **Pay Rent**

Observe the following about this transaction:

> ▷ **Cash** is **decreased** by $2,000 – a cash outflow.

> ▷ Office Rent Expense increased by $2,000 – this will cause **Net Income** to be **decreased** by $2,000.

> ▷ The effect on Cash and the effect on Net Income are the same—**decreased**.

> ▷ This transaction is an Operating Activity.

July 20 – Borrow Additional Cash from the Bank

The balance in *CCI*'s Cash account is down to only $1,900 as a result of the cash outflow from the two operating transactions on July 1. *CCI* determines that additional cash is required to finance the start-up of the business. On July 20, *CCI* borrows an additional $8,000 from the bank. The bank adds the additional borrowing to *CCI*'s 5 year long-term note.

🖱 Click **Borrow on N/P**

Cash is increased by $8,000 – a cash inflow.

The **S**ource of the cash inflow can be found in the change of the Note Payable Long-Term account in the General Ledger. This account changes from a $40,000 balance to a $48,000 balance. This increase of $8,000 in the Note Payable Long-Term account is the **S**ource of the $8,000 cash inflow.

This transaction is different than the two July 1 operating transactions. This transaction did **not** affect a revenue account or an expense account; thus it is **not** an operating activity. This transaction involves borrowing on a note from a creditor and affects the liability account Note Payable Long-Term.

As you will see when the Statement of Cash Flows is prepared:

> ▷ The **S**ource of this cash inflow will be identified by calculating the change in the Note Payable Long-Term line item on the Balance Sheet.

> ▷ The cash inflow from this transaction will be shown in the Financing Activities section of the Statement of Cash Flows.

July 31 – Pay Wages to Employees

On July 31, *CCI* pays $9,000 wages to its employees. This payment is for the work performed by the employees during the month of July to operate the business.

🖑 Click **Pay Wages**

Observe the following about this transaction:

▷ **Cash** is **decreased** by $9,000 – a cash outflow.

▷ Wages Expense is increased by $9,000 – this will cause **Net Income** to be **decreased** by $9,000.

▷ The effect on Cash and the effect on Net Income are the same—**decreased**.

▷ This transaction is an Operating Activity.

July 31 – Collect Cash for July Consulting Services

During the month of July, *CCI* performed consulting services for one client. On July 31, the client comes to *CCI*'s office and pays *CCI* $20,000, which is the amount due for the July consulting services.

🖑 Click **July Revenue**

Observe the following about this transaction:

▷ **Cash** is **increased** by $20,000 – a cash inflow.

▷ Consulting Revenue is increased by $20,000 – this will cause **Net Income** to be **increased** by $20,000.

▷ The effect on Cash and the effect on Net Income are the same—**increased**.

▷ This transaction is an Operating Activity.

July 31 – Pay Interest to the Bank for the Long-Term Note Payable

On July 31, *CCI* pays $300 interest to the bank. This payment is for the July interest on the 5 year long-term note that is due to the bank.

🖑 Click **Pay Interest**

Observe the following about this transaction:

▷ **Cash** is **decreased** by $300 – a cash outflow.

▷ Interest Expense is increased by $300 – this will cause **Net Income** to be **decreased** by $300.

▷ The effect on Cash and the effect on Net Income are the same—**decreased**.

▷ This transaction is an Operating Activity.

You might have thought that the payment of interest would be a Financing Activities transaction because it was for interest on the Long-Term Note Payable. The payment of interest is reported in the Operating Activities section because it is an expense transaction. The transaction increases Interest Expense, which will decrease Net Income. The cash flow effect of paying interest will always be reported in the Cash Flows from Operating Activities section of the Statement of Cash Flows.

Cash Flows from Operating Activities = Net Income (after 5 Operating Activity Transactions)

So far in July there have been five Operating Activity transactions. The following table lists the five transactions and the effect the transactions had on Cash Flows from Operating Activities and will have on Net Income:

Operating Activity Transaction or Adjusting Entry	Effect on Cash Flows from Operating Activities Inflow (Outflow)	Effect on Net Income Increase (Decrease)
Buy Supplies	$ (1,100)	$ (1,100)
Pay Office Rent	(2,000)	(2,000)
Pay Wages	(9,000)	(9,000)
Collect for Consulting Services	20,000	20,000
Pay Interest	(300)	(300)
Total	$ 7,600	$ 7,600

The table above shows that the net result of these five Operating Activity transactions is a $7,600 cash inflow. The table also shows that Net Income based on these five transactions will be $7,600. Cash Flows from Operating Activities and Net Income are equal because all five of the Operating Activity transactions resulted from either a cash inflow or a cash outflow. If the Statement of Cash Flows was prepared after these five Operating Activity transactions, Net Income would be shown as the **S**ource of the $7,600 Cash Flows from Operating Activities.

The final entry for July is the recording of depreciation. As you will see, the depreciation entry will affect the Net Income column in the table but will **not** affect the Cash Flows from Operating Activities column in the table.

July 31 – Depreciation Adjusting Entry

The monthly depreciation of the equipment is $1,000.

🖱 Click **Depreciation**

Observe the following about this adjusting entry:

   ▷ **Cash** is **not changed**.

   ▷ Accumulated Depreciation increased by $1,000.

   ▷ Depreciation Expense is increased by $1,000 – this will cause **Net Income** to be **decreased** by $1,000.

   ▷ The effect on Cash and the effect on Net Income are **not** the same.

   ▷ This is an Operating Activity adjusting entry.

The table above can now be updated for the depreciation adjusting entry.

Operating Activity Transaction or Adjusting Entry	Effect on Cash Flows from Operating Activities Inflow (Outflow)	Effect on Net Income Increase (Decrease)
Total from above	$ 7,600	$ 7,600
Depreciation	0	(1,000)
Total	$ 7,600	$ 6,600

The updated table shows that Net Income is now $1,000 less than cash inflow from Operating Activities. Net Income is $1,000 less because the depreciation entry **did** decrease Net Income, but **did not** decrease cash. When the July Statement of Cash Flows is prepared, the Net Income Source will have to be adjusted. The required adjustment will be an addition of $1,000 to the $6,600 of Net Income, to arrive at the $7,600 of Cash from Operating Activities. You will see this $1,000 adjustment when you prepare the July Statement of Cash Flows.

All of the July transactions and adjusting entries have been entered. The July financial statements can now be prepared.

⇨ PREPARE JULY's INCOME STATEMENT and BALANCE SHEET

◄► Scroll to position the Balance Sheets at the **right** edge of your screen.

✏ Click **Prepare the July Income Statement**

Observe that the balance in the revenue account and the balances in all of the expense accounts are used to prepare the Income Statement. Also observe that Net Income of $6,600 on the Income Statement matches the $6,600 Net Income amount in the table at the bottom of the previous page.

✏ Click **Prepare the July Balance Sheet**

Observe the following on the Balance Sheets:

▷ The Balance Sheet for the prior accounting period, June 30, is shown.

▷ The Retained Earnings amount on the July 31 Balance Sheet is:

Retained Earnings on the June 30 Balance Sheet	$ 0
Plus Net Income on the July Income Statement	6,600
Equals Retained Earnings as of July 31	$6,600

✏ Click **Close the Revenue and Expense Accounts**

Observe that the Ending Balance in the Retained Earnings account is the same $6,600 amount calculated above.

In this chapter and the next chapter, the entries in the General Journal to close the Revenue and Expense accounts will not be shown to save space. As you learned in previous chapters, Revenue and Expense accounts are always closed by first making entries in the General Journal and then posting those entries to the General Ledger.

⇨ PREPARE JULY's STATEMENT OF CASH FLOWS

You will now prepare *CCI*'s July Statement of Cash Flows using the Cash Flow Worksheet.

Step 1	Copy the Beginning and Ending Balance Sheets to the Worksheet

◄► Scroll to position the Balance Sheets at the left edge of your screen.

🖑 Click **Copy the 6/30 and 7/31 Balance Sheets to the Cash Flow Worksheet**

Step 2	Calculate the Change in Cash

◄► Scroll to position the Cash Flow Worksheet at the left edge of your screen.

🖑 Click **Calculate the Increase (Decrease) in Cash**

This calculation shows that cash increased by $15,600 from the end of the last accounting period, June 30, to the end of the current accounting period, July 31.

Step 3	Calculate the Change in All of the Balance Sheet Line Items (except cash)
	Assign an **S** or a **U** to the Changes

🖑 Click **For All Items (except cash) Calculate the Absolute Value**

Look at the Cash Flow Worksheet and observe the following about the changes in the Balance Sheet line items (except cash).

Accumulated Depreciation

Accumulated Depreciation changed by $1,000 and is assigned an **S**.

The $1,000 change in the Accumulated Depreciation line item is equal to the amount of Depreciation Expense[3] for July. The $1,000 of depreciation expense needs to be added back to the $6,600 of Net Income to arrive at the $7,600 of net cash inflow from Operating Activities. The amount of depreciation expense for the period will always need to be added back to Net Income in the Statement of Cash Flows; thus the change in Accumulated Depreciation will always[4] be assigned an **S**. The change in Accumulated Depreciation is an example of a line item change that is not really a Source of cash, but does need to be added back to Net Income. Thus for this type of line item change, think of the **S** as saying "**Add back to Net Income**" rather than saying "Source of cash."

[3,4]*The change in Accumulated Depreciation will not always be the same as the amount of Depreciation Expense for the period. If a Fixed Asset is disposed of during the period, and if that Fixed Asset had been previously depreciated, then the change in Accumulated Depreciation for the period will not be equal to Depreciation Expense for the period. CCI will not dispose of any Fixed Assets that have been previously depreciated. The homework problems will not contain any such Fixed Asset disposals. While this situation will not be presented, it can be easily handled using the Cash Flow Worksheet.*

Accumulated Depreciation is an example of a contra-asset. A contra-asset account has a normal credit balance and is shown as a negative amount on the Balance Sheet. When the credit balance in a contra-asset account increases, the amount shown on the Balance Sheet becomes more negative.

The following are the **S** and **U** rules for contra-assets:

Contra-Asset Line Items – Rules for Assigning an **S** or a **U** to the Change
▷ If a Contra-Asset line item becomes more negative from <u>Last</u> period to <u>This</u> period, then the change must be added back in the Statement of Cash Flows. The change is assigned an **S**. (For *CCI* this will always be the case for the contra-asset Accumulated Depreciation.)
▷ If a Contra-Asset line item becomes less negative from <u>Last</u> period to <u>This</u> period, then the change must be subtracted in the Statement of Cash Flows. The change is assigned a **U**.

Note Payable Long-Term

Note Payable Long-Term changed by $8,000 and is assigned an **S**. Per the rules on Pg 138, when a liability line item increases it is always assigned an **S**.

Retained Earnings

Retained Earnings changed by $6,600 and is assigned an **S**. Retained Earnings is part of owners' equity, and per the rules on Pg 138, when an owners' equity line item increases it is always assigned an **S**. (The arrows next to the $6,600 will be discussed in Step 5.)

Step 4	Total the **S**'s & **U**'s – Compare the Total to the Change in Cash

🖰 Click **Add-up all of the "S"s**

The **S**ources of cash and the **U**ses of cash were identified correctly because:

▷ The $15,600 total at the bottom of the <u>Source of Cash – Use of Cash</u> column matches the $15,600 amount at the bottom of the <u>Incr (Decr) Cash</u> column, and

▷ The net effect at the bottom of the <u>Source of Cash – Use of Cash</u> column is a net **S**ource of cash, which is consistent with an increase in cash.

Step 5   Combine – Break-Apart Amounts in the <u>S</u>ource of Cash – <u>U</u>se of Cash Column

---

🖯 Click **Break-Apart the Change in Retained Earnings into**

Two things cause Retained Earnings to change:

       ▷   Net Income increases Retained Earnings.

       ▷   Dividends decrease Retained Earnings.

Net Income is the first amount shown in the Cash Flows from Operating Activities section of the Statement of Cash Flows. As you will see in Step 6, the Net Income **S** will be moved to the Operating Activities column on the Cash Flow Worksheet.

In a later month you will learn: that Dividends are a cash outflow item, that Dividends are assigned a **U**, and that Dividends are moved to the Financing Activities column on the Cash Flow Worksheet.

Because Net Income and Dividends are shown in different activity sections on the Statement of Cash Flows, the change in Retained Earnings needs to be broken-apart into the Net Income **S** amount and the Dividends **U** amount.

CCI did not declare any dividends this period; thus all of the change in Retained Earnings is the result of Net Income. Net Income is $6,600 and is assigned an **S**.

Step 6   Move the **S**ources of Cash and the **U**ses of Cash to One of the Activities Columns

---

◀▶   Scroll to position the <u>NonCash Activities</u> column at the **right** edge of your screen.

🖯 Click **Move Depreciation to an Activity Column**

As previously indicated, Depreciation will be added back to Net Income in the Operating Activities section of the Statement of Cash Flows; thus the **S** $1,000 related to the change in the Accumulated Depreciation line item is moved to the Operating Activities column.

🖯 Click **Move Note Payable to an Activity Column**

Cash flow related to borrowing on a note from a creditor is categorized as a Financing Activity; thus the **S** $8,000 related to the change in the Note Payable Long-Term line item is moved to the Financing Activities column.

🖯 Click **Move Net Income to an Activity Column**

Net Income is the starting amount in the Operating Activities section of the Statement of Cash Flows; thus the Net Income **S** $6,600 is moved to the Operating Activities column.

You now have *CCI*'s July cash flows categorized by activity. To make sure that the amounts were moved correctly, each Activities Column is totaled, and the totals are netted together.

🖱 Click **Add-up all of the "S"s**

This final totaling process proves that our Cash Flow Worksheet still nets to **S** $15,600, which supports and explains the $15,600 increase in cash during the period.

The Cash Flow Worksheet is complete. Next you will prepare *CCI*'s July Statement of Cash Flows.

Step 7	Use the Activities Columns Amounts to Prepare the Statement of Cash Flows

◄► Scroll to position the <u>Information for the Line Item</u> column at the left edge of your screen.

All of the amounts needed to prepare *CCI*'s July Statement of Cash Flows are in the Activities Columns of the Cash Flow Worksheet.

Cash Flows from Operating Activities

The following is a review of some of the important points concerning the Cash Flows from Operating Activities section of the Statement of Cash Flows:

 ▷ The Indirect Method is used to prepare *CCI*'s Cash Flows from Operating Activities section of the Statement of Cash Flows.

 ▷ When the Indirect Method is used, the Cash Flows from Operating Activities section always starts with Net Income.

 ▷ Net Income is an accrual based amount.

 ▷ The Statement of Cash Flows is prepared on a cash basis.

 ▷ Thus, the Cash Flows from Operating Activities section:

  • Starts with Net Income—an accrual based amount.

  • Adjusts Net Income to eliminate the effects of non-cash transactions and non-cash adjusting entries.

  • Arrives at Cash Flows from Operating Activities—a cash based amount.

🖱 Click **Net Income**

Net Income is moved to *CCI*'s Statement of Cash Flows. As stated above, Net Income is always the starting amount in the Cash Flows from Operating Activities section when that section is prepared using the Indirect Method.

Next, Net Income needs to be adjusted for any items that caused Cash Flows from Operating Activities to be different than accrual based Net Income. As previously shown, the July Net Income amount and the July Cash Flows from Operating Activities amount were different by $1,000 as a result of the non-cash Depreciation adjusting entry; thus Depreciation needs to be added back to Net Income.

🖱 Click **Depreciation**

Observe how the Depreciation amount is shown on the statement.

🖰 Click **Operating Total**

The total of the Cash Flows from Operating Activities section shows that Operating Activities provided $7,600 of cash—positive cash flow of $7,600. The calculation of this amount was discussed in detail on Pgs 148 to 149.

Cash Flows from Investing Activities

🖰 Click **Investing Total**

As shown on the Statement of Cash Flows, there were no Investing Activities during July.

Cash Flows from Financing Activities

There was one Financing Activity during the month of July, and that activity was the additional borrowing from the bank on the 5 year note.

🖰 Click **Borrow on Bank Note**

This line item in the Financing Activities section shows the $8,000 cash inflow that resulted from the additional borrowing on the bank note.

🖰 Click **Financing Total**

The total of the Cash Flows from Financing Activities section shows that Financing Activities provided $8,000 of cash—positive cash flow of $8,000.

Completing the Totals at the Bottom of the Statement

The three activities sections (Operating, Investing, and Financing) of *CCI*'s Statement of Cash Flows are now complete. To finish the statement:

▷ The totals of the three sections are added-up to determine the Increase (Decrease) in Cash from July 1 to July 31, 2017.

▷ The Increase (Decrease) in Cash amount is then added to the Beginning Cash Balance to arrive at the Ending Cash Balance.

🖰 Click **Increase (Decrease) in Cash and Report Totals**

CCI's July Statement of Cash Flows is now complete.

Observe the following on *CCI*'s completed July Statement of Cash Flows:

▷ Depreciation is added back to accrual based Net Income to arrive at Cash Provided by Operating Activities—a cash based amount.

▷ The Cash Flows from Operating Activities section shows that by operating the business during the month of July, *CCI* produced net cash inflow of $7,600.

▷ *CCI* borrowed on a note an additional $8,000 to finance the consulting business.

▷ *CCI* started July with $5,000 of cash, increased cash by $15,600 during July, and ended July with $20,600 of cash.

You now have a basic understanding of the Statement of Cash Flows. In the next chapter, *CCI*'s months of August and September will be used to expand your knowledge of this statement.

Chapter 11 Homework

Larry's Landscaping, Inc. Starts Business

On January 1, 2017, Larry's Landscaping, Inc. started business. Larry's Landscaping was started by Larry Plant. To start the corporation, Larry Plant purchased $10,000 of Larry's Landscaping, Inc. Common Stock. The issuance of Common Stock by Larry's Landscaping, Inc. to Larry Plant was the only transaction in January 2017.

In February 2017, to continue the financing of the start-up of the business, Larry's Landscaping issued Common Stock to additional owners and borrowed on a long-term note from the bank. Also in February, Larry's Landscaping invested in various items of Property, Plant, & Equipment needed to operate the business. These items of Property, Plant, & Equipment were not placed into service until March 1; thus there will be no Depreciation recorded in the month of February.

In March 2017, Larry's Landscaping starting operating the business by performing landscaping services for customers.

Your homework for Chapter 11 will be to work four Statement of Cash Flow problems for Larry's Landscaping.

> ▷ The first three problems will be the preparation of <u>monthly</u> Statement of Cash Flows for January, February, and March. Note that the period of time covered by the Statement of Cash Flows for these three problems is <u>one month</u>.

> ▷ The fourth problem will be the preparation of a <u>quarterly</u> Statement of Cash Flows for the period January 1, 2017 to March 31, 2017. Note that the period of time covered by the Statement of Cash Flows for this problem is <u>three months</u> (a quarter of a year).

For each of the problems you will be given two Balance Sheets, one Balance Sheet for the end of the current period and one Balance Sheet for the end of the prior period. In addition to the two Balance Sheets, you will be given additional information that is needed to prepare the Statement of Cash Flows.

The process you will use to work each problem will be to prepare a Cash Flow Worksheet and then prepare a Statement of Cash Flows utilizing the data from your Cash Flow Worksheet.

> ▷ Included with your Solid Footing software is a workbook that contains a blank Cash Flow Worksheet. For each problem, you can either print a copy of the blank Cash Flow Worksheet and work it by hand, or you can complete the Cash Flow Worksheet using Excel and then print it out.

> ▷ There is a tear-out form in the back of the book for each of the required Statement of Cash Flows.

Use the workbook **11-12 Blank Cash Flow Worksheet** in the **Solid Footing 10e** folder.

The first homework problem for Chapter 11 starts on the next page.

Problem 11-1   Larry's Landscaping January Statement of Cash Flows

The following are the Balance Sheets for Larry's Landscaping as of December 31, 2016 (the end of last period) and January 31, 2017 (the end of this period):

Larry's Landscaping
Balance Sheets
as of the End of December 2016 and January 2017

	January 31, 2017	December 31, 2016
Assets		
Cash	$10,000	$0
Total Assets	$10,000	$0
Owners' Equity		
Common Stock	$ 1,000	$0
Paid-in Capital in Excess of Par Value ...	9,000	0
Total Equity	$10,000	$0

The following is additional information for the period January 1 to January 31, 2017:

▷ 1,000 shares of $1.00 par value common stock was issued at a price of $10.00 per share.

Use the following to complete this problem:

▷ A copy of the blank Cash Flow Worksheet located in the workbook named 11-12 Blank Cash Flow Worksheet. This workbook is located in the Solid Footing 10e folder.

▷ The form "Statement of Cash Flows for January 1 to January 31, 2017" located on Pg 237.

Requirement 1

Prepare a Cash Flow Worksheet for the period January 1 to January 31, 2017.

Tip: *The "This Period" Balance Sheet (January 31, 2017) is shown above on the left and the "Last Period" Balance Sheet (December 31, 2016) is shown on the right. When you put these Balance Sheets on your Cash Flow Worksheet, you should switch that order—that is, you should put the "Last Period" Balance Sheet on the Cash Flow Worksheet first and then put the "This Period" Balance Sheet to the right of the "Last Period" Balance Sheet.*

Requirement 2

Utilizing the data from the Cash Flow Worksheet prepared in Requirement 1 – prepare a Statement of Cash Flows for the period January 1 to January 31, 2017.

Problem 11-2   Larry's Landscaping February Statement of Cash Flows

The following are the Balance Sheets for Larry's Landscaping as of January 31, 2017 (the end of last period) and February 28, 2017 (the end of this period):

Larry's Landscaping
Balance Sheets
as of the End of January and February 2017

	February 28, 2017	January 31, 2017
Assets		
Cash	$ 15,000	$10,000
Total Current Assets	15,000	10,000
Equipment	25,000	0
Building	100,000	0
Land	20,000	0
Total Property, Plant & Equipment	145,000	0
Total Assets	$160,000	$10,000
Liabilities		
Note Payable Long-Term	$100,000	$ 0
Total Liabilities	100,000	0
Owners' Equity		
Common Stock	6,000	1,000
Paid-in Capital in Excess of Par Value	54,000	9,000
Total Owners' Equity	60,000	10,000
Total Liabilities and Equity	$160,000	$10,000

The following is additional information for the period February 1 to February 28, 2017:
   ▷ Equipment was purchased for $25,000 cash.
   ▷ A Building was purchased for $100,000 cash.
   ▷ Land was purchased for $20,000 cash.
   ▷ $100,000 cash was borrowed on a Long-Term Note from the bank.
   ▷ 5,000 shares of $1.00 par value common stock were issued at a price of $10.00 per share.

Use the following to complete this problem:
   ▷ The Cash Flow Worksheet in the workbook 11-12 Blank Cash Flow Worksheet
   ▷ The form "Statement of Cash Flows for February 1 to February 28, 2017" on Pg 238.

Requirement 1
Prepare a Cash Flow Worksheet for the period February 1 to February 28, 2017.

Requirement 2
Utilizing the data from the Cash Flow Worksheet prepared in Requirement 1 – prepare a Statement of Cash Flows for the period February 1 to February 28, 2017.

Problem 11-3   Larry's Landscaping March Statement of Cash Flows

The following are the Balance Sheets for Larry's Landscaping as of February 28, 2017 (the end of last period) and March 31, 2017 (the end of this period):

Larry's Landscaping
Balance Sheets
as of the End of February and March 2017

	March 31, 2017	February 28, 2017
Assets		
Cash	$ 17,500	$ 15,000
Total Current Assets	17,500	15,000
Equipment	40,000	25,000
Building	100,000	100,000
Accumulated Depreciation Equipment..	(500)	0
Accumulated Depreciation Building	(1,000)	0
Land	20,000	20,000
Total Property, Plant & Equipment	158,500	145,000
Total Assets	$176,000	$160,000
Liabilities		
Note Payable Long-Term	$110,000	$100,000
Total Liabilities	110,000	100,000
Owners' Equity		
Common Stock	6,000	6,000
Paid-in Capital in Excess of Par Value .	54,000	54,000
Retained Earnings	6,000	0
Total Owners' Equity	66,000	60,000
Total Liabilities and Equity	$176,000	$160,000

The following is additional information for the period March 1 to March 31, 2017:
- ▷ Additional Equipment was purchased for $15,000 cash.
- ▷ Depreciation was recorded for the Equipment and for the Building.
- ▷ $10,000 of additional cash was borrowed on the Long-Term Note from the bank.
- ▷ The Income Statement for March showed a Net Income of $6,000.
- ▷ No Dividends were declared during the month of March.

Use the following to complete this problem:
- ▷ The Cash Flow Worksheet in the workbook <u>11-12 Blank Cash Flow Worksheet</u>
- ▷ The form "Statement of Cash Flows for March 1 to March 31, 2017" on Pg 239.

Requirement 1

Prepare a Cash Flow Worksheet for the period March 1 to March 31, 2017.

Tip: *On your Cash Flow Worksheet, combine the two Accumulated Depreciation Source amounts into one Source amount. There will be only one Depreciation line item on your Statement of Cash Flows.*

Requirement 2

Utilizing the data from the Cash Flow Worksheet prepared in Requirement 1 – prepare a Statement of Cash Flows for the period March 1 to March 31, 2017.

Problem 11-4   Larry's Landscaping January to March Statement of Cash Flows

The following are the Balance Sheets for Larry's Landscaping as of December 31, 2016 (the end of last period) and March 31, 2017 (the end of this period):

Larry's Landscaping
Balance Sheets
as of the End of December 2016 and March 2017

	March 31, 2017	December 31, 2016
Assets		
Cash	$ 17,500	$0
Total Current Assets	17,500	0
Equipment	40,000	0
Building	100,000	0
Accumulated Depreciation Equipment	(500)	0
Accumulated Depreciation Building	(1,000)	0
Land	20,000	0
Total Property, Plant & Equipment	158,500	0
Total Assets	$176,000	$0
Liabilities		
Note Payable Long-Term	$110,000	$0
Total Liabilities	110,000	0
Owners' Equity		
Common Stock	6,000	0
Paid-in Capital in Excess of Par Value	54,000	0
Retained Earnings	6,000	0
Total Owners' Equity	66,000	0
Total Liabilities and Equity	$176,000	$0

The following is additional information for the period January 1 to March 31, 2017:
▷ Equipment was purchased for $40,000 cash.
▷ A Building was purchased for $100,000 cash.
▷ Land was purchased for $20,000 cash.
▷ Starting in March, Depreciation was recorded for the Equipment and for the Building.
▷ $110,000 cash was borrowed on a Long-Term Note from the bank.
▷ 6,000 shares of $1.00 par value common stock was issued at a price of $10.00 per share.
▷ The January 1 to March 31, 2017 Income Statement showed Net Income of $6,000.
▷ No Dividends were declared during the period January 1 to March 31, 2017.

Use the following to complete this problem:
▷ The Cash Flow Worksheet in the workbook 11-12 Blank Cash Flow Worksheet
▷ The form "Statement of Cash Flows for January 1 to March 31, 2017" on Pg 240.

Requirement 1
Prepare a Cash Flow Worksheet for the period January 1 to March 31, 2017.

Tip: For this Statement of Cash Flows the period of time is 3 months. The beginning of the period is January 1, 2017 and the end of the period is March 31, 2017.

Requirement 2
Utilizing the data from the Cash Flow Worksheet prepared in Requirement 1 – prepare a Statement of Cash Flows for the period January 1 to March 31, 2017.

NOTES

Chapter 12
Statement of Cash Flows Continued

In the previous chapter, you were introduced to the Statement of Cash Flows. In that chapter, you developed an understanding of the Statement of Cash Flows and you learned how to prepare the Statement of Cash Flows using a Cash Flow Worksheet. In this chapter, you will be working with *CCI*'s next two months—August and September.

⇨ **ADDITIONAL OPERATING ACTIVITIES – Month of August**

CCI's month of August will continue to use the workbook that you used in the previous chapter entitled "04-Connie's Consulting". If that workbook is not open on your computer, then do the following:

⇨ Open the workbook **04-Connie's Consulting** in the **Solid Footing 10e** folder

⇨ Enable Macros

To select the month that you will be using:

🖰 Click the **August** tab

You should see **Screen 12 A** in the upper left corner of the screen.

In *CCI*'s previous month of July, all of the Operating Activity transactions resulted from cash inflows and cash outflows and involved the Cash account and either a revenue or an expense account. Because of this, Cash Flows from Operating Activities and Net Income were equal after the five Operating Activity transactions. Only after making the depreciation adjusting entry did Cash Flows from Operating Activities and Net Income become different amounts.

In the month of August, there will be a total of nine transactions/adjusting entries, and all nine will be Operating Activities. What will make the August Statement of Cash Flows a little more complex to prepare is that six of the nine transactions/adjusting entries will have a different effect on the amount of Cash from Operating Activities than on the amount of Net Income.

As you will see, the Cash Flow Worksheet will enable you to easily handle this increased level of complexity.

August 1 – Buy Supplies

On August 1, *CCI* purchases $2,500 of supplies.

🖰 Click **Buy Supplies**

The quantity of supplies purchased will last for two or more months; thus *CCI* records the purchase as an asset in the Supplies account.

Observe the following about this transaction:

▷ **Cash** is **decreased** by $2,500 – a cash outflow.

▷ Supplies is increased by $2,500 – Supplies is a <u>current asset</u>.

▷ Supplies Expense is **not changed** – thus **Net Income** will **not be changed**.

▷ The effect on Cash and the effect on Net Income are **not** the same.

▷ This transaction is an Operating Activity.

August 1 – Pay the Office Rent for August

On August 1, *CCI* pays $2,000 to rent office space for the month of August.

🖰 Click **Pay Rent**

Observe the following about this transaction:

▷ **Cash** is **decreased** by $2,000 – a cash outflow.

▷ Office Rent Expense increased by $2,000 – this will cause **Net Income** to be **decreased** by $2,000.

▷ The effect on Cash and the effect on Net Income are the same—**decreased**.

▷ This transaction is an Operating Activity.

August 29 – Pay Wages to Employees

On August 29, *CCI* pays $8,000 wages to its employees. This payment is for the work performed by the employees during the first 29 days of August.

🖰 Click **Pay Wages**

Observe the following about this transaction:

▷ **Cash** is **decreased** by $8,000 – a cash outflow.

▷ Wages Expense is increased by $8,000 – this will cause **Net Income** to be **decreased** by $8,000.

▷ The effect on Cash and the effect on Net Income are the same—**decreased**.

▷ This transaction is an Operating Activity.

The employees will work on August 30 and 31. An adjusting entry will be made at the end of August to accrue the wages for August 30 and 31. The wages for these two days will be paid during the first week of September.

August 31 – Collect Cash from a Client for August Consulting Services

On August 31, *CCI*'s original consulting client comes to *CCI*'s office and pays *CCI* $22,000, which is the amount due for the August consulting services.

⏻ Click **Collect Cash**

Observe the following about this transaction:

  ▷ **Cash** is **increased** by $22,000 – a cash inflow.

  ▷ Consulting Revenue is increased by $22,000 – this will cause **Net Income** to be **increased** by $22,000.

  ▷ The effect on Cash and the effect on Net Income are the same—**increased**.

  ▷ This transaction is an Operating Activity.

August 31 – Invoice a New Client for August Consulting Services

During the month of August, *CCI* acquired a new client and performed $5,000 of consulting services for the new client. As of the end of the month, the new client has not paid; therefore on August 31, *CCI* invoices the new client for $5,000.

⏻ Click **Bill Client**

Observe the following about this transaction:

  ▷ **Cash** is **not changed**.

  ▷ Accounts Receivable is increased by $5,000 – Accounts Receivable is a <u>current asset</u>.

  ▷ Consulting Revenue is increased by $5,000 – this will cause **Net Income** to be **increased** by $5,000.

  ▷ The effect on Cash and the effect on Net Income are **not** the same.

  ▷ This transaction is an Operating Activity.

August 31 – Depreciation Adjusting Entry

The monthly depreciation of the equipment is $1,000.

⏻ Click **Depreciation**

Observe the following about this adjusting entry:

  ▷ **Cash** is **not changed**.

  ▷ Accumulated Depreciation is increased by $1,000.

  ▷ Depreciation Expense is increased by $1,000 – this will cause **Net Income** to be **decreased** by $1,000.

  ▷ The effect on Cash and the effect on Net Income are **not** the same.

  ▷ This is an Operating Activity adjusting entry.

August 31 – Supplies Adjusting Entry

On August 31, *CCI* determines that the amount of supplies on-hand is $1,300. The current balance in the Supplies asset account is $2,500; thus the Supplies account needs to be adjusted down by $1,200.

⏻ Click **Adj Supplies**

Observe the following about this adjusting entry:

> ▷ **Cash** is **not changed**.

> ▷ Supplies is decreased by $1,200 – Supplies is a <u>current asset</u>.

> ▷ Supplies Expense is increased by $1,200 – this will cause **Net Income** to be **decreased** by $1,200.

> ▷ The effect on Cash and the effect on Net Income are **not** the same.

> ▷ This is an Operating Activity adjusting entry.

August 31 – Interest Payable Adjusting Entry

On August 31, *CCI* calls the bank to find out the amount of interest owed to the bank for August on the 5 year long-term note. The bank indicates that the interest due for August is $400. The bank also indicates that *CCI* can wait until the beginning of September to actually pay the $400 of interest. To properly state liabilities on the Balance Sheet and expenses on the Income Statement, *CCI* records an adjusting entry to accrue the interest.

🖱 Click **Accrue Int.**

Observe the following about this adjusting entry:

> ▷ **Cash** is **not changed**.

> ▷ Interest Payable is increased by $400 – Interest Payable is a <u>current liability</u>.

> ▷ Interest Expense is increased by $400 – this will cause **Net Income** to be **decreased** by $400.

> ▷ The effect on Cash and the effect on Net Income are **not** the same.

> ▷ This is an Operating Activity adjusting entry.

August 31 – Wages Payable Adjusting Entry

When *CCI* paid wages to its employees on August 29, the payment was for work from August 1 to August 29. The employees did work on August 30 and 31. They are owed $1,100 for those two days. The wages for August 30 and 31 will be paid to the employees during the first week of September. To properly state liabilities on the Balance Sheet and expenses on the Income Statement, *CCI* records an adjusting entry to accrue the wages.

🖱 Click **Accrue Wages**

Observe the following about this adjusting entry:

> ▷ **Cash** is **not changed**.

> ▷ Wages Payable is increased by $1,100 – Wages Payable is a <u>current liability</u>.

> ▷ Wages Expense is increased by $1,100 – this will cause **Net Income** to be **decreased** by $1,100.

> ▷ The effect on Cash and the effect on Net Income are **not** the same.

> ▷ This is an Operating Activity adjusting entry.

Effects on Cash Flows from Operating Activities vs. Net Income

The following table lists the nine transactions/adjusting entries and the effect each had on Cash Flows from Operating Activities and will have on Net Income:

Operating Activity Transaction or Adjusting Entry	Effect on Cash Flows from Operating Activities Inflow (Outflow)	Effect on Net Income Increase (Decrease)
Buy Supplies	$ (2,500)	$ 0
Pay Office Rent	(2,000)	(2,000)
Pay Wages	(8,000)	(8,000)
Collect for Consulting Services	22,000	22,000
Invoice for Consulting Services	0	5,000
Depreciation adjusting entry	0	(1,000)
Supplies adjusting entry	0	(1,200)
Interest accrual adjusting entry	0	(400)
Wages accrual adjusting entry	0	(1,100)
Total	**$ 9,500**	**$13,300**

As you can see from the table, only three of the nine transactions/adjusting entries have the same effect on <u>Cash Flows from Operating Activities</u> and <u>Net Income</u>. Also, by looking at the table, you can see that there will need to be several adjustments made to the accrual based Net Income amount of $13,300 to arrive at the $9,500 of Cash Flows from Operating Activities. The Cash Flow Worksheet will make it easy to determine these required adjustments and to prepare the Cash Flows from Operating Activities section of the Statement of Cash Flows.

Before preparing the Statement of Cash Flows for August, you need to prepare the August Income Statement and Balance Sheet.

⇨ PREPARE AUGUST's INCOME STATEMENT and BALANCE SHEET

◄► Scroll to position the Balance Sheets at the **right** edge of your screen.

🖱 Click **Prepare the August Income Statement**

Observe that Net Income of $13,300 as shown on the Income Statement matches the Net Income amount shown in the table above.

🖱 Click **Prepare the August Balance Sheet**

Observe the following on the Balance Sheets:

▷ The Balance Sheet for the prior accounting period, July 31, is shown.

▷ The Retained Earnings amount on the August 31 Balance Sheet is:

Retained Earnings on the July 31 Balance Sheet	$ 6,600
Plus Net Income on the August Income Statement	13,300
Equals Retained Earnings as of August 31	$19,900

🖱 Click **Close the Revenue and Expense Accounts**

Observe that the Ending Balance in the Retained Earnings account is the same $19,900 amount calculated on the previous page.

⇨ **PREPARE AUGUST's STATEMENT OF CASH FLOWS**

You will now prepare *CCI*'s August Statement of Cash Flows using the Cash Flow Worksheet.

Step 1	Copy the Beginning and Ending Balance Sheets to the Worksheet

◄► Scroll to position the Balance Sheets at the left edge of your screen.

🖱 Click **Copy the 7/31 and 8/31 Balance Sheets to the Cash Flow Worksheet**

Step 2	Calculate the Change in Cash

◄► Scroll to position the Cash Flow Worksheet at the left edge of your screen.

🖱 Click **Calculate the Increase (Decrease) in Cash**

This calculation shows that cash increased by $9,500 from the end of the last accounting period, July 31, to the end of the current accounting period, August 31. This is the same amount that was shown in the table on Pg 165.

Step 3	Calculate the Change in All of the Balance Sheet Line Items (except cash) Assign an **S** or a **U** to the Changes

🖱 Click **For All Items (except cash) Calculate the Absolute Value**

Look at the Cash Flow Worksheet and observe the following about the changes in the Balance Sheet line items (except cash).

Accounts Receivable (current asset)

Accounts Receivable changed by $5,000 and is assigned a **U**. Per the rules for all Asset line items (except cash), when an asset line item increases it is always assigned a **U**. The increase in Accounts Receivable resulted from invoicing the new client. The table on Pg 165 shows that this transaction had $0 effect on cash and increased Net Income by $5,000; thus $5,000 needs to be subtracted from Net Income on the Statement of Cash Flows—that is what the Accounts Receivable **U** $5,000 will do.

The change in Accounts Receivable is an example of a line item change that is not really a **U**se of cash, but does need to be subtracted from Net Income. Thus, for this type of line item change think of the **U** as saying "**Subtract from Net Income**" rather than saying "Use of cash."

Supplies (current asset)

Supplies changed by $1,300 and is assigned a **U**. Per the rules for all Asset line items (except cash), when an asset line item increases it is always assigned a **U**. The $1,300 increase in Supplies resulted from the August 1 $2,500 purchase transaction increasing the Supplies account and the August 31, $1,200 adjusting entry decreasing the Supplies account.

The table below shows the two lines from the table on Pg 165 related to the <u>Buy Supplies</u> transaction and the <u>Supplies adjusting entry</u>. As the table shows, if you combine the Buy Supplies transaction and the Supplies adjusting entry, the net effects are a $2,500 decrease in Cash Flows from Operating Activities and a $1,200 decrease in Net Income. Cash Flows from Operating Activities has been decreased by $1,300 more than Net Income. On the Statement of Cash Flows, the adjustment to Net Income needs to be a subtraction of $1,300—that is what the Supplies **U** $1,300 will do.

Operating Activity Transaction or Adjusting Entry	Effect on Cash Flows from Operating Activities Inflow (Outflow)	Effect on Net Income Increase (Decrease)
Buy Supplies	$ (2,500)	$ 0
Supplies adjusting entry	0	(1,200)
Net Effect	$ (2,500)	$ (1,200)

Accumulated Depreciation (contra-asset)

Accumulated Depreciation changed by $1,000 and is assigned an **S**. See Pgs 150 to 151 for a detailed discussion of depreciation.

Interest Payable (current liability)

Interest Payable changed by $400 and is assigned an **S**. Per the rules for all Liability line items, when a liability line item increases it is always assigned an **S**. The increase in Interest Payable resulted from the accrual of interest related to the Long-Term Note Payable. The table on Pg 165 shows that this adjusting entry had $0 effect on cash and decreased Net Income by $400; thus $400 needs to be added back to Net Income on the Statement of Cash Flows—that is what the Interest Payable **S** $400 will do.

Wages Payable (current liability)

Wages Payable changed by $1,100 and is assigned an **S**. Per the rules for all Liability line items, when a liability line item increases it is always assigned an **S**. The increase in Wages Payable resulted from the accrual of wages for the last two days of August. The table on Pg 165 shows that this adjusting entry had $0 effect on cash and decreased Net Income by $1,100; thus $1,100 needs to be added back to Net Income on the Statement of Cash Flows—that is what the Wages Payable **S** $1,100 will do.

Retained Earnings (owners' equity)

Retained Earnings changed by $13,300 and is assigned an **S**. Per the rules for all Owners' Equity line items, when an Owners' Equity line item increases it is always assigned an **S**.

Step 4   Total the **S**'s & **U**'s – Compare the Total to the Change in Cash

---

🖰 Click **Add-up all of the "S"s**

The **S**ources of cash and the **U**ses of cash were identified correctly because:
- ▷ The $9,500 total at the bottom of the <u>Source of Cash – Use of Cash</u> column matches the $9,500 amount at the bottom of the <u>Incr (Decr) Cash</u> column, and
- ▷ The net effect at the bottom of the <u>Source of Cash – Use of Cash</u> column is a net **S**ource of cash, which is consistent with an increase in cash.

Step 5   Combine – Break-Apart Amounts in the <u>Source of Cash – Use of Cash</u> Column

---

🖰 Click **Break-Apart the Change in Retained Earnings into**

CCI did not declare any dividends this period; thus all of the change in Retained Earnings is the result of Net Income. Net Income is $13,300 and is assigned an **S**.

For a detailed discussion of the Net Income **S** and the Dividends **U**, see Pg 152.

Step 6   Move the **S**ources of Cash and the **U**ses of Cash to One of the Activities Columns

---

As you have previously seen, Net Income is the starting amount for the Cash Flows from Operating Activities section of the Statement of Cash Flows. Adjustment amounts are then added to or subtracted from Net Income to determine the Cash Flows from Operating Activities amount. If an **S** amount or a **U** amount is one of the required adjustments to Net Income, then that **S** amount or that **U** amount is moved to the Operating Activities column.

All of *CCI*'s **S** and **U** amounts for August are amounts needed to adjust Net Income to Cash Flows from Operating Activities. All of the August **S** and **U** amounts are adjustments to Net Income, because all of the August transactions and adjusting entries were Operating Activities. Thus all of the August **S** and **U** amounts will be moved to the Operating Activities column.

◀▶ Scroll to position the <u>NonCash Activities</u> column at the **right** edge of your screen.

🖰 Click **Move Accts. Rec. to an Activity Column**

The Accounts Receivable **U** $5,000 is moved to the Operating Activities column. Per the discussion under the <u>Accounts Receivable (current asset)</u> heading on Pg 166, the increase in Accounts Receivable will be subtracted from Net Income on the Statement of Cash Flows.

🖰 Click **Move Supplies to an Activity Column**

The Supplies **U** $1,300 is moved to the Operating Activities column. Per the discussion under the <u>Supplies (current asset)</u> heading on Pg 167, the increase in Supplies will be subtracted from Net Income on the Statement of Cash Flows.

🖱 Click **Move Depreciation to an Activity Column**

The Depreciation **S** $1,000 is moved to the Operating Activities column. See Pgs 150 to 151 for a detailed discussion of depreciation.

🖱 Click **Move Interest Pay. to an Activity Column**

The Interest Payable **S** $400 is moved to the Operating Activities column. Per the discussion under the Interest Payable (current liability) heading on Pg 167, the increase in Interest Payable will be added to Net Income on the Statement of Cash Flows.

🖱 Click **Move Wages Pay. to an Activity Column**

The Wages Payable **S** $1,100 is moved to the Operating Activities column. Per the discussion under the Wages Payable (current liability) heading on Pg 167, the increase in Wages Payable will be added to Net Income on the Statement of Cash Flows.

🖱 Click **Move Net Income to an Activity Column**

Net Income is the starting amount in the Cash Flows from Operating Activities section of the Statement of Cash Flows; thus the Net Income **S** $13,300 is moved to the Operating Activities column.

You now have *CCI*'s August cash flows categorized by activity. To make sure that the amounts were moved correctly, each Activities Column is totaled, and the totals are netted together.

🖱 Click **Add-up all of the "S"s**

This final totaling process proves that our Cash Flow Worksheet still nets to **S** $9,500, which supports and explains the $9,500 increase in cash during the period.

The Cash Flow Worksheet is now complete. Next you will prepare *CCI*'s August Statement of Cash Flows.

Step 7   Use the Activities Columns Amounts to Prepare the Statement of Cash Flows

---

◄► Scroll to position the Information for the Line Item column at the left edge of your screen.

All of the amounts needed to prepare *CCI*'s August Statement of Cash Flows are in the Activities Columns of the Cash Flow Worksheet.

Cash Flows from Operating Activities

🖰 Click **Net Income**

Net Income is moved to *CCI*'s Statement of Cash Flows. As previously indicated, Net Income is always the starting amount in the Cash Flows from Operating Activities section when that section is prepared using the Indirect Method.

Next, Net Income needs to be adjusted for items that caused Cash Flows from Operating Activities to be different than accrual based Net Income. To move all of the required adjustments from the Operating Activities column on the Cash Flow Worksheet to the Statement of Cash Flows:

🖰 Click: **Depreciation**
               increase Accts. Rec.
               increase Supplies
               increase Interest Pay.
               increase Wages Pay.

🖰 Click **Operating Total**

The total of the Cash Flows from Operating Activities section shows that Operating Activities provided $9,500 of cash—positive cash flow of $9,500.

The table on Pg 165 shows how the August Operating Activity transaction/adjusting entries resulted in Cash Flows from Operating Activities of $9,500 and Net Income of $13,300. Observe how the Cash Flows from Operating Activities section of the August Statement of Cash Flows starts with Net Income of $13,300 and then adjusts the Net Income amount to calculate Cash Provided by Operating Activities of $9,500. The Cash Flow Worksheet enabled you to determine all of the required adjustments to Net Income. The Depreciation adjustment came from the change in the Accumulated Depreciation line item. All of the other adjustments came from the changes in the Current Asset and the Current Liability line items.

Cash Flows from Investing Activities

🖰 Click **Investing Total**

As shown on the Statement of Cash Flows, *CCI* had no Investing Activities during the month of August.

Cash Flows from Financing Activities

🖰 Click **Financing Total**

As shown on the Statement of Cash Flows, *CCI* had no Financing Activities during the month of August.

Completing the Totals at the Bottom of the Statement

The three activities sections (Operating, Investing, and Financing) of *CCI*'s Statement of Cash Flows are now complete. To finish the statement:

> ▷ The totals of the three sections are added-up to determine the Increase (Decrease) in Cash from August 1 to August 31, 2017.

> ▷ The Increase (Decrease) in Cash amount is then added to the Beginning Cash Balance to arrive at the Ending Cash Balance.

🖱 Click **Increase (Decrease) in Cash and Report Totals**

CCI's August Statement of Cash Flows is now complete.

Observe the following on *CCI*'s completed August Statement of Cash Flows:

> ▷ The $5,000 increase in Accounts Receivable is the primary reason Cash Provided by Operating Activities is less than accrual based Net Income.

> ▷ *CCI* did produce a net cash inflow of $9,500 from operating the business.

> ▷ The $9,500 of Cash Provided by Operating Activities enabled *CCI* to end August with a $30,100 cash balance—compared to a $20,600 beginning cash balance.

You now have a greatly expanded understanding of the Cash Flows from Operating Activities section of the Statement of Cash Flows. Next, *CCI*'s month of September will enable you to apply all of your Statement of Cash Flows knowledge and introduce you to a few new cash flow topics.

⇨ UTILIZING YOUR NEW CASH FLOW TOOLS – Month of September

CCI's month of September will continue to use the workbook entitled "04-Connie's Consulting". If that workbook is not open on your computer, then do the following:

> ⇨ Open the workbook **04-Connie's Consulting** in the **Solid Footing 10e** folder

> ⇨ Enable Macros

To select the month that you will be using:

🖱 Click the **September** tab

◄► Scroll the screen all the way to the left. This will position the Transaction Buttons at the left edge of your screen.

You should see **Screen 12 B** in the upper left corner of the screen.

🖱 Click **Start Over**

CCI's month of September will enable you to apply all of your Statement of Cash Flows knowledge and tools. Plus, September will show you how to handle three new items on the Statement of Cash Flows. These three new items are:

   ▷ The declaration and payment of a dividend.

   ▷ A gain on the sale of a Property, Plant, & Equipment item.

   ▷ A NonCash Investing and Financing Activity.

Before we begin *CCI*'s month of September, let's summarize the rules that have been introduced to this point in Chapters 11 and 12.

S and U Rules for Balance Sheet Line Item Changes

Asset Line Items (except cash) – Rules for Assigning an **S** or a **U** to the Change

   ▷ If an Asset line item **Decreases** from Last period to This period, the change is assigned an **S**.

   ▷ If an Asset line item **Increases** from Last period to This period, the change is assigned a **U**.

Contra-Asset Line Items – Rules for Assigning an **S** or a **U** to the Change

   ▷ If a Contra-Asset line item becomes more negative from Last period to This period, the change is assigned an **S**.

   ▷ If a Contra-Asset line item becomes less negative from Last period to This period, the change is assigned a **U**.

Liability and **Owners' Equity** Line Items – Rules for Assigning an **S** or a **U** to the Change

   ▷ If a Liability or an Owners' Equity line item **Increases** from Last period to This period, the change is assigned an **S**.

   ▷ If a Liability or an Owners' Equity line item **Decreases** from Last period to This period, the change is assigned a **U**.

S and U Line Items to Combine or Break-Apart

   ▷ Issuance of Common Stock with a Par Value – The Common Stock line item **S** and the Paid-in Capital in Excess of Par Value line item **S** are combined into one **S** amount. This combined **S** amount is the amount of cash inflow that resulted from the issuance of the Common Stock.

   ▷ Change in Retained Earnings – The Retained Earnings line item **S** or **U** is broken-apart into a Net Income **S** and a Dividend **U**. In the months of July and August, *CCI* did not declare a dividend; thus the Dividend **U** was zero for both months. In September, *CCI* will declare and pay a dividend. This is one of the new items that will be introduced in September.

Rules for Moving Line Item S's and U's to an Activity Column

▷ Assets

- **Current Asset** line items move to the **Operating Activities** column.
  There are a few exceptions to this rule. There will <u>not</u> be any exceptions to this rule in *CCI's* four months or in the homework.

- **Accumulated Depreciation** line item moves to the **Operating Activities** column.
  See the footnote on Pg 150 for a discussion of an exception to this rule. There will <u>not</u> be any exceptions to this rule in *CCI's* four months or in the homework.

- **Property, Plant, & Equipment** line items move to the **Investing Activities** column.
  The exception to this rule is when a Property, Plant, or Equipment item is acquired in a non-cash exchange. This type of transaction involves the exchange of debt or equity for a Property, Plant, or Equipment item. You will see an example of this type of non-cash transaction in *CCI's* month of September, and the line item will be moved to the NonCash Activities column.

▷ Liabilities

- **Note Payable, Bond Payable, Mortgage Payable** line items move to the **Financing Activities** column.
  The exception to this rule is when debt is issued in exchange for a Property, Plant, or Equipment item. You will see an example of this type of non-cash transaction in *CCI's* month of September, and the line item will be moved to the NonCash Activities column.

- **Dividends Payable** line item is combined with the Dividends line item and moves to the **Financing Activities** column.
  There will <u>not</u> be a Dividends Payable line item in *CCI's* four months or in the homework.

- **All Other Liability** line items move to the **Operating Activities** column.
  There are a few exceptions to this rule. There will <u>not</u> be any exceptions to this rule in *CCI's* four months or in the homework.

▷ Owners' Equity

- **Net Income** (part of the change in Retained Earnings) moves to the **Operating Activities** column.

- **All Other Owners' Equity** line items move to the **Financing Activities** column.
  The exception to this rule is when equity is issued in exchange for a Property, Plant, or Equipment item, and the line item is moved to the NonCash Activities column. There will <u>not</u> be any of these types of non-cash transactions in *CCI's* four months or in the homework.

You will now work through *CCI's* month of September. Except for when the three new items are introduced, the explanations and discussions will be kept to a minimum because you are well on your way to becoming a Cash Flow expert.

September 1 – Pay the Interest Due to the Bank for the Month of August

At the end of August, *CCI* accrued $400 of interest due to the bank for the month of August. On September 1, *CCI* pays this interest.

🖱 Click **Pay Aug. Int.**

Observe the following about this transaction:

> ▷ **Cash** is **decreased** by $400 – a cash outflow.

> ▷ Interest Payable is decreased by $400 – Interest Payable is a <u>current liability</u>.

> ▷ Interest Expense is **not changed** – thus **Net Income** will **not be changed**.

> ▷ The effect on Cash and the effect on Net Income are **not** the same.

> ▷ This transaction is an Operating Activity.

September 1 – Pay the Office Rent for September

On September 1, *CCI* pays $2,000 to rent office space for the month of September.

🖱 Click **Pay Rent**

Observe the following about this transaction:

> ▷ **Cash** is **decreased** by $2,000 – a cash outflow.

> ▷ Office Rent Expense increased by $2,000 – this will cause **Net Income** to be **decreased** by $2,000.

> ▷ The effect on Cash and the effect on Net Income are the same—**decreased**.

> ▷ This transaction is an Operating Activity.

September 1 – Purchase Equipment

On September 1, *CCI* pays $7,000 cash for additional office equipment

🖱 Click **Buy Equipment**

Observe the following about this transaction:

> ▷ **Cash** is **decreased** by $7,000 – a cash outflow.

> ▷ **Equipment** is **increased** by $7,000 – Equipment is an item of Property, Plant, & Equipment. The increase in the Equipment account identifies the **U**se of cash.

> ▷ This transaction is an Investing Activity.

September 4 – Pay the Wages Due to the Employees for August 30 & 31

At the end of August, *CCI* accrued $1,100 of wages due to the employees for the last two days of August. On September 4, *CCI* pays these wages.

🖱 Click **Pay Aug. Wage**

Observe the following about this transaction:

> ▷ **Cash** is **decreased** by $1,100 – a cash outflow.

> ▷ Wages Payable is decreased by $1,100 – Wages Payable is a <u>current liability</u>.

> ▷ Wages Expense is **not changed** – thus **Net Income** will **not be changed**.

> ▷ The effect on Cash and the effect on Net Income are **not** the same.

> ▷ This transaction is an Operating Activity.

September 10 – Collect an Account Receivable

On August 31, *CCI* invoiced a new client for $5,000 of consulting services. On September 10, the client pays the invoice.

🖱 Click **Collect A/R**

Observe the following about this transaction:

> ▷ **Cash** is **increased** by $5,000 – a cash inflow.
>
> ▷ Accounts Receivable is decreased by $5,000 – Accounts Receivable is a <u>current asset</u>.
>
> ▷ Consulting Revenue is **not changed** – thus **Net Income** will **not be changed**.
>
> ▷ The effect on Cash and the effect on Net Income are **not** the same.
>
> ▷ This transaction is an Operating Activity.

September 15 – Sell Land

In June, *CCI* purchased land with the intention of building a new office building on the land. During September, *CCI* locates an existing office building that is for sale and sets September 30 as the date to purchase the building. *CCI* determines that they no longer need all of the land, and on September 15, *CCI* sells part of their land to a buyer. The buyer pays *CCI* $20,000 cash for the part of the land that is being sold. The part of the land that *CCI* is selling is a little less than half of *CCI*'s total land. Of the $30,000 total land cost, *CCI* allocates $14,000 to the part sold to the buyer.

The $20,000 selling price of the land is $6,000 greater than the $14,000 cost of the land; thus *CCI* has a $6,000 gain on the sale of the land.

🖱 Click **Sell Land**

Observe the following about this transaction:

> ▷ **Cash** is **increased** by $20,000 – a cash inflow.
>
> ▷ **Land** is **decreased** by $14,000 – Land is an item of Property, Plant, & Equipment.
>
> ▷ **Gain on Sale of Land**[1] is increased by $6,000 – this will cause **Net Income** to be **increased** by $6,000.
>
> ▷ This transaction is an Investing Activity.

The sale of land is an Investing Activity because land is an item of Property, Plant, & Equipment. Thus, the $20,000 cash inflow will be shown in the Cash Flows from Investing Activities section of the Statement of Cash Flows. When you prepare the Cash Flow Worksheet you will see that the **S**ource of the $20,000 Investing Activity cash inflow will come from two places—the $14,000 decrease in the Land item plus the $6,000 gain that is part of Net Income. Net Income is shown in the Operating Activities section of the Statement of Cash Flows; thus the $6,000 gain that is part of Net Income will have to be moved from the Operating Activities section to the Investing Activities section. When you prepare the Cash Flow Worksheet and the Statement of Cash Flows, you will see how this $6,000 move between sections is handled.

---

[1] The Gain on Sale of Land account is a type of revenue account. This account:
- Records an increase in owners' claims to assets.
- Is a temporary account that is closed to Retained Earnings.
- Has a normal credit balance.
- Is shown on the Income Statement.
- Increases Net Income.

September 18 – Payment to the Bank on the Note Payable

On September 18, *CCI* determines that the $44,600 balance in the Cash account is more cash than is required for the normal operation of the business. *CCI* uses $18,000 of its cash to pay-down the balance of the note payable due to the bank.

🖱 Click **Pmt. on Note**

Observe the following about this transaction:

 ▷ **Cash** is **decreased** by $18,000 – a cash outflow.

 ▷ **Note Payable Long-Term** is **decreased** by $18,000 – the decrease in the Note Payable Long-Term account identifies the **U**se of cash.

 ▷ This transaction is a Financing Activity.

September 20 – Pay Cash Dividend

On September 20, *CCI* declares and pays a $16,000 dividend. As introduced in Chapter 10, there are three dates associated with a dividend: Date of Declaration, Date of Record, and Date of Payment. *CCI* has only 5 stockholders; thus all three of these dates can be the same. Because the Date of Declaration and the Date of Payment are the same, the payment of cash to the stockholders takes place on the Date of Declaration, and the use of a Dividends Payable account is not needed.

🖱 Click **Pay Dividends**

Observe the following about this transaction:

 ▷ **Cash** is **decreased** by $16,000 – a cash outflow.

 ▷ **Retained Earnings** is **decreased** by $16,000.

 ▷ This transaction is a Financing Activity – see Pgs 140 to 141 for a discussion of Financing Activities.

This is the first time *CCI* has declared and paid a dividend. In the months of July and August, the change in Retained Earnings was totally the result of Net Income. The change in Retained Earnings for September will be the result of Net Income increasing Retained Earnings and the declaration of a dividend decreasing Retained Earnings.

September 30 – Collect Cash from a Client for September Consulting Services

On September 30, *CCI*'s original consulting client comes to *CCI*'s office and pays *CCI* $24,000, which is the amount due for September consulting services.

🖱 Click **Sept. Revenue**

Observe the following about this transaction:

 ▷ **Cash** is **increased** by $24,000 – a cash inflow.

 ▷ Consulting Revenue is increased by $24,000 – this will cause **Net Income** to be **increased** by $24,000.

 ▷ The effect on Cash and the effect on Net Income are the same—**increased**.

 ▷ This transaction is an Operating Activity.

September 30 – Pay Wages to Employees

On September 30, *CCI* pays $10,500 wages to its employees for the month of September.

🖱 Click **Pay Wages**

Observe the following about this transaction:

▷ **Cash** is **decreased** by $10,500 – a cash outflow.

▷ Wages Expense is increased by $10,500 – this will cause **Net Income** to be **decreased** by $10,500.

▷ The effect on Cash and the effect on Net Income are the same—**decreased**.

▷ This transaction is an Operating Activity.

September 30 – Pay Interest to the Bank for the Long-Term Note Payable

On September 30, *CCI* pays $450 interest to the bank. This payment is for the September interest on the long-term note.

🖱 Click **Pay Interest**

Observe the following about this transaction:

▷ **Cash** is **decreased** by $450 – a cash outflow.

▷ Interest Expense is increased by $450 – this will cause **Net Income** to be **decreased** by $450.

▷ The effect on Cash and the effect on Net Income are the same—**decreased**.

▷ This transaction is an Operating Activity.

September 30 – Purchase an Office Building by Issuing a Mortgage Note Payable

On September 30, *CCI* purchases an office building. *CCI* does not pay any cash to the seller of the building. *CCI* gives the seller a $95,000 Mortgage Note Payable in exchange for the $95,000 building.

🖱 Click **Purch. Building**

Observe the following about this transaction:

▷ **Cash** is **not** changed by this transaction.

▷ **Building** is increased by $95,000 – Building is an item of Property, Plant, & Equipment.

▷ **Mortgage Note Payable** is increased by $95,000 – Mortgage Note Payable is a liability that represents borrowing from a creditor.

▷ This transaction is a NonCash Activity.

If *CCI* had purchased the building by paying $95,000 cash to the seller, the building purchase would have been an Investing Activity transaction on the Statement of Cash Flows. If *CCI* had borrowed $95,000 cash from a creditor, the borrowing would have been a Financing Activity transaction on the Statement of Cash Flows. But there was no cash outflow or cash inflow related to this transaction because *CCI* issued the Mortgage Note Payable to the seller in exchange for the building. As you complete *CCI*'s month of September, you will see how this NonCash transaction will be handled on the Cash Flow Worksheet and shown on *CCI*'s Statement of Cash Flows.

September 30 – Depreciation Adjusting Entry

The monthly depreciation of the equipment is $1,200. The amount of depreciation for September increased because of the purchase of new equipment on September 1. The new office building will be placed into service on October 1; thus there is no September depreciation for the new building.

🖱 Click **Depreciation**

Observe the following about this adjusting entry:

▷ **Cash** is **not changed**.

▷ Accumulated Depreciation is increased by $1,200.

▷ Depreciation Expense is increased by $1,200 – this will cause **Net Income** to be **decreased** by $1,200.

▷ The effect on Cash and the effect on Net Income are **not** the same.

▷ This is an Operating Activity adjusting entry.

September 30 – Supplies Adjusting Entry

On September 30, *CCI* determines that the amount of supplies on-hand is $400. The current balance in the Supplies asset account is $1,300; thus the Supplies account needs to be adjusted down by $900.

🖱 Click **Adj Supplies**

Observe the following about this adjusting entry:

▷ **Cash** is **not changed**.

▷ Supplies is decreased by $900 – Supplies is a <u>current asset</u>.

▷ Supplies Expense is increased by $900 – this will cause **Net Income** to be **decreased** by $900.

▷ The effect on Cash and the effect on Net Income are **not** the same.

▷ This is an Operating Activity adjusting entry.

This completes *CCI*'s September transactions and adjusting entries. In terms of cash flow activity, September is *CCI*'s most complex month. You will easily be able to handle the September level of complexity by applying your cash flow knowledge and by using the Cash Flow Worksheet.

Before preparing the Statement of Cash Flows for September, you need to prepare the September Income Statement and Balance Sheet.

⇨ PREPARE SEPTEMBER's INCOME STATEMENT and BALANCE SHEET

◄► Scroll to position the Balance Sheets at the **right** edge of your screen.

🖱 Click **Prepare the Sept. Income Statement**

Observe how the **Gain on Sale of Land** is shown on the Income Statement.

🖱 Click **Prepare the Sept. Balance Sheet**

The Retained Earnings amount on the September Balance Sheet is:

Retained Earnings on the August 31 Balance Sheet	$19,900	
Less Dividends declared in September	(16,000)	
Equals Current Balance in Retained Earnings		3,900
Plus Net Income on the September Income Statement		14,950
Equals Retained Earnings on the September 30 Balance Sheet		$18,850

🖱 Click **Close the Revenue and Expense Accounts**

Observe that the Ending Balance in the Retained Earnings account is the same $18,850 amount calculated above.

⇨ PREPARE SEPTEMBER's STATEMENT OF CASH FLOWS

You will now prepare *CCI*'s September Statement of Cash Flows using the Cash Flow Worksheet.

Step 1	Copy the Beginning and Ending Balance Sheets to the Worksheet

◄► Scroll to position the Balance Sheets at the left edge of your screen.

🖱 Click **Copy the 8/31 and 9/30 Balance Sheets to the Cash Flow Worksheet**

Step 2	Calculate the Change in Cash

◄► Scroll to position the Cash Flow Worksheet at the left edge of your screen.

🖱 Click **Calculate the Increase (Decrease) in Cash**

This calculation shows that cash decreased by $6,450 from the end of the last accounting period, August 31, to the end of the current accounting period, September 30. The change in the cash balance is shown as a negative "( )" amount.

Step 3	Calculate the Change in All of the Balance Sheet Line Items (except cash)
	Assign an **S** or a **U** to the Changes

🖱 Click **For All Items (except cash) Calculate the Absolute Value**

S's and **U**'s are assigned to each line item change on the Cash Flow Worksheet using the rules on Pg 172 under the heading **S** and **U Rules for Balance Sheet Line Item Changes**.

Step 4	Total the **S**'s & **U**'s – Compare the Total to the Change in Cash

✐ Click **Add-up all of the "S"s**

The **S**ources of cash and the **U**ses of cash were identified correctly because:

▷ The $6,450 total at the bottom of the <u>Source of Cash – Use of Cash</u> column matches the $6,450 amount at the bottom of the <u>Incr (Decr) Cash</u> column, and

▷ The net effect at the bottom of the <u>Source of Cash – Use of Cash</u> column is a net **U**se of cash, which is consistent with the decrease in cash shown in the <u>Incr (Decr) Cash</u> column.

Step 5	Combine – Break-Apart Amounts in the <u>Source of Cash – Use of Cash</u> Column

✐ Click **Break-Apart the Change in Retained Earnings into**

As shown in the calculation of Retained Earnings at the top of Pg 179, the declaration of dividends caused Retained Earnings to decrease by $16,000, and Net Income caused Retained Earnings to increase by $14,950. The net result is that Retained Earnings decreased by $1,050; thus the Retained Earnings **U** $1,050.

Consistent with what you learned from working with *CCI*'s months of July and August, Net Income is always assigned an **S**; thus the Net Income **S** $14,950.

Dividends is assigned a **U** $16,000. This is consistent with the rule for equity accounts, if an equity account decreases then it is assigned a **U**. Dividends caused Retained Earnings, an equity account, to decrease; thus it is assigned a **U**. Assigning a **U** $16,000 to Dividends is also consistent with what happened when *CCI* declared and paid the dividend—a cash outflow of $16,000—a **U**se of $16,000 cash.

We will now handle *CCI*'s sale of land. Refer back to the discussion on Pg 175 under the heading **September 15 – Sell Land** to refresh your understanding of the land sale transaction. As noted in that discussion, the $6,000 Gain on Sale of Land became part of Net Income and needs to be moved out of Net Income and combined with the $14,000 change in the Land line item. The combination of the $6,000 Gain and the $14,000 change in Land explains the $20,000 cash inflow from the sale of land.

✐ Click **Move the "S" $6,000 Gain on Sale to the Land line**

The following is an explanation of the logic of how this is handled on the Cash Flow Worksheet:

▷ The Gain on Sale of Land **S** $6,000, which is part of the Net Income **S** $14,950, is moved up to the Land line item.

▷ To keep the Cash Flow Worksheet in balance, we could reduce the Net Income **S** $14,950 by the $6,000 that was moved to the Land line item. However we need the Net Income **S** $14,950 amount to start-off the Cash Flows from Operating Activities section of the Statement of Cash Flows; thus we cannot directly reduce the Net Income amount.

▷ Since we cannot directly reduce the Net Income amount, we put a **U** $6,000 amount next to the Net Income line item. This **U** $6,000 amount keeps our Cash Flow Worksheet in balance and will be used when we prepare the Operating Activities section of the Statement of Cash Flows.

▷ The **S** $14,000 Land amount is then combined with the **S** $6,000 Gain on Sale amount to arrive at the **S** $20,000 amount. The **S** $20,000 amount is the cash inflow that resulted from selling the land.

Step 6 Move the **S**ources of Cash and the **U**ses of Cash to One of the Activities Columns

◀▶ Scroll to position the <u>NonCash Activities</u> column at the **right** edge of your screen.

Review the rules for moving **S**'s and **U**'s on Pg 173 under the heading **Rules for Moving Line Item S's and U's to an Activity Column**. As you move each line item's **S** amount or **U** amount, the applicable rule that was used will be indicated.

🖱 Click **Move Accts. Rec. to an Activity Col.**

This line item follows the rule for <u>Assets</u> • **Current Asset**

🖱 Click **Move Supplies to an Activity Col.**

This line item follows the rule for <u>Assets</u> • **Current Asset**

You will now move the Building **U** $95,000 to an activity column. Refer back to the discussion on Pg 177 under the heading **September 30 – Purchase an Office Building by Issuing a Mortgage Note Payable** to refresh your understanding of the building purchase transaction.

🖱 Click **Move Building to an Activity Col.**

The change in the Building line item was the result of *CCI* acquiring the building in exchange for a Mortgage Note Payable—a non-cash transaction. Thus the Building line item is the exception shown under the <u>Assets</u> • **Property, Plant, & Equipment** rule. As noted in the exception, this line item is moved to the **NonCash Activities** column.

🖱 Click **Move Equipment to an Activity Col.**

This line item follows the rule for <u>Assets</u> • **Property, Plant, & Equipment**

🖱 Click **Move Depr. to an Activity Col.**

This line item follows the rule for <u>Assets</u> • **Accumulated Depreciation**

🖱 Click **Move Land to an Activity Col.**

This line item follows the rule for <u>Assets</u> • **Property, Plant, & Equipment**

🖱 Click **Move Int. Pay. to an Activity Col.**

This line item follows the rule for <u>Liabilities</u> • **All Other Liability**

🖱 Click **Move Wages Pay. to an Activity Col.**

This line item follows the rule for <u>Liabilities</u> • **All Other Liability**

🖱 Click **Move Note Pay. to an Activity Col.**

This line item follows the rule for <u>Liabilities</u> • **Note Payable, Bond Payable, Mortgage Payable**

You will now move the Mortgage Note Payable **S** $95,000 to an activity column. Refer back to the discussion on Pg 177 under the heading **September 30 – Purchase an Office Building by Issuing a Mortgage Note Payable** to refresh your understanding of this transaction.

🖱 Click **Move Mtg. Pay. to an Activity Col.**

The change in the Mortgage Note Payable line item was the result of *CCI* acquiring a building in exchange for a Mortgage Note Payable—a non-cash transaction. Thus the Mortgage Note Payable line item is the exception shown under the <u>Liabilities</u> • **Note Payable, Bond Payable, Mortgage Payable** rule. As noted in the exception, this line item is moved to the **NonCash Activities** column.

🖱 Click **Move Net Income to an Activity Col.**

This line item follows the rule for <u>Owners' Equity</u> • **Net Income**

You will now move to an activity column the **U** $6,000 amount that is next to Net Income. Refer back to the bottom of Pg 180, for a discussion of the logic related to this item.

🖱 Click **Move U 6,000 Gain to an Activity Col.**

The **U** $6,000 amount is moved to the Operating Activities column and is placed just under the **S** $14,950 Net Income amount. The **U** $6,000 amount is an offset against the **S** $14,950 Net Income amount. The reason this offset is required is because $6,000 of the Net Income **S**ource amount was moved to the sale of Land line item that is in the Investing Activities column.

🖱 Click **Move Dividends to an Activity Col.**

This line item follows the rule for <u>Owners' Equity</u> • **All Other Owners' Equity**

You now have *CCI*'s September cash flows categorized by activity. To make sure that the amounts were moved correctly, each Activities Column is totaled, and the totals are netted together.

🖰 Click **Add-up all of the "S"s**

This final totaling process proves that our Cash Flow Worksheet still nets to **U** $6,450, which supports and explains the $6,450 decrease in cash during the period.

Observe that the NonCash Activities column nets to "0". The NonCash Activities column will always net to "0" because the **S**ource amount(s) will always equal the **U**se amount(s).

The Cash Flow Worksheet is now complete. Next you will prepare *CCI*'s September Statement of Cash Flows.

Step 7	Use the Activities Columns Amounts to Prepare the Statement of Cash Flows

◀▶ Scroll to position the Information for the Line Item column at the left edge of your screen.

All of the amounts needed to prepare *CCI*'s September Statement of Cash Flows are in the Activities Columns of the Cash Flow Worksheet.

Cash Flows from Operating Activities

🖰 Click **Net Income**

Net Income is moved to *CCI*'s Statement of Cash Flows.

🖰 Click **Gain on Sale of Land**

The $6,000 Gain on Sale of Land is included in the $14,950 Net Income amount. The $6,000 Gain on Sale of Land will also be included in the $20,000 Cash Provided by the Sale of Land amount in the Investing Activities section. The $6,000 is subtracted from Net Income to keep the Gain amount from being double counted.

Next, Net Income needs to be adjusted for items that caused Cash Flows from Operating Activities to be different than accrual based Net Income. To move all of the required adjustments from the Operating Activities column on the Cash Flow Worksheet to the Statement of Cash Flows:

🖰 Click: **Depreciation**
             decrease Accounts Rec.
             decrease Supplies
             decrease Interest Pay.
             decrease Wages Pay.

🖰 Click **Operating Total**

The total of the Cash Flows from Operating Activities section shows that Operating Activities provided $14,550 of cash—positive cash flow of $14,550.

Cash Flows from Investing Activities

🖰 Click **Purchase Equipment**

In September, *CCI* paid $7,000 cash to purchase additional office equipment—an Investing Activity—a $7,000 cash outflow.

🖰 Click **Sale of Land**

This is the $20,000 cash that *CCI* received from the sale of land. As previously discussed, the $20,000 includes a $6,000 gain that *CCI* realized when they sold the land. The $6,000 gain is also included in the $14,950 Net Income amount in the Operating Activities section. The (6,000) shown just under Net Income removes the $6,000 gain from the Operating Activities section and avoids double counting the $6,000 gain.

🖰 Click **Investing Total**

The Cash Flows from Investing Activities section on the Statement of Cash Flows is now complete. Notice that the total line reads **Cash Provided by Investing Activities**. The word "Provided" indicates that there was an inflow of cash associated with the Investing Activities for the period. There was a cash inflow of $13,000 from Investing Activities because the $20,000 cash received from the sale of land was greater than the $7,000 cash used to purchase office equipment.

Cash Flows from Financing Activities

🖰 Click **Payment on Note Pay.**

In September, *CCI* paid $18,000 cash to the bank to pay-down a portion of the note due to the bank—a Financing Activity—an $18,000 cash outflow.

🖰 Click **Pay Dividends**

In September, *CCI* declared and paid a $16,000 cash dividend to stockholders—a Financing Activity—a $16,000 cash outflow.

🖰 Click **Financing Total**

The Cash Flows from Financing Activities section on the Statement of Cash Flows is now complete. Notice that the total line reads **Cash Used by Financing Activities**. The word "Used" indicates that there was an outflow of cash associated with the Financing Activities for the period. Both Financing Activities during the period were uses of cash.

Completing the Totals at the Bottom of the Statement

🖱 Click **Increase (Decrease) in Cash and Report Totals**

Observe that there was a $6,450 decrease in cash for the month of September. There was a decrease in cash because the Cash Used by Financing Activities was greater than the combined Cash Provided by Operating Activities + Cash Provided by Investing Activities. *CCI* started September with $30,100 of cash and ended September with $23,650 of cash.

NonCash Investing and Financing Activities

As previously discussed, *CCI* purchased a building by giving the seller a $95,000 Mortgage Note Payable in exchange for the building. Because this transaction did not involve any cash outflow or any cash inflow, it is not reported in either the Cash Flows from Investing Activities section or the Cash Flows from Financing Activities section.

Because this was a significant transaction for *CCI*, it will be shown in a note at the bottom of the Statement of Cash Flows.

🖱 Click **NonCash Bldg. Purchase**

Observe how the amounts in the NonCash Activities column on the Cash Flow Worksheet are used to prepare the note.

This completes the two Solid Footing chapters devoted to the Statement of Cash Flows (Indirect Method). While we have not covered all possible cash flow items, you now have a solid understanding of the Statement of Cash Flows and the tools to be able to handle most cash flow situations.

As previously indicated, there is another method that can be used to prepare the Cash Flows from Operating Activities section of the Statement of Cash Flows. This other method is called the **Direct Method**. The Direct Method is used by only about one percent of all companies; thus it has not been shown in the two cash flow chapters. The next page contains a one page appendix describing the Direct Method.

⇨ Statement of Cash Flows Appendix – DIRECT METHOD

🖰 Click the **Direct Method** tab in the Connie's Consulting workbook.

You should see **Screen 12 C** in the upper left corner of the screen.

The statement on the right is a copy of the September Statement of Cash Flows you prepared for *CCI*. This statement was prepared using the **Indirect Method**. The statement on the left is *CCI*'s September Statement of Cash Flows prepared using the **Direct Method**. Observe what is the same on both statements:

- ▷ The Cash Provided by Operating Activities total of $14,550.
- ▷ All of the Cash Flows from Investing Activities section.
- ▷ All of the Cash Flows from Financing Activities section.
- ▷ The Decrease in Cash from Sept. 1 to Sept. 30, 2017.
- ▷ The September Beginning and Ending Cash Balances.
- ▷ The NonCash Investing and Financing Activities footnote.

The <u>only</u> difference between a Statement of Cash Flows prepared using the Indirect Method and one prepared using the Direct Method is how the amount of Cash Provided (Used) by Operating Activities is determined. As you learned in Chapters 11 and 12, the Indirect Method starts with accrual based Net Income and adjusts that amount to determine the cash based Cash Flows from Operating Activities. As you can see, the Direct Method simply lists the operating cash inflows and the operating cash outflows to determine the amount of Cash Provided (Used) by Operating Activities.

CCI had only twelve transactions during the month of September, and of those twelve transactions the following seven were operating transactions:

- ▷ Sept 1   Pay .... $400 cash for interest
- ▷ Sept 1   Pay .... $2,000 cash for rent
- ▷ Sept 4   Pay .... $1,100 cash for wages
- ▷ Sept 10   Collect ..... $5,000 cash from client
- ▷ Sept 30   Collect ... $24,000 cash from client
- ▷ Sept 30   Pay .... $10,500 cash for wages
- ▷ Sept 30   Pay .... $450 cash for interest

By looking at these seven transactions, you can see how the cash inflows and cash outflows shown in *CCI*'s Direct Method Operating Activities section were calculated. If you click back to *CCI*'s month of September, you will see these seven transactions in the General Journal.

Even a medium size company has tens of thousands of operating transactions during its accounting period; thus it is not practical to review all of the operating transactions to determine the cash inflows and cash outflows for the Direct Method Operating Activities section. A greatly expanded version of the Cash Flow Worksheet you learned in Chapters 11 and 12 can be used to prepare a Statement of Cash Flows using the Direct Method, but the amount of work, analysis, and time required are very significant. **The high cost and extensive effort required to prepare a Direct Method Statement of Cash Flows are the major reasons that less than 1% of all companies use the Direct Method.**

The purpose of this short appendix was to make you aware of the Direct Method that can be used to prepare the Operating Activities section of the Statement of Cash Flows. Because so few companies use the Direct Method, the emphasis in Chapters 11 and 12 was on the method used by 99%+ of all companies—the **Indirect Method**.

Chapter 12 Homework

Problem 12-1   Larry's Landscaping April Statement of Cash Flows

The homework problems for Chapter 12 will use Larry's Landscaping. To refresh your knowledge of Larry's Landscaping, see the heading "Larry's Landscaping, Inc. Starts Business" on Pg 155.

The following are the Balance Sheets for Larry's Landscaping as of March 31, 2017 (the end of last period) and April 30, 2017 (the end of this period):

	April 30, 2017	March 31, 2017
Assets		
Cash	$ 21,000	$ 17,500
Supplies	1,500	0
Prepaid Insurance	3,300	0
Total Current Assets	25,800	17,500
Equipment	40,000	40,000
Building	100,000	100,000
Accumulated Depreciation Equipment	(1,000)	(500)
Accumulated Depreciation Building	(2,000)	(1,000)
Land	20,000	20,000
Total Property, Plant & Equipment	157,000	158,500
Total Assets	$182,800	$176,000
Liabilities		
Interest Payable	$ 550	$ 0
Total Current Liabilities	550	0
Note Payable Long-Term	110,000	110,000
Total Liabilities	110,550	110,000
Owners' Equity		
Common Stock	6,000	6,000
Paid-in Capital in Excess of Par Value	54,000	54,000
Retained Earnings	12,250	6,000
Total Owners' Equity	72,250	66,000
Total Liabilities and Equity	$182,800	$176,000

The following is additional information for the period April 1 to April 30, 2017:
▷ The Income Statement for April showed a Net Income of $6,250.
▷ No Dividends were declared during the month of April.

Use the following to complete this problem:
▷ The Cash Flow Worksheet in the workbook 11-12 Blank Cash Flow Worksheet
▷ The form "Statement of Cash Flows for April 1 to April 30, 2017" on Pg 241.

Requirement 1
Prepare a Cash Flow Worksheet for the period April 1 to April 30, 2017.
Tip: On your Cash Flow Worksheet, combine the two Accumulated Depreciation Source amounts into one Source amount—there should be only one Depreciation line on your Statement of Cash Flows.

Requirement 2
Utilizing the data from the Cash Flow Worksheet prepared in Requirement 1 – prepare a Statement of Cash Flows for the period April 1 to April 30, 2017.

Problem 12-2   Larry's Landscaping May Statement of Cash Flows

The following are the Balance Sheets for Larry's Landscaping as of April 30, 2017 (the end of last period) and May 31, 2017 (the end of this period):

	May 31, 2017	April 30, 2017
Assets		
Cash	$ 18,000	$ 21,000
Accounts Receivable	6,000	0
Supplies	1,100	1,500
Prepaid Insurance	3,000	3,300
Total Current Assets	28,100	25,800
Equipment	44,000	40,000
Building	100,000	100,000
Accumulated Depreciation Equipment ..	(1,600)	(1,000)
Accumulated Depreciation Building	(3,000)	(2,000)
Land	20,000	20,000
Total Property, Plant & Equipment	159,400	157,000
Total Assets	$187,500	$182,800
Liabilities		
Wages Payable	$ 1,500	$ 0
Interest Payable	0	550
Total Current Liabilities	1,500	550
Note Payable Long-Term	105,000	110,000
Total Liabilities	106,500	110,550
Owners' Equity		
Common Stock	6,000	6,000
Paid-in Capital in Excess of Par Value ..	54,000	54,000
Retained Earnings	21,000	12,250
Total Owners' Equity	81,000	72,250
Total Liabilities and Equity	$187,500	$182,800

The following is additional information for the period May 1 to May 31, 2017:
  ▷ Additional Equipment was purchased for $4,000 cash.
  ▷ A $5,000 cash payment was made to pay down the Note Payable.
  ▷ The Income Statement for May showed a Net Income of $8,750.
  ▷ No Dividends were declared during the month of May.

Use the following to complete this problem:
  ▷ The Cash Flow Worksheet in the workbook 11-12 Blank Cash Flow Worksheet
  ▷ The form "Statement of Cash Flows for May 1 to May 31, 2017" on Pg 242.

Requirement 1
Prepare a Cash Flow Worksheet for the period May 1 to May 31, 2017.

Tip: *On your Cash Flow Worksheet, combine the two Accumulated Depreciation Source amounts into one Source amount. There will be only one Depreciation line item on your Statement of Cash Flows.*

Requirement 2
Utilizing the data from the Cash Flow Worksheet prepared in Requirement 1 – prepare a Statement of Cash Flows for the period May 1 to May 31, 2017.

Problem 12-3   Larry's Landscaping June Statement of Cash Flows

The following are the Balance Sheets for Larry's Landscaping as of May 31, 2017 (the end of last period) and June 30, 2017 (the end of this period):

	June 30, 2017	May 31, 2017
Assets		
Cash	$ 25,000	$ 18,000
Accounts Receivable	9,500	6,000
Supplies	1,600	1,100
Prepaid Insurance	2,700	3,000
Total Current Assets	38,800	28,100
Equipment	94,000	44,000
Building	100,000	100,000
Accumulated Depreciation Equipment	(2,200)	(1,600)
Accumulated Depreciation Building	(4,000)	(3,000)
Land	17,000	20,000
Total Property, Plant & Equipment	204,800	159,400
Total Assets	$243,600	$187,500
Liabilities		
Wages Payable	$ 0	$ 1,500
Interest Payable	500	0
Total Current Liabilities	500	1,500
Note Payable Long-Term	105,000	105,000
Note Payable for Equipment	50,000	0
Total Liabilities	155,500	106,500
Owners' Equity		
Common Stock	6,000	6,000
Paid-in Capital in Excess of Par Value	54,000	54,000
Retained Earnings	28,100	21,000
Total Owners' Equity	88,100	81,000
Total Liabilities and Equity	$243,600	$187,500

The following is additional information for the period June 1 to June 30, 2017:
▷ $50,000 of Equipment was purchased by issuing a Note to the equipment vendor. No cash was paid to the vendor.
▷ Land was sold for $5,000 cash. The land had a cost of $3,000; thus there was a $2,000 gain on the sale of the land. The $2,000 gain is included in Net Income.
▷ The Income Statement for June showed a Net Income of $15,100.
▷ An $8,000 dividend was declared and paid in June.

Use the following to complete this problem:
▷ The Cash Flow Worksheet in the workbook 11-12 Blank Cash Flow Worksheet
▷ The form "Statement of Cash Flows for June 1 to June 30, 2017" on Pg 243.

Requirement 1
Prepare a Cash Flow Worksheet for the period June 1 to June 30, 2017.
Tip: On your Cash Flow Worksheet, combine the two Accumulated Depreciation Source amounts.

Requirement 2
Utilizing the data from the Cash Flow Worksheet prepared in Requirement 1 – prepare a Statement of Cash Flows for the period June 1 to June 30, 2017.

Problem 12-4 Larry's Landscaping April to June Statement of Cash Flows

The following are the Balance Sheets for Larry's as of March 31, 2017 and June 30, 2017:

Assets	June 30, 2017	March 31, 2017
Cash	$ 25,000	$ 17,500
Accounts Receivable	9,500	0
Supplies	1,600	0
Prepaid Insurance	2,700	0
Total Current Assets	38,800	17,500
Equipment	94,000	40,000
Building	100,000	100,000
Accumulated Depreciation Equipment	(2,200)	(500)
Accumulated Depreciation Building	(4,000)	(1,000)
Land	17,000	20,000
Total Property, Plant & Equipment	204,800	158,500
Total Assets	$243,600	$176,000
Liabilities		
Wages Payable	$ 0	$ 0
Interest Payable	500	0
Total Current Liabilities	500	0
Note Payable Long-Term	105,000	110,000
Note Payable for Equipment	50,000	0
Total Liabilities	155,500	110,000
Owners' Equity		
Common Stock	6,000	6,000
Paid-in Capital in Excess of Par Value	54,000	54,000
Retained Earnings	28,100	6,000
Total Owners' Equity	88,100	66,000
Total Liabilities and Equity	$243,600	$176,000

The following is additional information for the period April 1 to June 30, 2017:
▷ $50,000 of Equipment was purchased by issuing a Note to the equipment vendor. No cash was paid to the vendor.
▷ $4,000 of Equipment was purchased for $4,000 cash.
▷ Land was sold for $5,000 cash. The land had a cost of $3,000; thus there was a $2,000 gain on the sale of the land. The $2,000 gain is included in Net Income.
▷ A $5,000 cash payment was made to pay down the Note Payable Long-Term.
▷ The April 1 to June 30, 2017 Income Statement showed Net Income of $30,100.
▷ An $8,000 dividend was declared and paid during the period April 1 to June 30, 2017.

Use the following to complete this problem:
▷ The Cash Flow Worksheet in the workbook 11-12 Blank Cash Flow Worksheet
▷ The form "Statement of Cash Flows for April 1 to June 30, 2017" on Pg 244.

Requirement 1
Prepare a Cash Flow Worksheet for the period April 1 to June 30, 2017.

Tips: For this Statement of Cash Flows the period of time is 3 months—April 1 to June 30, 2017.
On your Cash Flow Worksheet, split the Equipment U 54,000 into a U 50,000 and a U 4,000.
On your Cash Flow Worksheet, combine the two Accumulated Depreciation Source amounts.

Requirement 2
Prepare a Statement of Cash Flows for the period April 1 to June 30, 2017.

Name: _____   Section: _____   #: _____

Forms for: Problem 1-1 – The Coffee Can Accounting System

_____   =   _____   +   _____

Trial Balance

Name: _____   Section: _____   #: _____

Answer Sheet for: Problem 1-2   True / False Questions for Chapter 1 _____

Circle **T**rue or **F**alse for each question:

1. True   False

2. True   False

3. True   False

4. True   False

5. True   False

6. True   False

7. True   False

8. True   False

9. True   False

10. True   False

Name: _____   Section: _____   #: _____

Forms for: Problem 2-1 – OverPriced Jeans, Inc. Starts Business

General Journal

Date	Account	Debit	Credit

Name: _____   Section: _____   #: _____

Forms for: Problem 2-1 – OverPriced Jeans, Inc. Starts Business

General Journal

Date	Account	Debit	Credit

Forms for: Problem 2-1   (continued)

Trial Balance

Account Name	Debit	Credit
Total		

Assets:

	$
	$

Liabilities:

	$

Equity:

	$

Name: _____ Section: _____ #: _____

Forms for: Problem 2-1 (continued)

———————————————————— **General Ledger** ————————————————————

| **Assets** | = | **Liabilities** | + | **Owners' Equity** |

	Dr.	Cr.

	Dr.	Cr.

	Dr.	Cr.

	Dr.	Cr.

	Dr.	Cr.

	Dr.	Cr.

	Dr.	Cr.

Name: _____   Section: _____   #: _____

Answer Sheet for: Problem 2-2   True / False Questions for Chapter 2

Circle **T**rue or **F**alse for each question:

1.   True   False

2.   True   False

3.   True   False

4.   True   False

5.   True   False

6.   True   False

7.   True   False

8.   True   False

9.   True   False

10.   True   False

11.   True   False

12.   True   False

13.   True   False

14.   True   False

Name: _____ Section: _____ #: _____

Forms for: Problem 3-1 – OverPriced Jeans, Inc. Rips-Off Its First Customers

General Journal

Date	Account	Debit	Credit

Forms for: Problem 3-1 (continued)

Trial Balance

Account Name	Debit	Credit
Cash - Big Bank		
Cash - Little Bank		
Accounts Receivable		
Inventory		
Equipment		
Note Payable - Big Bank		
Note Payable - Little Bank		
Interest Payable - Big Bank		
Interest Payable - Little Bank		
Common Stock		
Retained Earnings		
Total		

What Caused the Change
in Retained Earnings
during the Period Feb. 1 to Feb. 28, 2017

Sale of Inventory to Customers	$
Less: Cost of Inventory Sold to Customers	
Assets Consumed for Rent	
Assets Consumed for Wages	
Increase in Big & Little Banks' Claims to Assets for Interest	
Increase in the Owners' Claim to the Assets during February	$

Name: _____   Section: _____   #: _____

Forms for: Problem 3-1 (continued)

───────────────────────── **General Ledger** ─────────────────────────

Assets	=	**Liabilities**	+	**Owners' Equity**

	Cash	
	Dr. Big Bank	Cr.
Beg. Balance	35,000	
Ending Balance		

	Cash	
	Dr. Little Bank	Cr.
Beg. Balance	20,000	
Ending Balance		

	Accounts	
	Dr. Receivable	Cr.
Beg. Balance	0	
Ending Balance		

	Dr. Inventory	Cr.
Beg. Balance	85,000	
Ending Balance		

	Dr. Equipment	Cr.
Beg. Balance	60,000	
Ending Balance		

	Note Payable	
	Dr. Big Bank	Cr.
Beg. Balance		65,000
Ending Balance		

	Note Payable	
	Dr. Little Bank	Cr.
Beg. Balance		60,000
Ending Balance		

	Interest Payable	
	Dr. Big Bank	Cr.
Beg. Balance		0
Ending Balance		

	Interest Payable	
	Dr. Little Bank	Cr.
Beg. Balance		0
Ending Balance		

	Common	
	Dr. Stock	Cr.
Beg. Balance		75,000
Ending Balance		

	Retained	
	Dr. Earnings	Cr.
Beg. Balance		0
Ending Balance		

Forms for: Problem 3-1 (continued)

Assets:

	$
	$

Liabilities:

	$

Equity:

	$

Name: _____   Section: _____   #: _____

Answer Sheet for: Problem 3-2   True / False Questions for Chapter 3

Circle **T**rue or **F**alse for each question:

1.	True	False
2.	True	False
3.	True	False
4.	True	False
5.	True	False
6.	True	False
7.	True	False
8.	True	False
9.	True	False
10.	True	False

Blank Page for Miscellaneous Calculations

Name: _____   Section: _____   #: _____

Forms for: Problem 4-1 – OverPriced Jeans, Inc. Revenue and Expense Accounts

General Journal

Date	Account	Debit	Credit

Forms for: Problem 4-1 (continued)

Pre-Closing Trial Balance		
Account Name	Debit	Credit
Cash - Big Bank		
Cash - Little Bank		
Accounts Receivable		
Inventory		
Equipment		
Note Payable - Big Bank		
Note Payable - Little Bank		
Interest Payable - Big Bank		
Interest Payable - Little Bank		
Common Stock		
Retained Earnings		
Sales Revenue		
Cost of Goods Sold		
Rent Expense		
Wages Expense		
Interest Expense		
Total		

Income Statement	
	$
Net Income	$

Name: _____   Section: _____   #: _____

Forms for: Problem 4-1 (continued)

──────────── **General Ledger** ────────────

| **Assets** | = | **Liabilities** | + | **Owners' Equity** |

Assets

Cash		
Dr.	Big Bank	Cr.
Beg. Balance	35,000	
Ending Balance		

Cash		
Dr.	Little Bank	Cr.
Beg. Balance	20,000	
Ending Balance		

Accounts		
Dr.	Receivable	Cr.
Beg. Balance	0	
Ending Balance		

Inventory		
Dr.		Cr.
Beg. Balance	85,000	
Ending Balance		

Equipment		
Dr.		Cr.
Beg. Balance	60,000	
Ending Balance		

Liabilities

Note Payable		
Dr.	Big Bank	Cr.
Beg. Balance		65,000
Ending Balance		

Note Payable		
Dr.	Little Bank	Cr.
Beg. Balance		60,000
Ending Balance		

Interest Payable		
Dr.	Big Bank	Cr.
Beg. Balance		0
Ending Balance		

Interest Payable		
Dr.	Little Bank	Cr.
Beg. Balance		0
Ending Balance		

Owners' Equity

Common		
Dr.	Stock	Cr.
Beg. Balance		75,000
Ending Balance		

Retained		
Dr.	Earnings	Cr.
Beg. Balance		0
Current Balance		

Sales		
Dr.	Revenue	Cr.
Beg. Balance		0
Ending Balance		

Cost of Goods		
Dr.	Sold	Cr.
Beg. Balance	0	
Ending Balance		

Rent		
Dr.	Expense	Cr.
Beg. Balance	0	
Ending Balance		

Wages		
Dr.	Expense	Cr.
Beg. Balance	0	
Ending Balance		

Interest		
Dr.	Expense	Cr.
Beg. Balance	0	
Ending Balance		

Forms for: **Problem 4-1** (continued)

Calculation of
Retained Earnings as of
Feb. 28 for the Balance Sheet

OverPriced Jeans, Inc.
Balance Sheet
as of February 28, 2017

Assets:

Cash - Big Bank	$
Cash - Little Bank	
Accounts Receivable	
Inventory	
Equipment	
Total Assets	$

Liabilities:

Note Payable - Big Bank	$
Note Payable - Little Bank	
Interest Payable - Big Bank	
Interest Payable - Little Bank	
Total Liabilities	

Equity:

Common Stock	
Retained Earnings	
Total Equity	
Total Liabilities and Equity	$

Name: _____   Section: _____   #: _____

Answer Sheet for: Problem 4-2   True / False Questions for Chapter 4

Circle **T**rue or **F**alse for each question:

                            1.   True   False

                            2.   True   False

                            3.   True   False

                            4.   True   False

                            5.   True   False

                            6.   True   False

                            7.   True   False

                            8.   True   False

                            9.   True   False

                            10.   True   False

Blank Page for Miscellaneous Calculations

Name: _____   Section: _____   #: _____

Forms for: Problem 5-1 – OverPriced Jeans, Inc. Closing Entries for February

General Journal

Date	Account	Debit	Credit

Forms for: Problem 5-1 (continued)

Post-Closing Trial Balance		
Account Name	Debit	Credit
Cash - Big Bank		
Cash - Little Bank		
Accounts Receivable		
Inventory		
Equipment		
Note Payable - Big Bank		
Note Payable - Little Bank		
Interest Payable - Big Bank		
Interest Payable - Little Bank		
Common Stock		
Retained Earnings		
Sales Revenue		
Cost of Goods Sold		
Rent Expense		
Wages Expense		
Interest Expense		
Total		

Name: _____   Section: _____   #: _____

Forms for: Problem 5-1   (continued)

General Ledger

Assets	=	Liabilities	+	Owners' Equity

Assets

Cash — Big Bank

	Dr.	Cr.
Beg. Balance	35,000	
Feb 01		4,000
Feb 04	62,000	
Feb 22		17,000
Ending Balance	76,000	

Cash — Little Bank

	Dr.	Cr.
Beg. Balance	20,000	
Feb 07		10,000
Feb 18	40,000	
Feb 27		23,000
Ending Balance	27,000	

Accounts Receivable

	Dr.	Cr.
Beg. Balance	0	
Feb 15	88,000	
Feb 18	70,000	
Ending Balance	158,000	

Inventory

	Dr.	Cr.
Beg. Balance	85,000	
Feb 04		16,000
Feb 15		22,000
Feb 18		28,000
Feb 22	17,000	
Ending Balance	36,000	

Equipment

	Dr.	Cr.
Beg. Balance	60,000	
Ending Balance	60,000	

Liabilities

Note Payable — Big Bank

	Dr.	Cr.
Beg. Balance		65,000
Ending Balance		65,000

Note Payable — Little Bank

	Dr.	Cr.
Beg. Balance		60,000
Ending Balance		60,000

Interest Payable — Big Bank

	Dr.	Cr.
Beg. Balance		0
Feb 28		600
Ending Balance		600

Interest Payable — Little Bank

	Dr.	Cr.
Beg. Balance		0
Feb 28		450
Ending Balance		450

Owners' Equity

Common Stock

	Dr.	Cr.
Beg. Balance		75,000
Ending Balance		75,000

Retained Earnings

	Dr.	Cr.
Beg. Balance		0
Ending Balance		

Sales Revenue

	Dr.	Cr.
Beg. Balance		0
Feb 04		62,000
Feb 15		88,000
Feb 18		110,000
Ending Balance		260,000
After Close Bal.		

Cost of Goods Sold

	Dr.	Cr.
Beg. Balance	0	
Feb 04	16,000	
Feb 15	22,000	
Feb 18	28,000	
Ending Balance	66,000	
After Close Bal.		

Rent Expense

	Dr.	Cr.
Beg. Balance	0	
Feb 01	4,000	
Ending Balance	4,000	
After Close Bal.		

Wages Expense

	Dr.	Cr.
Beg. Balance	0	
Feb 07	10,000	
Feb 27	23,000	
Ending Balance	33,000	
After Close Bal.		

Interest Expense

	Dr.	Cr.
Beg. Balance	0	
Feb 28	600	
Feb 28	450	
Ending Balance	1,050	
After Close Bal.		

Name: _____   Section: _____   #: _____

Answer Sheet for: Problem 5-2   True / False Questions for Chapter 5 _____

Circle **T**rue or **F**alse for each question:

1.   True   False

2.   True   False

3.   True   False

4.   True   False

5.   True   False

6.   True   False

7.   True   False

8.   True   False

9.   True   False

10. True   False

Name: _____ Section: _____ #: _____

Forms for: Problem 7-1   Purchase and Depreciate a New Delivery Truck

Requirement 1 – March 1 truck purchase

Date	Account Name	Debit	Credit

Requirement 2 – Monthly depreciation

$ _____

Requirement 3 – March 31 depreciation adjusting entry

Date	Account Name	Debit	Credit

Requirement 4 – Balance in <u>Accumulated Depreciation – Truck</u> after 18 months

$ _____

Requirement 5 – Monthly depreciation if life was 4 years

$ _____

Blank Page for Miscellaneous Calculations

Name: _____ Section: _____ #: _____

Forms for: Problem 7-2 **Purchase and Depreciate Two Items of Property, Plant, & Equipment**

Requirement 1 – April 1 office building purchase

Date	Account Name	Debit	Credit

Requirement 2 – Monthly depreciation for the office building

$

Requirement 3 – April 30 depreciation adjusting entry for the office building

Date	Account Name	Debit	Credit

Requirement 4 – May 1 computer system purchase

Date	Account Name	Debit	Credit

Forms for: Problem 7-2 (continued)

Requirement 5 – Monthly depreciation for the computer system

$

Requirement 6 – May 31 depreciation adjusting entry for the computer system

Date	Account Name	Debit	Credit

Requirement 7 – May 31 depreciation adjusting entry for the office building

Date	Account Name	Debit	Credit

Requirement 8 – Total Depreciation Expense on the May Income Statement

$

Name: _____   Section: _____   #: _____

**Forms for: Problem 7-3   Purchasing Supplies and the
Monthly Supplies Adjusting Entry**

Requirement 1 — July 1 purchase of supplies

Date	Account Name	Debit	Credit

Requirement 2 — July 31 supplies on-hand

$

Requirement 3 — "T" Account Analysis for July 31 adjusting entry

"T" Account Analysis for Asset and Liability Accounts		
Account Name →	**Supplies** (asset account)	
	Debit	**Credit**
(1) What is the <u>current</u> balance?		
(3) What adjustment is required to adjust from the <u>current</u> balance to the <u>should be</u> balance?		
(2) What <u>should be</u> the balance?		

Requirement 4 — July 31 supplies adjusting entry

Date	Account Name	Debit	Credit

Forms for: Problem 7-3 (continued)

Requirement 5 – August 31 supplies on-hand

$ [   ]

Requirement 6 – "T" Account Analysis for August 31 adjusting entry

"T" Account Analysis for Asset and Liability Accounts		
Account Name →	**Supplies** (asset account)	
	Debit	**Credit**
(1) What is the <u>current</u> balance?		
(3) What adjustment is required to adjust from the <u>current</u> balance to the <u>should be</u> balance?		
(2) What <u>should be</u> the balance?		

Requirement 7 – August 31 supplies adjusting entry

Date	Account Name	Debit	Credit

Requirement 8 – Total dollar amount of supplies consumed during first two months of operation

$ [   ]

Name: _____   Section: _____   #: _____

**Forms for: Problem 7-4   Paying Rent in Advance and the
Monthly Prepaid Rent Adjusting Entry**

Requirement 1 – June 20 advance payment of rent

Date	Account Name	Debit	Credit

Requirement 2 – Prepaid Rent timeline

In the boxes above the timeline, indicate the amount of remaining Prepaid Rent for each date on the timeline.

Note that the amounts of Prepaid Rent for June 20 (the date the contract was signed) and for October 31 (the last day of the four month rental period) have already been entered.

In the boxes below the timeline, indicate the amount of Prepaid Rent that expires (is used-up) during each of the four months.

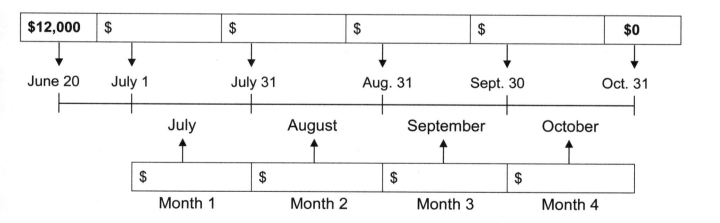

Forms for: Problem 7-4 (continued)

Requirement 3 – "T" Account Analysis for the July 31 adjusting entry

"T" Account Analysis for Asset and Liability Accounts		
Account Name →	**Prepaid Rent**	
	Debit	**Credit**
(1) What is the <u>current</u> balance?		
(3) What adjustment is required to adjust from the <u>current</u> balance to the <u>should be</u> balance?		
(2) What <u>should be</u> the balance?		

Requirement 4 – July 31 Prepaid Rent adjusting entry

Date	Account Name	Debit	Credit

Requirement 5

Amount of Prepaid Rent on the August 31 Balance Sheet

$

Amount of Rent Expense on the August 1 to August 31 Income Statement

$

Name: _____ Section: _____ #: _____

Forms for: Problem 7-5   Prepaid Insurance and the
Monthly Prepaid Insurance Adjusting Entry

Requirement 1 – September 1 advance payment of the two insurance policies

Date	Account Name	Debit	Credit

Requirement 2 – **Auto and Truck** Prepaid Insurance timeline

In the boxes above the timeline, indicate the amount of remaining Prepaid Insurance related to the **Auto and Truck** insurance policy for each date on the timeline.

In the boxes below the timeline, indicate the amount of Prepaid Insurance that expires (is used-up) during each of the three months.

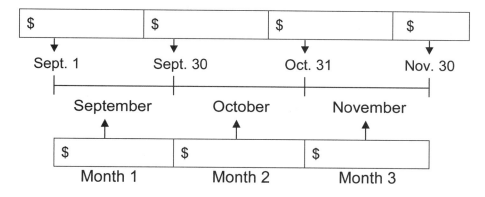

Requirement 3 – **Business Liability** Prepaid Insurance timeline

In the boxes above the timeline, indicate the amount of remaining Prepaid Insurance related to the **Business Liability** insurance policy for each date on the timeline.

In the boxes below the timeline, indicate the amount of Prepaid Insurance that expires (is used-up) during each of the four months.

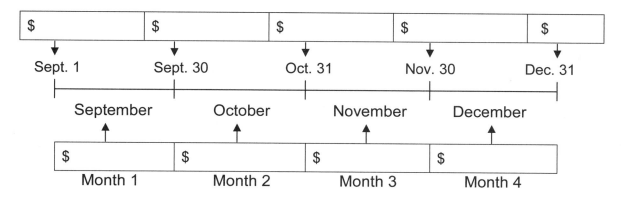

Forms for: Problem 7-5 (continued)

Requirement 4 – "T" Account Analysis for the September 30 Prepaid Insurance adjusting entry

Note that the Prepaid Insurance account contains the total amount of prepaid insurance for both the **Auto and Truck** insurance policy and the **Business Liability** insurance policy.

"T" Account Analysis for Asset and Liability Accounts		
Account Name →	Prepaid Insurance	
	Debit	**Credit**
(1) What is the <u>current</u> balance?		
(3) What adjustment is required to adjust from the <u>current</u> balance to the <u>should be</u> balance?		
(2) What <u>should be</u> the balance?		

Requirement 5 – September 30 Prepaid Insurance adjusting entry

Date	Account Name	Debit	Credit

Requirement 6

Amount of Prepaid Insurance on the October 31 Balance Sheet

$

Amount of Insurance Expense on the October 1 to October 31 Income Statement

$

Name: _____ Section: _____ #: _____

**Forms for: Problem 7-6   Weekly Wage Payment Entries and the
Month-End Wages Payable Adjusting Entry**

Requirement 1 – Wage payment on Friday June 25th

Date	Account Name	Debit	Credit
6/25/xx			

Requirement 2

Total amount earned by the employees for:
Monday June 28th + Tuesday June 29th + Wednesday June 30th

$

Requirement 3 – June 30 Wages Payable adjusting entry

Date	Account Name	Debit	Credit
6/30/xx			

Requirement 4 – Wage payment on Friday July 2nd

Date	Account Name	Debit	Credit
7/02/xx			

Blank Page for Miscellaneous Calculations

Name: _____ Section: _____ #: _____

Forms for: Problem 7-7   Take-Out a Loan
Accrue Interest on the Loan – Pay Interest

Requirement 1 – April 1 get the loan from the bank

Date	Account Name	Debit	Credit

Requirement 2 – April 30 interest accrual adjusting entry

Date	Account Name	Debit	Credit

Requirement 3 – May 31 interest accrual adjusting entry

Date	Account Name	Debit	Credit

Requirement 4 – Payment of the April, May, and June interest to the bank

Date	Account Name	Debit	Credit

Name: _____   Section: _____   #: _____

Forms for: Problem 7-8   Accrue Rent Payable – Pay Rent the Following Month

Requirement 1 – September 1 entry to record signing the contract

Date	Account Name	Debit	Credit

Requirement 2 – September 30 rent payable accrual adjusting entry

Date	Account Name	Debit	Credit

Requirement 3 – October 5 payment of September's rent

Date	Account Name	Debit	Credit

Name: _____ Section: _____ #: _____

Forms for: Problem 8-1   Collecting Rent In Advance and the Monthly Adjusting Entry

Requirement 1 – January 1 receive $21,000 advance payment for rent

Date	Account Name	Debit	Credit

Requirement 2 – "T" Account Analysis for the January 31 adjusting entry

"T" Account Analysis for Asset and Liability Accounts		
Account Name →	**Unearned Rent Revenue**	
	Debit	**Credit**
(1) What is the <u>current</u> balance?		
(3) What adjustment is required to adjust from the <u>current</u> balance to the <u>should be</u> balance?		
(2) What <u>should be</u> the balance?		$14,000

Bldg #1 $6,000 (Feb. & March) + Bldg #2 $8,000 (Feb. & March) = $14,000

Requirement 3 – January 31 Unearned Rent Revenue adjusting entry

Date	Account Name	Debit	Credit

Forms for: Problem 8-1 (continued)

Requirement 4 – "T" Account Analysis for the February 28 adjusting entry

"T" Account Analysis for Asset and Liability Accounts		
Account Name →	*Unearned Rent Revenue*	
	Debit	**Credit**
(1) What is the <u>current</u> balance?		
(3) What adjustment is required to adjust from the <u>current</u> balance to the <u>should be</u> balance?		
(2) What <u>should be</u> the balance?		

Requirement 5 – February 28 Unearned Rent Revenue adjusting entry

Date	Account Name	Debit	Credit

Requirement 6

Amount of Unearned Rent Revenue on the February 28, 2017 Balance Sheet

$

Amount of Rent Revenue on the February 1 to February 28, 2017 Income Statement

$

Name: _____   Section: _____   #: _____

Forms for: Problem 8-2   Collect Cash for Season Tickets and
                          the Monthly Adjusting Entry

Requirement 1 – September's season ticket sales

Date	Account Name	Debit	Credit

Requirement 2 – "T" Account Analysis for the October 31 adjusting entry

"T" Account Analysis for Asset and Liability Accounts		
Account Name →	**Unearned Ticket Revenue**	
	Debit	**Credit**
(1) What is the current balance?		
(3) What adjustment is required to adjust from the current balance to the should be balance?		
(2) What should be the balance?		

Calculation of Unearned Ticket Revenue as of October 31

Package	Total Season Ticket Sales	x	% of Games in the Package to be Played in Nov. + Dec.	=	Unearned Ticket Revenue
#1	$250,000	x	80%	=	$200,000
#2	$30,000	x	60%	=	$18,000
#3	$75,000	x	100%	=	$75,000
				Total	$293,000

Requirement 3 – October 31 Unearned Ticket Revenue adjusting entry

Date	Account Name	Debit	Credit

Forms for: Problem 8-2 (continued)

Requirement 4 – "T" Account Analysis for the November 30 adjusting entry

"T" Account Analysis for Asset and Liability Accounts		
Account Name →	**Unearned Ticket Revenue**	
	Debit	**Credit**
(1) What is the <u>current</u> balance?		
(3) What adjustment is required to adjust from the <u>current</u> balance to the <u>should be</u> balance?		
(2) What <u>should be</u> the balance?		

Calculation of Unearned Ticket Revenue as of November 30

Package	Total Season Ticket Sales	x	% of Games in the Package to be Played in December	=	Unearned Ticket Revenue
#1	$	x	%	=	$
#2	$	x	%	=	$
#3	$	x	%	=	$
				Total	$

Requirement 5 – November 30 Unearned Ticket Revenue adjusting entry

Date	Account Name	Debit	Credit

Requirement 6

Amount of Unearned Ticket Revenue on the November 30 Balance Sheet

$

Amount of Ticket Revenue on the November 1 to November 30 Income Statement
Remember that this includes $650,000 "day-of-the-game" ticket sales.

$

Name: _____ Section: _____ #: _____

Forms for: Problem 8-3   Loan Money – Accrue Monthly Interest – Collect Interest

Requirement 1 – July 1 MegaMoney making the loan to SOC

Date	Account Name	Debit	Credit

Requirement 2 – July 31 Interest Receivable adjusting entry

Date	Account Name	Debit	Credit

Requirement 3 – August 31 Interest Receivable adjusting entry

Date	Account Name	Debit	Credit

Requirement 4 – September 30 receipt of cash by MegaMoney for July, August, and September interest

Date	Account Name	Debit	Credit
9/30/17	Cash		
	Interest Receivable		
	Interest Revenue		
	Collect July, August, and September Interest		

Name: _____   Section: _____   #: _____

Forms for: Problem 8-4   Accrue Monthly Rent Receivable – Collect Rent

Requirement 1 – May 31 Rent Receivable adjusting entry

Date	Account Name	Debit	Credit

Requirement 2

Amount of Rent Receivable shown on Office Rental Inc.'s Balance Sheet as of May 31, 2017

$ _____

Amount of Rent Revenue on Office Rental Inc.'s Income Statement for the period May 1 to May 31, 2017

$ _____

Requirement 3 – June 30 receipt of cash by Office Rental, Inc. from Watson for the January through June rent

Date	Account Name	Debit	Credit
06/30/17	Cash		
	Rent Receivable		
	Rent Revenue		
	Collect 6 months of rent – January to June		

Name: _____   Section: _____   #: _____

Answer Sheet for: Problem 9-1   True / False Questions
Timing Issues Related to Adjusting Entries

Circle **T**rue or **F**alse for each question:

1.   True   False

2.   True   False

3.   True   False

4.   True   False

5.   True   False

6.   True   False

7.   True   False

8.   True   False

9.   True   False

10.   True   False

11.   True   False

12.   True   False

Blank Page for Miscellaneous Calculations

Name: _____   Section: _____   #: _____

Forms for: Problem 10-1   Recording Dividends

Requirement 1

A. August 15 Dividend declaration entry

Date	Account Name	Debit	Credit

B. After posting the above entry the Current Balances in the Dividends Payable account and the Retained Earnings account

Current Balance in the **Dividends Payable** account as of August 15	Current Balance in the **Retained Earnings** account as of August 15
$	$

Requirement 2

A. Calculation of Retained Earnings as of August 31 for the Balance Sheet

Calculation of
Retained Earnings as of
August 31 for the Balance Sheet

B. Dividends Payable shown on EasyMoney's August 31 Balance Sheet

Dividends Payable on the August 31 Balance Sheet
$

Forms for: Problem 10-1 (continued)

Requirement 3

A. September 20 Dividend payment entry

Date	Account Name	Debit	Credit

B. After posting the above entry the Current Balance in the Dividends Payable account

Current Balance in the **Dividends Payable** acccount as of Sept. 20
$

Name: _____　Section: _____　#: _____

Problem 11-1　Statement of Cash Flows for January 1 to January 31, 2017

Larry's Landscaping
Statement of Cash Flows (Indirect Method)
for the Period January 1 to January 31, 2017

Cash Flows from Operating Activities

Net Income	$
Cash Provided by Operating Activities	

Cash Flows from Investing Activities

Cash Provided (Used) by Investing Activities	

Cash Flows from Financing Activities

Cash Provided by Financing Activities	

Increase in Cash from January 1 to January 31, 2017	$

Beginning Cash Balance January 1, 2017	$
Increase in Cash from January 1 to January 31, 2017	
Ending Cash Balance January 31, 2017	$

Name: _____   Section: _____   #: _____

Problem 11-2   Statement of Cash Flows for February 1 to February 28, 2017

Larry's Landscaping
Statement of Cash Flows (Indirect Method)
for the Period February 1 to February 28, 2017

<u>Cash Flows from Operating Activities</u>

Net Income	$
Cash Provided by Operating Activities	

<u>Cash Flows from Investing Activities</u>

Cash Used by Investing Activities	

<u>Cash Flows from Financing Activities</u>

Cash Provided by Financing Activities	

Increase in Cash from February 1 to February 28, 2017	$

Beginning Cash Balance February 1, 2017	$
Increase in Cash from February 1 to February 28, 2017	
Ending Cash Balance February 28, 2017	$

Name: _____   Section: _____   #: _____

Problem 11-3   Statement of Cash Flows for March 1 to March 31, 2017

Larry's Landscaping
Statement of Cash Flows (Indirect Method)
for the Period March 1 to March 31, 2017

Cash Flows from Operating Activities

Net Income	$
Cash Provided by Operating Activities	

Cash Flows from Investing Activities

Cash Used by Investing Activities	

Cash Flows from Financing Activities

Cash Provided by Financing Activities	

Increase in Cash from March 1 to March 31, 2017	$

Beginning Cash Balance March 1, 2017	$
Increase in Cash from March 1 to March 31, 2017	
Ending Cash Balance March 31, 2017	$

Name: _____   Section: _____   #: _____

Problem 11-4   Statement of Cash Flows for January 1 to March 31, 2017 _____

Larry's Landscaping
Statement of Cash Flows (Indirect Method)
for the Period January 1 to March 31, 2017

Cash Flows from Operating Activities

Net Income	$
Cash Provided by Operating Activities	

Cash Flows from Investing Activities

Cash Used by Investing Activities	

Cash Flows from Financing Activities

Cash Provided by Financing Activities	

Increase in Cash from January 1 to March 31, 2017	$

Beginning Cash Balance January 1, 2017	$
Increase in Cash from January 1 to March 31, 2017	
Ending Cash Balance March 31, 2017	$

Name: _____   Section: _____   #: _____

Problem 12-1   Statement of Cash Flows for April 1 to April 30, 2017

Larry's Landscaping

Statement of Cash Flows (Indirect Method)

for the Period April 1 to April 30, 2017

Cash Flows from Operating Activities

Net Income	$
Cash Provided by Operating Activities	

Cash Flows from Investing Activities

Cash Provided (Used) by Investing Activities	

Cash Flows from Financing Activities

Cash Provided (Used) by Financing Activities	
Increase in Cash from April 1 to April 30, 2017	$

Beginning Cash Balance April 1, 2017 $

Increase in Cash from April 1 to April 30, 2017

Ending Cash Balance April 30, 2017 $

Name: _____   Section: _____   #: _____

Problem 12-2   Statement of Cash Flows for May 1 to May 31, 2017

Larry's Landscaping
Statement of Cash Flows (Indirect Method)
for the Period May 1 to May 31, 2017

Cash Flows from Operating Activities

Net Income	$

Cash Provided by Operating Activities	

Cash Flows from Investing Activities

Cash Used by Investing Activities	

Cash Flows from Financing Activities

Cash Used by Financing Activities	

Decrease in Cash from May 1 to May 31, 2017	$

Beginning Cash Balance May 1, 2017	$
Decrease in Cash from May 1 to May 31, 2017	
Ending Cash Balance May 31, 2017	$

Name: _____   Section: _____   #: _____

Problem 12-3   Statement of Cash Flows for June 1 to June 30, 2017

Larry's Landscaping
Statement of Cash Flows (Indirect Method)
for the Period June 1 to June 30, 2017

Cash Flows from Operating Activities

Net Income	$

Cash Provided by Operating Activities

Cash Flows from Investing Activities

Cash Provided by Investing Activities

Cash Flows from Financing Activities

Cash Used by Financing Activities

Increase in Cash from June 1 to June 30, 2017 $

Beginning Cash Balance June 1, 2017 $
Increase in Cash from June 1 to June 30, 2017
Ending Cash Balance June 30, 2017 $

NonCash Investing and Financing Activities

Name: _____   Section: _____   #: _____

Problem 12-4   Statement of Cash Flows for April 1 to June 30, 2017

Larry's Landscaping
Statement of Cash Flows (Indirect Method)
for the Period April 1 to June 30, 2017

Cash Flows from Operating Activities

Net Income	$
Cash Provided by Operating Activities	

Cash Flows from Investing Activities

Cash Provided by Investing Activities	

Cash Flows from Financing Activities

Cash Used by Financing Activities	

Increase in Cash from April 1 to June 30, 2017	$

Beginning Cash Balance April 1, 2017	$
Increase in Cash from April 1 to June 30, 2017	
Ending Cash Balance June 30, 2017	$

NonCash Investing and Financing Activities

Glossary of Terms / Subject Index

Account – A place in the general ledger where the dollar balance of an asset, liability, equity, revenue, expense, or dividend is kept. (Pg. 4)

Accounting Cycle – The nine step accounting process that a business entity goes through each accounting period. The cycle begins with recording transactions and ends with closing the temporary accounts. (Pgs. 21, 50, 54)

Accounting Equation
Assets = Liabilities + Owners' Equity (Pgs. 4, 7)

Accounting Period – The period of time covered by the financial statements. The period of time during which the business entity goes through the entire Accounting Cycle. (Pgs. 21, 68)

Accounts Payable – The claims of an entity's vendors to the entity's assets. The amount of money owed to vendors for the purchase of services, supplies, and inventory. (Pg. 53)

Accounts Payable account – A liability account that tracks the amount owed to vendors. The normal balance is a credit. (Pgs. 53, 56)

Accounts Receivable – The amount owed to the business entity by customers who have purchased services or products on credit. (Pg. 28)

Accounts Receivable account – An asset account that tracks the amount owed to the entity by its customers. The normal balance is a debit. (Pgs. 28, 55)

Accrual Basis of Accounting – The basis of accounting under which business transactions are recorded in the accounting period in which they take place even if <u>no</u> cash is received or paid out. (Pg. 21)

Accrued Asset – An asset that has been earned but not previously recorded in the accounts. An adjusting entry is required to record this asset prior to the preparation of financial statements. (Pgs. 105, 116, 117)

Accrued Expense – Another name for an Accrued Liability. (Pgs. 81, 114, 117)

Accrued Liability – A liability that has been incurred and is owed to an outside entity, but that has not been previously recorded in the accounts. An adjusting entry is required to record this liability prior to the preparation of financial statements. (Pgs. 81, 114, 117)

Accrued Revenue – Another name for an Accrued Asset. (Pgs. 105, 116, 117)

Accumulated Depreciation account – A contra-asset account that tracks the amount of previously recorded depreciation on the asset the account is contra to. The normal balance is a credit. (Pgs. 71, 72, 113, 150)

Adjusting Entries – Journal entries that are required to tune-up the balances in the accounts prior to the preparation of financial statements. (Pgs. 30, 67, 75, 79, 117)

Asset – Something that is owned by the entity and will provide future benefit to the entity. (Pg. 7)

Asset Account – An account that tracks the dollar amount of a resource owned by the entity. Asset accounts are increased by a debit and decreased by a credit. The normal balance is a debit. Also see Contra-Asset. (Pgs. 8, 11)

Balance of an Account – The amount in an account that results from the beginning balance and the debits and credits entered into the account during the accounting period. (Pg. 13)

Balance Sheet – The financial statement that reports the assets, liabilities, and owners' equity of an entity at a point in time. (Pgs. 5, 20, 62)

Cash account – An asset account that tracks the amount of cash owned by the entity. The normal balance is a debit. (Pg. 18)

Chart of Accounts – A listing of all the accounts in a company's general ledger. (ACP Project – Chart Accts tab)

Closing Entries – Entries made in the general journal at the end of the accounting cycle to move the balances in the temporary accounts (revenues and expenses) into Retained Earnings. The resulting balances in the revenue and expense accounts are zero. (Pgs. 47, 48, 63, 123)

Closing Process – The process completed at the end of each accounting cycle to zero-out the temporary accounts and move their balances to the Retained Earnings account. (Pg. 47)

Common Stock – The basic class of stock of a corporation. The owners of a corporation are issued shares of Common Stock to evidence their ownership interest in the corporation. (Pg. 18)

Common Stock account – An equity account that tracks the amount of the owners' claim to assets as a result of the owners putting money into the business. The normal balance is a credit. (Pgs. 18, 26, 133)

Contra-Asset Account – A negative asset account that tracks the dollar amount that has been recorded as an offset against a related asset account. The account is increased by a credit and decreased by a debit. The normal balance is a credit. (Pgs. 71, 113, 151)

Corporation – A legal entity that is separate from its owners. The assets owned by a corporation belong to the corporation—not to the individual owners. (Pg. 17)

Cost of Goods Sold account – An expense account that tracks the reduction in the owners' claim to assets during an accounting period— that results from the consumption of inventory when that inventory is sold to a customer. The normal balance is a debit. (Pgs. 36, 37)

Cost Principle – This principle states that a transaction will be recorded at the dollar cost of the asset received, or given-up, on the date of the transaction. (Pg. 22)

Credit – The right side of all accounts. (Pg. 11)

Current Asset – An asset that will turn into cash in the next 12 months or be consumed in the next 12 months. (ACP Project – BalSht tab)

Current Liability – A liability that must be paid in the next 12 months. (ACP Project – BalSht tab)

Debit – The left side of all accounts. (Pg. 11)

Deferred Expense – Another name for a Prepaid Asset. (Pgs. 76, 113, 117)

Deferred Revenue liability – Another name for an Unearned Revenue liability. (Pgs. 100, 115, 117)

Depreciation – The process of allocating the cost of Property, Plant, & Equipment to the accounting periods in which these assets are used. (Pg. 70)

Depreciation Expense account – An expense account that tracks the reduction in the owners' claim to assets during an accounting period— that results from the consumption of Property, Plant, & Equipment in the operation of the business. The normal balance is a debit. (Pgs. 71, 72)

Direct Method – The method that shows gross cash receipts less gross cash payments to calculate Cash Provided by Operating Activities on the Statement of Cash Flows. (Pgs. 142, 186)

Dividend – The distribution of some of the assets, normally cash, to the owners of the business. (Pg. 119, 176)

Dividends Payable account – A liability account that tracks the amount owed to the owners of a business as a result of the declaration of a dividend. The normal balance is a credit. (Pgs. 120, 121)

Entity Assumption – This assumption states that only transactions that involve the business being accounted for—will be recorded in that business's accounts. (Pg. 21)

Equipment – A physical asset used by a business to produce or deliver the business's products or services. (Pg. 19)

Equipment account – An asset account that tracks the original cost of equipment purchased by a business. The normal balance is a debit. (Pg. 19)

Equity – The owners' claim to the entity's assets. (Pg. 7)

Expense Account – An account that tracks the reduction in the owners' claim to assets as a result of the operation of the business. Expense accounts are increased by a debit and decreased by a credit. The normal balance is a debit. (Pgs. 37, 43)

Financing Activities – Cash flows that result from transactions with owners, or from borrowing on notes or bonds from creditors. (Pg. 140)

Fixed Assets – Another name for Property, Plant, & Equipment. (Pgs. 70, 113)

General Journal – The area in the accounting system where the accounts affected by a transaction and the dollar amount of the effect are first recorded. The amounts are then posted from the General Journal to the General Ledger accounts. (Pg. 17)

General Ledger – The collection of all of the accounts in the accounting system. (Pg. 14)

Going Concern Assumption – The assumption that an entity will continue in business for an extended period of time. (Pg. 21)

Gross Profit – Sales less Cost of Goods Sold (Pg. 42)

Income Statement – The financial statement that reports the change in the owners' claim to assets that results from the operation of the business. The Income Statement is a period-of-time report—the period of time reported on is the accounting period. (Pgs. 32, 41, 60)

Indirect Method – The method that starts with accrual based Net Income and then adjusts that amount to calculate Cash Provided by Operating Activities on the Statement of Cash Flows. (Pg. 142)

Interest Expense account – An expense account that tracks the reduction in the owners' claim to assets during an accounting period— that results from the cost of using money borrowed from non-owners. The normal balance is a debit. (Pgs. 36, 40, 58)

Interest Payable account – The claims of the entity's creditors to the entity's assets—for interest due that has not yet been paid. The normal balance is a credit. (Pgs. 30, 41, 58, 81, 114)

Interest Receivable account – An asset account that tracks the amount of interest owed to the entity by companies or individuals. The normal balance is a debit. (Pgs. 105, 116)

Inventory – Items held for sale to an entity's customers. (Pg. 19)

Inventory account – An asset account that tracks the cost of inventory that has been purchased or manufactured and held for sale to customers. The normal balance is a debit. (Pg. 20)

Investing Activities – Cash outflows and cash inflows that result from the purchase or the sale of long-lived productive assets, or from the purchase or the sale of securities of other companies. (Pg. 140)

Journal Entry – An entry in the General Journal to record the effects of a transaction on the entity's accounts. (Pg. 17)

Liabilities – The claims of non-owners to the entity's assets. (Pgs. 7)

Liability Account – An account that tracks the dollar amount of non-owners claims to assets. Liability accounts are increased by a credit and decreased by a debit. The normal balance is a credit. (Pgs. 9, 12)

Matching Principle – The concept of matching revenues and expenses in the same accounting period. If an expense is related to the generation of revenue then the expense should be recorded in the same period as the related revenue. (Pg. 80)

Merchandising Company – A company that buys items from another company that manufacturers the items—and then sells those items to a consumer. (Pg. 17)

Monetary Unit Assumption – Only economic events that can be stated in terms of a monetary unit (e.g. dollars) are recorded in an entity's accounting system and thus reported in the entity's financial statements. (Pg. 21)

Net Income – When all revenues for the accounting period less all expenses for the accounting period result in a positive amount, that amount is called Net Income. Net Income is reported on an entity's Income Statement. Net Income is also called Net Profit. (Pgs. 42, 43)

Net Loss – When all revenues for the accounting period less all expenses for the accounting period result in a negative amount, that amount is called Net Loss. Net Loss is reported on an entity's Income Statement. (Pg. 43)

NonCash Activity – A transaction that involves both an Investing Activity and a Financing Activity – and no cash outflow or cash inflow. (Pg. 177)

Note Payable – The claim of a non-owner to the entity's assets that results from the non-owner loaning money to the entity. The loan is evidenced by a contract called a Note. (Pgs. 7, 18)

Note Payable account – A liability account that tracks the principal amount owed on a note to a creditor. The normal balance is a credit. (Pgs. 7, 19)

Operating Activities – Cash inflows and cash outflows that result from transactions affecting Net Income. (Pg. 140)

Owners' Equity – The claim of the owners of the entity to the entity's assets. (Pgs. 7)

Period of Time Assumption – The assumption that the life of an entity can be broken into periods of time and those periods of time reported on in the financial statements. (Pg. 21)

Permanent Accounts – These are the accounts in the General Ledger that are never closed. The Permanent Accounts are the: Asset accounts, Liability accounts, Common Stock account, and the Retained Earnings account. (Pg. 49)

Post-Closing Trial Balance – A listing that is prepared after all temporary accounts have been closed. The listing shows all of the accounts in the General Ledger and their ending balances. The purpose of the Post-Closing Trial Balance is to determine if the General Ledger is in balance and ready to start a new Accounting Cycle. (Pgs. 49, 64)

Posting -- The moving of the journal entry amounts from the General Journal to each account in the General Ledger affected by the entry. (Pg. 17)

Pre-Closing Trial Balance – A listing that is prepared after all adjusting entries have been made. The listing shows all of the accounts in the General Ledger and their ending balances. The purpose of the Pre-Closing Trial Balance is to determine if the General Ledger is in balance prior to preparing the financial statements. (Pgs. 41, 60, 122)

Prepaid Asset – An item or service that is purchased in the current accounting period, and is not totally consumed in the current accounting period, and the item or service will benefit one or more future accounting periods. (Pgs. 76, 113, 117)

Prepaid Insurance – An asset in the Prepaid Asset category that occurs when insurance is purchased and the coverage will benefit one or more future accounting period. (Pg. 114)

Prepaid Maintenance – An asset in the Prepaid Asset category that occurs when maintenance coverage is purchased that will benefit one or more future accounting period. (Pg. 114)

Prepaid Rent – An asset in the Prepaid Asset category that occurs when rent is paid that will benefit one or more future accounting period. (Pg. 114)

Property, Plant, & Equipment – Long-term assets that are used in the operation of the business. Examples are: land, buildings, equipment, autos, and trucks. (Pgs. 70, 113, 117)

Rent Expense account – An expense account that tracks the reduction in the owners' claim to assets during an accounting period—that results from the cost of renting an item for use in the business. The normal balance is a debit. (Pgs. 36, 38)

Rent Payable account – A liability account that tracks the amount owed to a landlord. The normal balance is a credit. (Pg. 81)

Rent Receivable account – An asset account that tracks the amount of rent owed to the entity by tenants. The normal balance is a debit. (Pgs. 105, 116)

Retained Earnings account – An equity account that tracks the amount of the owners' claim to assets that results from the operation of the business. The normal balance is a credit. (Pgs. 26, 32, 42, 61, 122)

Revenue account – An account that tracks the increase in the owners' claim to assets as a result of the operation of the business. Revenue accounts are increased by a credit and decreased by a debit. The normal balance is a credit. (Pg. 43)

Sales Revenue account – The revenue account for a merchandising company or a manufacturing company. The normal balance is a credit. (Pgs. 36, 37, 43)

Service Company – A company that earns its revenue by providing services to its customers. (Pg. 67)

Service Revenue account – The revenue account for a service company. The normal balance is a credit. (Pg. 69)

Statement of Cash Flows – The financial statement that reports the cash inflows and cash outflows of a business entity. The Statement of Cash Flows is a period-of-time report—the period of time reported on is the accounting period. (Pg. 131)

Statement of Stockholders' Equity – The financial statement that shows what caused the changes in the Stockholders' Equity amounts during the current accounting period. (ACP Project – IS & SEquity tab)

Stockholders' Equity – See Owners' Equity.

Straight-Line Method of Depreciation – A method of depreciation that results in the same amount of depreciation expense each accounting period. (Pg. 70)

Supplies account – An asset account that tracks the cost of supplies that have been purchased for use in the business. The normal balance is a debit. (Pgs. 74)

Supplies Expense account – An expense account that tracks the reduction in the owners' claim to assets during an accounting period—that results from the consumption of the supplies asset. The normal balance is a debit. (Pgs. 69, 76)

T Account Analysis – An analysis process that utilizes a "T" account format and a three step process to determine the required amount of an adjusting entry. (Pgs. 79, 80, 98)

Temporary Accounts – These are the accounts in the General Ledger that are closed each accounting period to Retained Earnings. The Temporary Accounts are the Revenue accounts and the Expense accounts. (Pgs. 49, 53)

Trial Balance – A listing that shows all of the accounts in the General Ledger and their ending balances. The purpose of a Trial Balance is to determine if the General Ledger is in balance. Also see Pre-Closing Trial Balance and Post-Closing Trial Balance. (Pgs. 13, 20)

Unearned Revenue – A liability that is the result of cash being received from a customer in one accounting period, and all of the goods or services not being delivered to the customer in that same accounting period, and the undelivered goods or services will be delivered to the customer in some future accounting period. (Pgs. 95, 115, 117)

Unearned Revenue account – A liability account that tracks the amount owed to a customer, when that customer has made an advance payment for goods or services and all or part of those goods or services has not been delivered to the customer. The normal balance is a credit. (Pgs. 95, 98)

Wage Expense account – An expense account that tracks the reduction in the owners' claim to assets during an accounting period—that results from the cost of wages earned by employees working for the business. The normal balance is a debit. (Pgs. 36, 38)

Wages Payable account – A liability account that tracks the amount owed to employees. The normal balance is a credit. (Pg. 80, 96, 114)

NOTES

NOTES

Solid Footing 10e

Software ID Code
Permanent Record Slip

**Do not remove this
slip from your book**

Your Software ID Code

27424838

You will use your
Software ID Code to:

1. Download your
Solid Footing software

2. Activate your
OPJ Mini-Project

3. Activate your
Accounting Cycle Project

Solid Footing 10e

Accounting Cycle Project
Registration Slip

As directed by your instructor:

1. Fill in your information below

2. Remove this slip

3. Turn in this slip

Software ID Code
27424838

Your Name:

Seat or ID#:

Instructor:

Class Time:

Section:

Solid Footing 10e

OPJ Mini-Project
Registration Slip

As directed by your instructor:

1. Fill in your information below

2. Remove this slip

3. Turn in this slip

Software ID Code
27424838

Your Name:

Seat or ID#:

Instructor:

Class Time:

Section: